FROM
STRESS
TO
STRENGTH

ALSO BY ROBERT S. ELIOT, M.D.

Is It Worth Dying For?

FROM
STRESS
TO
STRENGTH

HOW TO LIGHTEN YOUR LOAD
AND SAVE YOUR LIFE

5-24-94

ROBERT S. ELIOT, M.D.

To Marc
with best wishes!

Robert S. Eliot M.D.

BANTAM BOOKS
NEW YORK · TORONTO · LONDON · SYDNEY · AUCKLAND

FROM STRESS TO STRENGTH
A Bantam Book / February 1994

Abdominal/Gluteal Ratio chart, p. 195, from Bray, G.A., and
D.S. Gray, "Obesity: Part I. Pathogenesis," *Western Journal of
Medicine,* 149, page 432. Reprinted by permission of the *Western
Journal of Medicine* and George A. Bray, M.D. Copyright ©
1988. Body Mass Index Nomogram, p. 197, reprinted by
permission of George A. Bray, M.D. Copyright © 1978.

Book design by Michael Mendelsohn of MM Design 2000, Inc.

Library of Congress Cataloging-in-Publication Data

Eliot, Robert S.
   From stress to strength : how to lighten your load and save
your life / Robert S. Eliot.
      p.   cm.
   Includes index.
   ISBN 0-553-07117-3
   1. Stress management.   2. Cardiac arrest—Prevention.
   3. Cardiovascular system—Diseases—Prevention.   I. Title.
RA785.E443   1993
155.9'042—dc20   92-28739
                                                            CIP

Published simultaneously in the United States and Canada

Bantam Books are published by Bantam Books, a division of Bantam
Doubleday Dell Publishing Group, Inc. Its trademark, consisting of
the words "Bantam Books" and the portrayal of a rooster, is
Registered in U.S. Patent and Trademark Office and in other
countries. Marca Registrada. Bantam Books, 1540 Broadway, New
York, New York 10036.

PRINTED IN THE UNITED STATES OF AMERICA

BVG   0   9   8   7   6   5   4   3   2   1

To Bruce K. Munro, Ph.D.
... a gifted behaviorist, respected anthropologist, and
irreplaceable friend

CONTENTS

PART III

THE HABITS OF HEALTH

ACKNOWLEDGMENTS

Over the five years this book has been in progress, the major catalyst has been my cousin and remarkable friend, Dr. Bruce K. Munro. His extensive background in behavioral medicine and fellowship in the Royal Anthropological Society of London are coupled with a brisk command of the "Queen's English." His energy, enthusiasm, and commitment were major dynamic forces. I am deeply indebted to Evelyn M. Munro as well, whom I have known since college days. She occasionally hosted some of our multiday editorial sessions and tolerated Bruce's absences for "the cause."

Toni Burbank, Executive Editor, Bantam Books, was a gifted guiding force from the beginning, to and through publication. She has been a supportive, constructive, and intuitive influence in the development of the focus of this book. A great contributor was my delightful, indefatigable, talented administrative assistant, Cathy Eikenhorst. Linda Perigo Moore affably and competently condensed the manuscript into a more readable, practical, and accessible form.

The research and editing was enhanced by Hugo M. Morales, M.D., FACC; Esther Adler; Jacqueline Hooper, D.H.Sc.; Ellen S. Wingard, M.Ed.; Patricia St. Germain, M.A.; Renee Shamroth; Inger and Bob Koedt; David and Lynda Tews; Steve Chiccehitto; Dr. Merlin and Paulina Kampfer; Dr. Bob and Jackie Rosenlof; Emily W. Betts; Marge and Bill Raymond; Dean Ornish, M.D.; Brendan P. Phibbs, M.D., FACC; C. Wayne Callaway, M.D., George Washington University; Wilson S. Leach; Leonard S. Wojnowich, M.D.; Bruce B. Baker, M.D.; Dr. Richard A. Lippin, M.D.; Wesley E. Sime, Ph.D.; Kathryn Raymer, Ph.D.; and Cousin Betty Ehrlich.

I extend my appreciation to those who have supported the basic research and clinical foundation of this book, including the National Institutes of Health for the study of the mechanisms of sudden cardiac death, the Canaveral Heart Association, the American Heart Association, the Florida Heart Association, the International Stress Foundation, the Research Division of the Veterans Administration,

Physicians Mutual Insurance Company, the Paavo Nurmi Foundation, and many other private foundations and donors.

My gratitude also extends to the people of Nebraska who, through their legislators, passed a special bill (LB-1054), thereby generously providing funds to begin and sustain the first academic Department of Preventive and Stress Medicine in conjunction with a multidisciplinary cardiovascular center. I also wish to acknowledge the pragmatism of the administration and the dedicated, outstanding faculty and staff who made it happen.

Special acknowledgment is owed for the support and encouragement from my many friends and colleagues in the American College of Cardiology who, over the past few years, have elected me Chairman of the Board of Governors, member of the Board of Trustees, and member of the Executive Committee, the Long-Range Planning Committee, and the Prevention Committee, among others.

Another significant catalyst was the Academy of Behavioral Medicine Research, which made me a charter member. The varied backgrounds of this remarkable group of professionals permit active interdisciplinary discussions critical to an accurate and balanced blending of the diverse fields represented in this book.

Many of my medical and scientific colleagues urged me to provide our comprehensive observations and methods in a practical way for nonmedical audiences. I have been stimulated and often encouraged by: William D. Nelligan, CAE, FACC, former Executive Vice President, American College of Cardiology; Henry McIntosh, M.D., Past President and Chairman, Prevention Committee, American College of Cardiology; Stephen M. Weiss, Ph.D., former Chief, Behavioral Medicine Branch, Division of Epidemiology and Clinical Applications, National Heart, Lung and Blood Institute (NHLBI), Department of Health & Human Services, National Institutes of Health; William P. Castelli, M.D., Medical Director, Framingham Heart Study, NHLBI; Dean Ornish, M.D., Executive Director, Preventive Medical Research Institute; Fred W. Lyons, Jr., President and CEO, J. Michael Gorman, Director of Professional Services, David Katterhenrich, Director of Research, Warren Anderson, and Patricia I. Ross of Marion Merrell Dow Inc.; the late Howard Baer, Senior Vice President, Ciba-Geigy Pharmaceutical Company; H. Weston Moses, M.D., FACC; Naresh Kumar, M.D., Whitby Cardiovascular Center,

Toronto; Margaret A. Chesney, Ph.D., University of California, San Francisco; Redford B. Williams, Jr., M.D., Duke University; General W. Russell Dougherty (Ret.), former Commander-in-Chief, Strategic Air Command; Leonard R. Kowalski, M.D., Medical Director, Denver Aeronautics Groups, Martin Marietta Corporation; Michael Quatrella, M.D., Medical Director, Irene A. Chow, Ph.D., Senior Vice President, Elaine Snowhill, Ph.D., Executive Director, Susan Smith, R.N., and Judith Kostrowski of Ciba-Geigy Pharmaceutical Company; Madeline Weinstein, First Vice President, Merrill Lynch; Robert E. Windom, M.D., former Assistant Secretary for Health, Department of Health & Human Services; Michael E. DeBakey, M.D., Baylor University; Jesse E. Edwards, M.D., cardiac pathologist; Neal Miller, Ph.D.; Laurent P. LaRoche, M.D., former Medical Director, Cape Kennedy; Giorgio Baroldi, M.D., cardiac pathologist; Paul Dudley White, M.D., the father of cardiology; and the late Norman Cousins, author, editor, and lecturer.

A special note of appreciation is owed to the "father of stress," Dr. Hans Selye, who encouraged me to translate his animal studies into practical methods that could be used in the clinical measurement of stress. He emphasized that these measurements must be objective. Although he indicated that *he* could not think of a way of doing it, he knew research was essential if a bridge of knowledge was to be built between animal studies and patient management.

My friends and colleagues James C. Buell, M.D., Chief, Cardiology Department, Texas Tech University, and Robert Royce deserve the credit for developing much of the instrumentation that has made this work possible.

I want to thank our children, William and Susan, for their technical and editorial assistance.

Finally my wife, Phyllis, provided many dimensions in this work. Among many other things, she was a writer (the chapter on nutrition), editor, innkeeper, major adviser, unique and loving wife, and *very* patient.

Robert S. Eliot, M.D., FACC
Institute of Stress Medicine
Jackson Hole, Wyoming
September 1993

INTRODUCTION

Should I Read This Book?

Quickly scan the following statements and respond with the first thought that comes to mind.

	Yes	No
1. I am generally pretty healthy.	___	___
2. I've had a heart attack and/or bypass surgery and my doctor tells me I need to control my stress level.	___	___
3. There are not enough hours in the day.	___	___
4. My blood pressure has always been normal.	___	___
5. My blood pressure is currently being treated with medication.	___	___
6. I find that I sometimes have trouble controlling my anger or my anxiety.	___	___
7. I have trouble watching my weight.	___	___
8. My boss is a jerk and/or I work with jerks.	___	___
9. I have experienced a tension headache or nervous indigestion within the past month.	___	___
10. Often I find that a drink or a cigarette can calm my nerves.	___	___
11. At night I have trouble forgetting the problems of the day.	___	___
12. My family could drive anybody nuts.	___	___

Scoring:
   If you answered "yes" to:
   1–2 statements. Select another book.
   3–9 statements. This book was written with you in mind.
   10–12 statements. I'd make notes in the margins.

As life's pressures mount and your burdens increase, the resulting stress can have a catastrophic impact on your health and physiology. Usually attacking the weakest part of your body, stress can impair your respiratory system, gastrointestinal tract, or immune system. As a cardiologist, I see the devastation created when stress attacks the cardiovascular system. Coronary heart disease, high blood pressure, sudden cardiac death, heart attack, and strokes can be related directly to the levels of stress you experience and to how your body processes these events.

Today's American health care system can be likened to 240 million people living on the edge of a cliff. Every week, thousands fall off. At the bottom is a nearly trillion-dollar team of remarkable medical specialists and state-of-the-art facilities expertly applying the latest in high tech to repair the damage. Someone like me comes along and says, "Why not build a fence?" The response: "We can't afford it; we're spending all our money down there."

This book is designed to help you build your own fence until our health care system recognizes and fulfills this need. It provides medicine before the fact, not after the fact.

The Institute of Stress Medicine is a private facility in which the services, research, and educational programs were originally developed during my academic career as Professor of Medicine at the University of Nebraska, as Director of the Cardiovascular Center, and as Chairman of the Department of Preventive and Stress Medicine. During the last 20 years, we have evaluated and treated thousands of patients, both at our clinic and through "house calls" to dozens of corporations and other organizations.

Many of my patients come to me after a stroke, heart attack, or bypass surgery. They have been brushed by death, and they are often terrified. My role is to teach these highly motivated individuals how to regain control of their lives and their health by turning stresses into strengths. If you are such a person, this book is for you.

However, I'm also concerned with a second, not-so-obvious group I've come to call the Walking Worried Well. Even if you have never been treated for heart disease or high blood pressure, you too may be a candidate for a stress-related catastrophe. On the surface your medical history may be gloriously dull reading:

- You have no previous heart condition; no family tendencies toward hypertension. You pass every physical examination with flying colors, and your blood pressure has always been well within the normal range or elevated only at times.

• You live in a stress-filled world, but then, who doesn't? You have deadlines to meet, people who need you. Sometimes you're so busy you miss lunch. Even when life's at its most hectic, you manage to maintain control—you are certainly not one of those hostile Type-A personalities.

• Nor are you obese. You may be carrying a few extra pounds, but you've been buying low-cholesterol margarine for years, and most of the time you eat chicken or fish.

• You don't smoke. You used to exercise, and you've been meaning to get back to something as soon as you get caught up.

All in all, you're doing okay.

Don't count on it.

You could drop dead today—unaware that for years you've had a time bomb strapped to your heart.

> **Often the first indication of heart disease is *sudden death*.**

AMERICA'S LEADING CAUSE OF DEATH

Sudden cardiac death (SCD) is the term describing an unexpected fatal heart attack—an abrupt end to a seemingly healthy existence. An estimated 520,000 Americans succumb to SCD every year, making it this nation's leading cause of death. In the time it took you to decide whether or not to read this book, SCD claimed another life.

> **520,000 sudden cardiac deaths per year**
> **1,425 deaths each day**
> **59 deaths per hour**
> **1 death almost every minute**

In most cases of SCD, death is the only warning signal; an autopsy, the only proof of a lifetime of damage accumulated within the heart tissue or throughout the vascular network. I have devoted thirty years of clinical and laboratory research to this mystery. My conclusion is that SCD occurs, in part, because of the way some individuals react to the rigors of daily stress. My studies revealed that when they were exposed to the standard challenges of daily activities, approximately one in every five apparently healthy individuals had surges in blood pressure to rival those expected in mortal combat.

I called these individuals *Hot Reactors*. Moreover, I was surprised to discover that their at-rest blood pressure readings (such as those taken in a physician's office) in no way reflected the remarkable degree of elevation that occurred in the "real world." Since my initial findings, experts from around the world have demonstrated that this real-world stress-induced blood pressure most accurately predicts the primary risks of high blood pressure: coronary heart disease, sudden death or heart attack, and stroke.

Importantly, however, learning methods for managing stress can help turn you from a Hot to a Cool Reactor. This is not hypothesis; it is something we can measure routinely in the laboratory or in the real world.

This conclusion was the impetus for my first book, *Is It Worth Dying For?* There I explained how the heart works and what we knew about the relationship between stress and cardiovascular malfunction. The book has reached (and, it is hoped, influenced) more than half a million readers; however, since its initial publication, we've continued testing our theories—and we have come across even more startling information. These new discoveries are the subject of *From Stress to Strength*.

WHAT WE DIDN'T KNOW TEN YEARS AGO

• Hot Reactors are more numerous than we had first suspected. One out of every five apparently healthy individuals responds to stress in this destructive manner. The ratio is even higher (greater than 50 percent) in those who already have high blood pressure.

• Women are catching up with men. As American women en-

4

deavor to fulfill so many different roles, stress has become their number-one health problem.

• Physicians are now combating the physiological effects of stress in children. One study concluded that by the age of six, many children have already laid the groundwork for severe hypertension.

• Our legal system now recognizes stress as a consequence of criminal acts, as courts have verified that a crime victim literally can be "scared to death."

• Stress causes cholesterol to rise as much or *more* than does diet.

• It is the "working," not the standardized "at rest" blood pressure, that predicts disasters. This means that the reading taken in your doctor's office often does not represent your true blood pressure and your true risk.

• Of those patients currently taking medications for hypertension, an astonishing six out of seven are taking the wrong medication or the wrong dosage, or are using the medication improperly.

• We can now verify a strong relationship between stress and increases in both immune system disorders and cancer.

• Many driven, so-called Type-A personalities are outliving seemingly calmer Type-B personalities.

• You can teach yourself to have high blood pressure. And in many cases, you can unlearn it!

• We can now predict if you are apt to develop high blood pressure long before the condition manifests itself.

• Your neighborhood community, and/or job can contribute to high blood pressure and its complications. We have found companies and organizations in which workers display three times the normal incidence of high blood pressure.

• Job status and social cohesiveness influence health and life expectancy.

• Individual metabolic fluctuations (and thus a person's ability to control weight) are greatly influenced by stress.

• Coronary obstruction can be reversed by diet, minimal exercise, and stress control.

• You can overdo physical fitness.

• Control over the most important events in your life is critical to controlling the complications of stress.

ARE YOU READY TO LIGHTEN YOUR LOAD?

Stress has been called the silent killer, attacking those who had no previous warning. That's why the Institute of Stress Medicine's program is designed to help those who think: "It'll never happen to me. It always happens to someone else." "Death is optional!" "I'm going to leave the planet alive!" or "I give stress. I don't get it!"

In fact, people with such attitudes are often the very individuals who seem to turn stress inward in a self-destructive manner.

I tell my patients to imagine stress as a heavy knapsack that has some of its compartments filled with sand. It makes your trip difficult and more burdensome than necessary, especially if you are carrying 75 or 100 pounds of the stuff. It puts tremendous strain on your heart, which often responds as if it were carrying this load physically. My work demonstrates that there are as many as 40 different compartments for the sand, but you can't tell which ones are filled when it's all in a lump on your back. The Quality of Life Index used in our program will help you find the compartments with sand, dump them, and go on your way with a much lighter load.

From Stress to Strength will show you:

- how stress may affect you
- how we can measure your physiological reactions to stress
- how you can turn harmful stress into strength

My goal is to teach you how to make the principles and practices of Stress Medicine work as well for you as they have for me and my patients.

PART I

A FENCE AT THE EDGE
OF THE CLIFF

CHAPTER 1

THE HOT REACTORS
WHO DIES FROM STRESS?

More than twenty years ago I was the typical Hot Reactor. This fact came to my attention when I eluded sudden death by surviving a heart attack. At the time my physicians and I even went so far as to label it a "totally unpredictable heart attack." Unpredictable, because I was, after all, a cardiologist—someone skilled in the detection and prevention of heart disease. I had a good family history. I didn't smoke. I had neither diabetes nor high cholesterol. I wasn't overweight; nor had I ever been told that I had high blood pressure. Many people thought I was a classic Type-B personality: calm, cool, and collected. That was on the outside. On the inside, however, my own physical reactions to stress were killing me.

Wise men speak of the moment of clarity—that instant when absolute knowledge presents itself. My moment of clarity came as I was doubled up in a bathroom at a Nebraska community hospital two hundred miles from home. Earlier that morning, after conducting grand rounds in the facility's coronary care unit, I had participated in a cardiology conference before my peers. My lecture had been on heart attacks and sudden death. I had experienced some discomfort during the program but dismissed it as indigestion—or, at worst, a bout with my gallbladder.

It had been a hectic week. The day before the conference, back at my own hospital, I had argued both vehemently and unsuccessfully with administrators over the budget, manpower, and timing regarding a planned cardiovascular center. Two days before that I had flown back from an exhausting lecture series in New Orleans—where, once again, I had been the so-called expert on sudden cardiac death.

9

In that bathroom, the first symptom I noticed was intense pressure. It began near my breastbone; shot up into my shoulders, neck, and jaws; and surged down again through both of my arms. It was as if an elephant had plopped down on my chest. I could barely catch my breath. I started sweating. I began getting bowel cramps and then overwhelming nausea. Immediately I diagnosed my own condition: myocardial infarction. Later, as the nurses helped me into a hospital bed, I remember saying with astonishment, "I'm having a heart attack." I was forty-four years old.

During my recovery I realized my professional life had become a joyless treadmill. I had worked tirelessly for acceptance within the medical community and yet efforts to establish my own cardiovascular center had failed. This was a bitter pill for someone who had always defined life in terms of victory or defeat. My disillusionment was compounded by the knowledge that I had brought promising associates into this seemingly futile situation. I've since described my state of mind as *invisible entrapment*.

I didn't like being on the wrong side of the sheets in a coronary care unit. Something had to change; and I asked myself, "Is any of this worth dying for?" Fortunately for me, my answer was "No!" I had looked into the abyss and decided to stop sweating the small stuff. Pretty soon, I saw that it was *all* small stuff.

> **I had discovered for myself that it's not *what* you do, but *how* you do it that matters.**

The irony of my own self-induced heart attack had an even greater twist because earlier in my career, I'd been a part of the pioneering research that now defines the physiology of stress.

SUDDEN DEATH AT NASA

In 1968, I was asked to be a cardiovascular consultant to the National Aeronautics and Space Administration's installation at Cape Canaveral.

To be blunt, NASA had discovered a fatal side effect to the space program—strong, healthy aerospace engineers and scientists, most between the ages of twenty-eight and thirty-five, were dropping dead—for no apparent reason. My task was to investigate the puzzling rise in the numbers of people suffering SCD (sudden cardiac death) at the Space Center.

An examination of the medical histories of the NASA workers revealed only a normal incidence of traditional risk factors: family history of heart disease, chronic high blood pressure, high cholesterol, diabetes, obesity, or smoking—nothing to explain why the rate of SCD was so high.

Surprised by this finding, I began by analyzing autopsies of the former space workers. Even though their coronary arteries were rarely blocked, mysterious microscopic lesions appeared in the fibers of the heart muscles themselves. I wondered if these lesions could have led to electrical short circuits and fatal heart rhythms. Years later, in my laboratory at the University of Nebraska, my theories were confirmed when I discovered that large doses of adrenalinelike chemicals normally released during stressful situations could produce these lesions (now labeled *contraction band lesions*).

As I broadened my search for risk factors, I discovered that environmental instability was the only factor all the workers had in common. During the height of the space program, Cape Canaveral families led the nation in drinking, drug addiction, and divorce. But further analysis showed that for most of the SCD victims, the greatest source of instability came from the work site.

At this time, the customary procedure at NASA was to reduce staff drastically as soon as a rocket program was completed. Typically, 15 percent of those specialized aerospace workers who had made the launch possible were laid off. The technical expertise these engineers possessed was of no value outside the space program; and so in order to feed their families, they were forced either to move from the area or to accept substantially lower-paying jobs. In field investigations, I found astrophysicists and jet propulsion experts taking tickets at Disney World, delivering newspapers, repairing television sets, and pumping gas while hoping to catch a ride on the next space program. This sense of impending personal catastrophe, coupled with the rigors of the work itself, meant that these engineers and scientists were

11

living in a work environment characterized by a loss of control. Anxiety, depression, anger, and a sense of helplessness were their daily companions. Both laid-off workers *and* the managers who had to do the firing were dying. Our conclusion was that they were dying from stress.

ISN'T STRESS PART OF A NORMAL LIFE?

Physical and biochemical reactions to stress are an essential part of surviving life challenges. I'll describe these reactions in more detail in Chapter 2. To understand Hot Reacting, you need to know only the two major ways the body responds to stress.

First, there is the *acute alarm reaction* in which your body prepares for fight or flight. This is a time of emergency. Your heart pumps blood faster and with greater force; your blood pressure elevates abruptly; and your lungs respond by delivering more oxygen to muscle tissue. Simultaneously your brain writes a prescription for powerful adrenalinelike chemicals called *catecholamines,* so that you have the option of confronting the danger or getting the heck out of there. Whether grappling for food on the savannah or avoiding an oncoming freight train, this ability to fight or flee for life has been a pillar of our survival as a species. In modern life, it has been credited with everything from propelling an athlete through the Olympic high jump to enabling a department manager to address the corporate board.

The second response to stress is *chronic vigilance,* in which the body prepares for long-term challenge. Among our early ancestors, this was most often the response to climatic catastrophe, the depletion of vital resources, or any type of long-term struggle or displacement. Vigilance is the biologic response to a loss of control; and in our modern societies, it is this kind of *sustained* vigilance that can have the most destructive consequences.

Tokyo: The Ministry of Health has identified *karoshi* as the second leading cause of death in Japan.

Officially defined as a fatal mix of apoplexy, high blood pressure, and stress, *karoshi* strikes primarily middle managers in their forties and fifties who are characterized as being *moretsu sha-in* (fanatical workers) and *yoi kigyo senshi* (good corporate soldiers).[1]

During vigilance your brain prescribes another powerful chemical called *cortisol*. In response, your blood pressure rises slowly and steadily; you begin to retain vital chemicals, such as sodium; metabolism drops and gastric acid increases to maximize the calories you get from food; high-energy fats and blood clotting agents are released into your bloodstream—just in case they might be needed; energy is diverted from your immune system; and "nonessentials," such as the sex hormones, are dramatically suppressed. Your body is prepared for the long haul.

For most of us, real physical danger or real environmental deprivation are rare events. Nevertheless, Hot Reactors encode *every* stress as if it were a saber-toothed tiger or a threat of starvation. Daily challenges—the completion of a work assignment, friendly competition in leisure activities, a disagreement with a neighbor, dealing with the kids, child rearing, or caring for aging parents—trigger astronomical blood pressure levels.

HOW DO WE DETECT HOT REACTORS?

Hot Reactors are those individuals who exhibit extreme cardiovascular arousal in response to standardized stress tests. Specifically, in Hot Reactors these tests evoke dramatic and rapid increases in blood pressure (the force with which blood pushes against the walls of the blood vessels). As the heart beats and pumps blood into your arteries, the pressure rises to a peak; this peak is called the *systolic* pressure. As the heart relaxes between beats, the pressure falls to its lowest point, or the *diastolic* pressure.

> **Most of the time blood pressure is being monitored the same way it was one hundred years ago. What else in medicine has been so stagnant?**

To help illustrate how blood pressure can become elevated, think of your cardiovascular system as a garden hose in which water pressure may be increased in one of three ways:

1. by opening the faucet and increasing the flow
2. by restricting the flow with a nozzle or a clamp
3. by a combination of the first two methods

The open faucet is a metaphor for what can happen when the heart pumps too much blood through the system. Medically, the amount pumped is called the *cardiac output*. The second metaphor illustrates the kind of pressure resulting when blood vessels become clamped down. Medically, this constriction results in elevated *total systemic resistance*. Like the pressure in a garden hose, blood pressure also can increase because of a combination of both processes.

Stress can cause all three increases; and whether you're talking about water in a hose, or blood in your body, too much pressure will tax the system—weakening or even rupturing the pipes, while also putting an unhealthy strain on the pump.

After working with over 11,000 subjects in the past decade, my associates and I have made some surprising discoveries about Hot Reactors.

Of those apparently healthy subjects tested, one in five was found to be a Hot Reactor. It's important to note that this was regardless of how an individual may have previously reacted to standard at-rest blood pressure readings. Hot Reacting is determined by the degree to which a person's physiology is aroused by stress tests that reflect the challenges you face in the real world.

For Hot Reactors, stress doesn't have to be earth-shattering. I discussed earlier how a surge in catecholamines can produce lesions within the muscle fiber of the heart itself. These chemicals can destroy thousands of heart muscle cells within minutes, and catecholamine lesions are found in 86 percent of autopsies following sudden cardiac death. Some have called catecholamines the *cardiac knockout punch*.

Squandering doses of these powerful substances on mundane episodes such as missing a green light, standing in a grocery line, or running out of dental floss is a symptom in the pathology of the Hot Reactor.

> **These walking time bombs burn a dollar's worth of energy for a dime's worth of trouble.**

Hot Reactors are often cool on the outside. In 1974 Drs. Meyer Friedman and Ray Rosenman published *Type A Behavior and Your Heart* and thus proposed the link between heart disease and the way an individual responds to life.[2] They defined the Type-A and Type-B personalities with a series of observable traits. Type-A's were said to exhibit both verbal and nonverbal impatience and hostility, including fidgeting, eye-blinking, interrupting, sitting on the edge of their chairs, finger-tapping, grimacing, or filling in during pauses in a conversation. The Type-B personality, on the other hand, displayed a much different behavior pattern: appearing to be more relaxed, listening more intently, rarely if ever interrupting, and so on.

Friedman and Rosenman found that 15 percent of Type-A's had heart attacks while 7 percent of Type-B's suffered the same fate. Subsequent research reaffirmed these general ratios, and in 1980 a panel convened by the National Institutes of Health concluded that Type-A behavior is a risk factor in coronary heart disease.

However, a risk factor merely denotes general patterns seen in large population groups. It cannot tell us if an individual person is or is not likely to develop pathology. Being classified as a Type-A personality is not a death sentence. Indeed, follow-up of the original study reveals that many cantankerous old Type-A's fidget through the funerals of their younger Type-B friends and relatives.

It has been my experience that personality traits do not correlate significantly with Hot Reacting. Hot Reactors may be hard-driving Type-A personalities, or they may be more placid Type-B's. In fact, some of the *Hottest* Reactors have been as cool as cucumbers on the surface and as hot as chili peppers underneath. One explanation may be that placid-appearing individuals are often unassertive and possibly afraid to say what they really think. Such individuals essentially function as human pressure cookers with stuck safety valves; and they literally stew in their own juices—the internal chemicals they produce in response to stress. While they may *appear* calm, Type-B personalities often have difficulty surviving rush-hour traffic in Manhattan or confronting a boisterous Type-A who pushes ahead in a supermarket line. Conversely, the angry or aggressive behavior exhibited by a Type-A individual might be either an *appropriate* response (specifically, when survival is a consideration) or of little physiological harm to him- or herself. And so we often find that as they go about life annoying everyone else, Cool-Reactor Type-A personalities may be causing themselves no great physical distress. They can be like cars without mufflers. Noisy and unpleasant to others, but as long as the drivers obey the traffic laws and keep from riding the brake, they'll get to where they're going with little damage. Meanwhile, their Hot-Reactor Type-B companions may be dying as they calmly burn rubber at every intersection.

For Hot Reactors, perceived control over their environment is a major life and health issue. Psychiatrists have long accepted that when people feel in control of their own future, they are more likely to be psychologically healthy. In our study of the young aerospace workers at Cape Canaveral, we learned that there is also a vital mind/body connection that can sometimes produce fatal *physical* consequences. Many other studies have since confirmed that men and women who have experienced severe loss of control over their personal and professional futures are at high risk for illness. Hot Reactors are particularly prone to perceive any gap between their expectations and reality as a personal defeat, a threat to their identity and self-esteem.

We have nicknamed this crucial form of stress the FUD factor—short for Fear, Uncertainty, and Doubt. One of our primary interventions with Hot Reactors is helping to reduce the FUD factor in their lives.

Physical fitness does not automatically protect against Hot Reacting. One surprise that resulted from our clinical research was that fitness and health are clearly *not* the same thing. A physically fit person—one with a strong musculature, good lung capacity, and stamina—can also overreact dramatically to uncontrolled mental stress.

Physical fitness does not guarantee mental fitness; just the opposite is true. In fact, one of the hottest of Hot Reactors ever to come through our clinic was the fitness director for a renowned health spa.

When it comes to heart disease and Hot Reacting, women are catching up with men. Heart disease has become the number-one killer of women in the United States. Out of 520,000 deaths from heart attack each year, 257,000 are women. Strokes kill 90,000 women a year. In contrast, approximately 44,000 women die each year from lung cancer and 42,000 die annually from breast cancer. In women, the total number of deaths from all combinations of heart and blood vessel disease is nearly 500,000, while the combined deaths from all forms of cancer number 220,000.[3]

Ten years ago our Hot Reactor clinical testing showed a 40 percent lower incidence of Hot Reacting in women. Today women who are screened have caught up with men, with one out of five also showing up as a Hot Reactor. We also have seen an alarming increase in lifestyle habits such as smoking, excessive drinking, and compulsive overeating accompanying the Hot Reactor status.

Sudden cardiac death is not the only risk for the Hot Reactor. Hot Reacting to stress is often associated with a separate phenomenon called *chronic hypertension,* which is fixed high blood pressure at rest. Because of the inaccuracy of primary measurement techniques, Hot Reacting and chronic hypertension are easily and often clinically confused. However, they are not the same.

The causes of chronic hypertension are many—genetic predisposition, too much body weight, and too much salt in the diet, to name a few. Some Hot Reactors never develop this condition. However, our research is leading us to conclude that for many Hot Reactors, repeated surges in blood pressure under stress precede fixed high

17

blood pressure. The body's natural tendency toward adaptation probably causes this chronic hypertension to occur. In other words, the body tends to adjust upward and thus tolerate higher and higher resting levels of blood pressure. In this frightening cycle, Hot Reactors' blood pressure may rise thirty or forty times a day, thus boosting the body's tolerance higher and higher for longer periods of time. The higher the pressure goes—without causing a cardiac arrest or stroke—the more the body will adapt and the greater the risk of eventual overload to the system. Their bodies literally teach themselves to become hypertensives.

In addition to increased blood pressure, Hot Reactors also evoke dangerous chemical changes within their bodies that can increase the chance of chaotic heart rhythms. Destructive reactions to stress also can trigger other far-reaching calamities, such as stroke and debilitating heart disease.

TEN POSSIBLE COMPLICATIONS OF HOT REACTING

1. Permanent high blood pressure
2. Damaged blood vessel linings
3. Atherosclerosis
4. Accelerated blood clotting
5. Ruptured heart muscle fibers (contraction band lesions)
6. Heart rhythm disturbances
7. Kidney and heart failure
8. Heart attack
9. Stroke
10. Sudden death

FINDING DISORDERS BEFORE THEY BECOME DISASTERS

After my own heart attack, I developed a personal connection with those aerospace workers I had first identified as Hot Reactors; and for twenty years, while on faculty at the universities of Minnesota, Florida, and Nebraska, I participated in developing the interdisciplinary approach now known as Stress Medicine. During that time, all of my efforts were directed toward teaching and research.

It is important that you not confuse Stress Medicine with the superficial, unsubstantiated theories of stress management that are now rampant in our society. Such simplistic schemes are often a single idea pushed to its extreme by a single individual. I've learned that because stress and our physiological reactions to it are so complex, simple solutions rarely work. Instead, the practitioners of Stress Medicine approach the problem of stress from a medical viewpoint—physical, psychological, nutritional, and behavioral.

This interdisciplinary solution is at the heart of my organization, the Institute of Stress Medicine (ISM). At ISM, we have quantified the significant physical impact that lifestyle behavior—and, in particular, excessive stress—can have on the human body.

We have developed a portable program that analyzes both psysiological dangers and self-destructive attitudes, behaviors, and life situations; and we use these data to reach those individuals who are now charging through life, completely unaware of the time bombs ticking away inside their chests. Our patients include corporate leaders, engineers, physicians, educators, football players and coaches, media celebrities, homemakers, politicians, sales professionals, law enforcement agents, airline pilots, billionaires, firefighters, government officials, future and current admirals and generals, as well as many others. In a nutshell, we see everybody. In twenty years, three hundred peer review papers and five medical textbooks have confirmed our clinical results.

> **We now know that often we can *teach* rather than *treat*. Nobody ever told me that in medical school!**

Our comprehensive program evaluates individuals in three steps:

1. *We screen individuals by means of noninvasive technology.*
   As I explained earlier, blood pressure can be elevated by increased cardiac output (such as the water flow at a faucet), total

systemic resistance (such as a nozzle or clamp on a hose), or both. Determining *which* of these three mechanisms actually caused the elevation in blood pressure has traditionally been a painful, costly, and risky procedure that required invasive techniques, such as the placement of tubes (catheters) in various chambers of the heart and major blood vessels.

Our sophisticated diagnostic measures are noninvasive. This means no needles, no catheters, no pain, and no radiation. The screening system simulates daily stress while recording heart rate and blood pressure response. When we find a Hot Reactor or a hypertensive, we electronically monitor blood pressure, cardiac output, and total systemic resistance during standardized physical and mental challenges. Specialized computer software instantaneously analyzes the data. When tested against invasive measurements, this system provides an accuracy rate of 90 percent.

Aside from being informative and individualized, our information is provided at a very low cost.

2. *We stratify the risk.*

As Johnny Carson used to say, "How hot was it?" We make such determinations. We do this not with the typical five-minute medical history but with an intense physical, psychological, nutritional, and behavioral analysis. Essential to that process is our 40-item Quality of Life Index, which identifies your particular stresses and strengths. You will begin by examining your gut-level reactions to queries about your daily life, and you will progress to identify the areas that most need improvement. Finally, you will be taught how best to focus wasted energies and thus turn stress *into* strength.

3. *We prioritize intervention.*

Steps 1 and 2 provide us with a means for identifying a Hot Reactor. We then teach such an individual how to make immediate, manageable, long-term lifestyle changes and which should be addressed first. If you have a history of stress-related pathology (cardiovascular or otherwise), this phase of our program can help you prevent your disorder from progressing further.

Risk-reduction is extremely difficult for a person with serious heart disease; we sometimes refer patients for immediate medical treatment. Conversely, not everyone with blocked coronary vessels needs open heart surgery. And even more options are open to those whose disorders have not yet reached disaster level. In the last twenty years we have learned how to identify those with a potential for cardiac disaster and how to teach them the ways to control the destructive factors in their lives.

Prioritizing intervention also means identifying those things people are *most likely* to do for their own health. The world's best prevention techniques mean nothing if a person won't take time to integrate them into his or her life. It is not the quick fix but the enduring change that we seek.

CHAPTER 2

THE KILLER WITHIN

HOW YOUR BODY RESPONDS TO STRESS

For our ancient ancestors, survival depended on two key biological reactions to stress. As I outlined in Chapter 1, the first was an *alarm reaction,* a short-term fight-or-flight response that prepared them for all-out, often mortal struggle with fellow human beings, predatory animals, or extreme physical danger. The second was called the *vigilance reaction,* and it involved the ability to deal with prolonged stress.

> **Today we are living in the bodies of our ancestors in a world they never dreamed would exist. We inherited the adaptive responses that enabled them to survive attacks of wild beasts, weather extremes, food deprivation, and environmental catastrophes.**

THE ALARM REACTION

The alarm reaction begins deep within the hypothalamic region of your brain when perception of imminent danger triggers the body into action. The message then travels along the sympathetic nervous system to the inner part (medulla) of the small adrenal glands—perhaps better called the survival glands—located on top of each kidney. Upon receiving the alarm message, the adrenal glands immediately release into the bloodstream a family of hormones called the *catecholamines.* Among these powerful stimulants are adrenaline and its

22

chemical cousin, noradrenaline. Adrenaline levels are at their highest at the initial perception of danger—when you become anxious or when you need to call up additional physical energy for some sudden or strenuous physical activity. By contrast, noradrenaline is released later, during the stressful event that follows—as your emotions progress from initial fear to anger or the impulse to fight.

Both of these powerful hormones act immediately and simultaneously with other physiologic reactions to create the complex network of survival. Some of the more important reactions are:

- surges in heart rate that increase the heart's pumping ability, thus delivering additional power and blood volume at a moment's notice
- elevated blood sugar levels that supply instant muscle energy in times of emergency
- diversion of blood from the digestive organs to the skeletal muscles, allowing for a quick getaway or knockout blow
- faster blood clotting, to reduce the likelihood of bleeding to death from wounds
- the widening of the eye's pupil, so as to admit more light and thus heighten visual acuity and awareness
- increased breathing rate, so that more oxygen is available to the body's vital organs

In addition to the catecholamines, the alarm reaction also stimulates production of other substances such as endorphins, which decrease the body's sensitivity to pain; and hormones, which can increase both visual and auditory acuity.

During the alarm reaction, the body is preparing for an anticipated physical challenge. In order to do this, it conserves its resources for any eventuality. This state of readiness means neglect of other bodily functions, such as upkeep and repair. If you live in a prolonged state of alarm, you will become vulnerable in areas where you have previously sustained an injury (perhaps in your heart or blood vessels), or where you have a constitutionally inherited weakness. This is similar to what happens to the fighter who, after being weakened by six rounds of pounding punches, suddenly collapses under a comparatively minor blow. A chill from a rainstorm may escalate into pneumonia. An argument may result in a heart attack.

The survival hormones themselves also carry the potential for destruction. For example, in a rare medical condition known as *pheochromocytoma,* a tumor of the adrenal medulla produces excessive amounts of catecholamines, which can result in death due to blood pressure surges, stroke, or heart attack. My own research, described later in this chapter, documents a direct link between stress-induced catecholamines and fatal heart damage. Catecholamines can save our lives in the short run, and kill us in the long run.

THE VIGILANCE REACTION

The vigilance reaction is activated by the perception of an impending and/or long-term, persistent danger. In the bodies of our ancestors, vigilance provided the staying power necessary to exist on marginal food, salt, and water supplies during both frigid winters and summer droughts. The brain prescriptions for this response come mainly from the pituitary (or "master") gland, which is located at the base of the brain. In turn, this gland stimulates the outside (cortex) of the adrenal glands to release cortisol into the bloodstream. Like constant low-voltage electricity, cortisol works slowly and steadily to cause a series of physical changes that include:

- irritability and hyperalertness
- fat storage for both insulation and energy reserves
- salt retention
- blood pressure elevation
- loss of essential minerals such as potassium and magnesium
- erratic heart rhythms
- increased fats and cholesterol in the bloodstream
- suppression of the sex hormones
- increased gastric acid

In the cardiovascular system, cortisol increases the tendency of small "controller" blood vessels (arterioles) to overcontract. During periods of sudden or maximal physical activity, contraction of these

24

small blood vessels protects your skeletal muscles from hemorrhage and subsequent flooding of blood. Cortisol also increases the number of blood-clotting elements (platelets), and it slows the heartbeat. The result of these actions is to increase the efficiencies of those systems that can absorb and utilize energy—thus your body prepares for the long haul. In addition, cortisol initially stimulates and then chronically depresses the immune system by the way in which it reduces the effectiveness of the white blood cells (lymphocytes) and other immune phenomena.

The physical effects of vigilance have been chronicled by many physicians, including Brendan P. Phibbs, who wrote of his experiences as a front-line military surgeon in an excellent book called *The Other Side of Time*.[1] Phibbs observed that when troops engaged in battle were warned about drinking from streams and eating contaminated food, the soldiers simply laughed off the advice and went about their rigorous deadly tasks. Sick call was a breeze. Within two days after peace was declared, Phibbs recorded that 50 percent of his troops had developed infectious diseases. As long as vigilance had been directed toward perceived control and victory, the soldiers' immune systems seemed to be enhanced. When the challenge disappeared, overstimulation of the body's natural resistance ceased.

Other rare physical conditions also illustrate the effects of excessive cortisol on the body and help us understand how long-term doses of this hormone can affect otherwise healthy human beings. For example, Cushing's syndrome is an extreme condition resulting when a tumor of the adrenal cortex causes chronic overproduction of cortisol. The three major complications and eventual causes of death in individuals suffering from this condition are atherosclerosis, high blood pressure, and suicide.

SURVIVAL REACTIONS IN MODERN BODIES

The alarm and vigilance reactions provoked profound adaptations in our ancient metabolism and physiology; and for those of our ancestors who survived the rigors of their environment, these adaptations

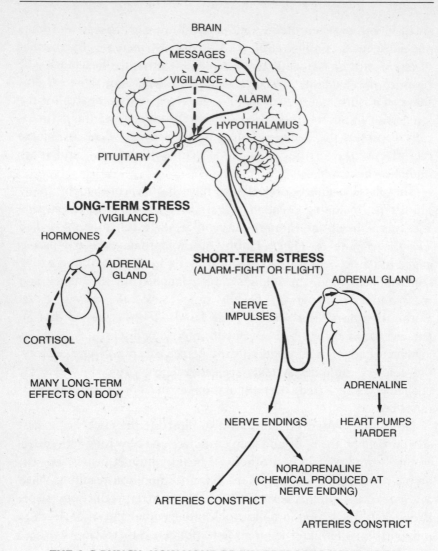

THE 1–2 PUNCH: HOW YOUR BRAIN PREPARES YOUR BODY FOR STRESS

became a part of their automatic bodily functions. We exist as present-day benefactors of that selective process.

Today, however, our bodies use these essential physiological tools—once required for fight, flight, or endurance—differently. Ordinarily, the threats we face from nature are infrequent and brief. Even those requiring vigilance usually have a foreseeable time limit.

26

Certainly, in some circumstances, modern men and women do use the powerful hormones (collectively called *neuropeptides*) as our ancient forefathers did—although today it might more often be dodging an oncoming car than fleeing an attack by wild animals. However, most of us live our entire lives never facing a charging tiger or even a rabid dog.

We live in bodies designed to respond to physical stress; and yet our present-day challenges generally involve the emotional and abstract mental conflicts arising from professional competition, bureaucratic hassles, interpersonal discord, financial insecurities, deadlines, and demanding telephones. You may disagree with your boss, but you probably won't wrestle him or her to the ground. Nevertheless, just thinking about the problem may invisibly evoke the ancestral physiology of all-out, mortal combat.

> **For Hot Reactors, the alarm reaction triggers a bigger bang for their catecholamine bucks. Instead of a nudge, they get a shove. Instead of a firecracker, they get a bomb.**

Our physical problems begin when we use our natural survival mechanisms as an overresponse to circumstances that are not really life-threatening. As a result, more than one out of five of us are now using catecholamines and cortisol to hamper rather than to insure survival. If you put your body on live-or-die alert thirty times a day when the only predator you face is an offensive neighbor or a missed deadline, you are carrying many times the load of stress that our ancestors did. If your hormones have organized your body for a winter on the tundra, or if you are reacting with ferocity as you merely remove the crabgrass from your front lawn, you are overusing your body's physiological resources. Your alarm and vigilance defense systems are probably becoming overloaded and confused. Speaking metaphorically, your body finally rebels against being uselessly switched on and off by remaining stuck in the *on* position. Your brain writes hormonal prescriptions that are archaic—perfect for situations of real physical stress, but noxious and perilous when summoned inappropriately.

ALARM AND VIGILANCE IN THE LABORATORY

Laboratory animals provide an invaluable tool in the search for knowledge about the human condition. We know through observation and study of other creatures how the stress hormones work both in their bodies and in our own.

For example, we have learned that entrapped animals that repeatedly trigger their alarm reactions—and that have no means to either fight or flee—will develop extreme metabolic and physiological changes. These changes invariably place the animals on a self-destructive, downward spiral. Sometimes the stress will lower the animals' resistance, making them susceptible to many infectious diseases and cancer. Sometimes, within days or weeks of having been entrapped, animals simply roll over and die. The cause of death is usually high blood pressure and its associated complications of stroke, heart attack, kidney failure, and sudden death.

Most research into hypertension involves the Spontaneous Hypertensive Rat (SHR), an animal bred by consistently exposing three or four generations to long-term, inescapable stress. However, a limited number of significant studies have involved other species. One such experiment was conducted in the Soviet Union and used the hamadryas baboon, a generally monogamous species that mates for life. The researchers used this characteristic as a catalyst for extreme stress by separating mated pairs of baboons and placing them in adjacent cages. Then in full view of the original male, the female was introduced to a new mate. Immobilized behind bars, the ostracized males were prevented from exercising their instincts to intervene. Within six to twelve months, all displaced male baboons became ill or died from complications involving high blood pressure and heart attacks.[2]

Other scientists utilized a similar predicament to illustrate the destructive potential of vigilance. For this experiment, they selected tree shrews, a primate species in which males defend territory from one another in an aggressive fight to the death. After placing pairs of male tree shrews together in a cage, experimenters halted the resultant combat as soon as one shrew had established dominance over the other. The animals were then placed into adjacent cages where a transparent screen prevented physical contact but allowed the animals to see and smell one another. On one side was the dominant animal and on the other was the submissive animal. Most interesting to the researchers was the physiological reaction of the submissive shrews. With tail hairs held rigidly erect, these animals constantly watched their former conquerors. After a week or two of such unremitting tension, the subordinate shrews invariably died. As with the hamadryas baboons, death was from complications of high blood pressure.[3]

CARDIOVASCULAR DAMAGE—THE MOST COMMON PHYSICAL RESULT OF STRESS

Stress is like electricity entering a fuse box. Too many appliances, too much overload, and the fuse blows. Physiologically, this can mean an "overheating" and resultant breakdown of the body's weakest system. In our society, the heart and blood vessels are the systems most often attacked and weakened.

Constant unresolved distress occurs when you perceive one anxiety-producing situation after another. As a result, your body deteriorates under the strain. While our ancestors most certainly experienced fear, uncertainty, and doubt, their anxieties were of a different kind. Anthropologists tell us that conflict with a tiger or other predator happened only occasionally. As I implied earlier, today's tigers are paper ones; and they are more numerous. Our encounters come in the form of reports, speeding tickets, deadlines, divorce decrees, and other life-diminishing or frustrating situations. More events are packed into shorter time periods; and unlike what occurred among our ancestors, there is no rest between such assaults. The commonest phrase I hear in today's corporate corridors is "I have to work twice as hard just to stay even." Physiologically our alarm reactions are brought into operation and given little or no time to cool off before the next alarming incident.

This constant turning on of the alarm reaction sets in motion the pile-driving, punishing surges of blood pressure that silently cause so much damage. Specifically, these surges pummel and progressively weaken the delicate, protective inner linings of the arteries (the endothelium).

When damage to the endothelium occurs and the lining is roughened, fats are deposited within the arteries. This narrows the lumen (inside space) of the blood vessels. Gradually the accumulated deposits slow blood circulation to a sluggish flow, setting up the high probability of future blood clot formation.

The likelihood of this happening is high because, under the influence of stress chemicals, platelets (clotting elements in the blood) collect against the roughened tissue edge inside the arteries. In their efforts to heal, these platelets cannot tell if the damaged area leads to the outside of the body or not. They cannot determine if a potentially dangerous hemorrhage has occurred, or if the rough spot is an internal problem better left alone. They have just one function—to form a clot.

It's like a David and Goliath story. Little David is the endothelium. Goliath is the surges of blood pressure and the substances in the bloodstream that the endothelium has to fight off. Stress ties David's arms behind his back.

Once platelets are mobilized to the damaged endothelium, a "healing process" begins that permits the invasion of fatty material. As these fatty plaques are deposited at the injury site, the vessels become rigid and inflexible. Consecutive layers are added over time, due to fatty meals and stress. Current theories suggest that another mechanism for blockage occurs as the artery loses its elastic flexibility at those spots. Hemorrhage can result under this plaque because of its rigidity compared to the elasticity of the normal adjacent arterial wall. The wall then distends to variable degrees like a weakened inner tube or a ballooning hose.

The rest is a predictable chain of events.

• Surges in blood pressure cause distentions that can distort and rip the inflexible border on the underside of the plaque.

• The underside levels contain tiny nutrient blood vessels; and when these arteries are ripped, they bleed into the softer, surrounding tissues below the plaque, thus dislodging it.

• Once dislodged, the rigid, fatty plaque is extruded into the arterial lumen, causing instantaneous obstruction in a previously narrowed but still open pathway.

• Finally, under command signals from the brain, the remaining flexible sections of the arterial wall may constrict, thus further precipitating the occlusion (blockage) of a sizable length of the artery itself.

Such catastrophes are among the greatest potential dangers for the Hot Reactor.

The typical heart attack, or *coagulation necrosis* (*necrosis* means death; *coagulation* refers to oxygen deprivation) occurs when the heart muscle is literally starved of oxygen. This type of heart attack occurs when the coronary arteries become blocked by any of the previously described mechanisms. If the artery is merely narrowed, stress and exertion may cause transient lack of oxygen to heart muscle causing chest pain without a full-blown heart attack. Such pain is called *angina pectoris.*

The important point for you to remember is: *Emotional stress can and does trigger this sequence of events.*

ANOTHER KIND OF HEART ATTACK

For the pathologist, evidence of coagulation necrosis, the typical heart attack, is confirmed when specific types of inflammation and white blood cells are found in the heart muscle tissue. By contrast, heart attacks brought on by contraction band lesions (the fibers that caused most of the sudden deaths at Cape Canaveral) leave an entirely different physical trail of evidence.

If the brain prescribes excess catecholamines, these powerful stress chemicals can produce lesions in many of the tiny muscle fibers that cause the main pumping chambers of the heart to overcontract. Within minutes (time and intensity vary with each individual case),

31

the damaged muscle fibers respond with millions of microscopic electrical short circuits, which then travel chaotically throughout the entire heart.

You can think of this as a brownout in the nervous system governing the heartbeat. The result is very often an "electrical storm" (*ventricular fibrillation*), in which the heart, instead of beating firmly at normal intervals and pumping its blood effectively, quivers and flails uselessly. It then resembles a writhing bag of worms. Pumping action falters and fails.

Without treatment (in the form of massage, electrical shock, or a rhythm-controlling injection), ventricular fibrillation usually results in sudden death. The link between ventricular fibrillation, sudden death, and contraction band lesions is a strong one. In fact, the hearts of 86 percent of the victims of SCD show extensive evidence of these contraction band lesions.

As I frequently explain at medical meetings, Professor Giorgio Baroldi of Milan reported this 86 percent figure after he had studied the hearts of 208 consecutive victims of sudden death. In each case, death had been witnessed by a competent observer; however, due to some extenuating circumstance, such as the remoteness of the victim's location, no cardiopulmonary resuscitation (CPR) attempts could be made.[4]

This fact is important, because mechanical heart compression from CPR was once thought to be a possible postmortem cause of the lesions.

Not only did Baroldi prove that CPR did not cause contraction band lesions, but further microscopic studies also demonstrated that even if someone with the lesions survives for twenty-four hours after collapse and resuscitation, the heart muscle has already been so damaged that it literally will begin to dissolve and disappear.

It also has been found that if someone with contraction band lesions dies seventy-two hours after collapse and resuscitation, some heart muscle sheaths will be entirely empty. Upon observing this condition, earlier pathologists called it *fallout necrosis*. To them, it looked as if the heart muscle fibers had literally fallen out of their sheaths; and again, this is quite different from the typical postmortem findings of heart attack due to oxygen deprivation.

Finally, if a person with contraction band lesions survives for ten days after collapse and resuscitation, only patchy areas of fibrosis (scarring) will appear interspersed among normal heart muscle fibers; no evidence of either inflammation or coagulation necrosis will be found. At this stage, the findings resemble the dilemma often faced by a forest ranger examining acres of ashes and burned-out tree stumps. Whether caused by a cigarette, lightning, or a careless camper, the end result of a forest fire looks the same.

In time the patchy areas of heart fibrosis may become so extensive that the heart beats in an abnormal (dyskinetic) fashion. That is to say, its normal regular pumping becomes a series of irregular, ineffective, wiggly, uncoordinated pulsations. Physicians refer to such conditions as *cardiomyopathies* (diseases that alter the muscle of the heart). Again, because the last stages of many heart disease processes look like cardiomyopathies, the initiating cause remains a mystery.[5]

THE FINAL PIECE OF THE PUZZLE

In 1983, sixteen years after confronting the damage done by contraction band lesions at Cape Canaveral, my colleagues and I were able to confirm their cause. More important, we determined that these ruptures in the heart muscle were preventable!

We began our experiments at the University of Nebraska in the College of Medicine's Cardiovascular Center. Under my direction were Drs. Gordon Todd, Jimmy Salhany, and Galen Pieper, assisted by Frank Clayton and several others. Later Dr. Baroldi reviewed and confirmed the pathological changes we were to observe.

The anecdotal evidence we had gathered at NASA and the implications of Dr. Baroldi's work had suggested to us that the alarm reaction was somehow involved; but we needed documentation that an overdose of powerful survival chemicals could actually *produce* contraction band lesions. Our tests involved administering increasing doses of catecholamines to anesthetized animals and then examining the condition of their heart muscle tissues. We confirmed that the number of contraction band lesions did increase proportionately with the amount of catecholamines administered. We were amazed that the destruction took less than five minutes, whereas it takes more than six hours in heart attacks caused by coronary blockage.

We then hypothesized that if we could block the development of

33

contraction band lesions, we could stop the onset of fatal heart rhythms. And so we decided to pretreat the next group of animals with beta blockers or calcium channel blockers. (These two drugs block or blunt the effects of catecholamines and are routinely administered to patients with various types of hypertension and coronary heart disease.)

Our hunch was correct. The treatment worked, greatly reducing contraction band lesions and their complications and thus preventing the potentially fatal heart rhythms.

We were in for an even greater surprise. Later experiments revealed that contraction band lesions occurred in the presence of a full oxygen supply to the heart muscle. To construct this experiment, we isolated hearts and mechanically maintained them with all the needed oxygen, fluids, and nutrients. As observed in the intact animals, contraction band lesions still occurred when catecholamines were introduced. Remarkably, the heart muscle was dying in the presence of plenty of oxygen. *This was different from anything we had ever seen before.*

Our final verification came when we tied off the coronary arteries of laboratory animals, thus producing an oxygen-deprived situation (*ischemia*) in a technique known to produce a "typical" heart attack. Throughout the resulting coagulation necrosis, the heart muscle was free from contraction band lesions. We had confirmed that heart attacks due to coronary blockage and those due to catecholamines were completely different in cause and postmortem appearance.

All of these findings lead us to an inescapable conclusion: Surges of catecholamines can quickly overwhelm the heart, thus causing it to overcontract. Therefore, our ancestral, life-saving chemicals, when overused, can lose their beneficial effects and become toxic or even fatal.

YOU MAY *DIE* WITHIN *FIVE* MINUTES AFTER A CATECHOLAMINE OVERDOSE

The facts are pure and simple.

Within five minutes after excessive catecholamines are produced in your body, contraction band lesions may form. Four hours later the muscle fibers in your heart will actually begin to dissolve. Gradually your body will begin replacing healthy heart muscle with patchy areas of scar tissue. If you survive and continue Hot Reacting, catecholamines will intermittently take tiny "bites" out of the muscle as your heart steadily weakens. Over time (a matter of days or years), it will beat in an ineffective fashion; and it will become progressively more vulnerable to potentially fatal heart rhythms and heart failure.

CONTRACTION BAND LESIONS MAKE LEGAL HISTORY

In 1985 the prosecuting attorney for the state of Maryland called me with the following question: "Can a piece of paper and a paper bag be instruments of death—even when there has been no weapon or physical violence?"

He went on to relate the story of Mrs. Perle Pizzamiglia, a sixty-year-old desk clerk at a motel in Chevy Chase, Maryland. One night, shortly after she had come on duty, two men came into the motel lobby. One remained at the front door, while the second approached Mrs. Pizzamiglia with a piece of paper and a paper bag. With what she later described as a menacing look, the second man handed her a note that read, "Put all the money in the paper bag and nobody will get hurt." She complied and gave the thieves $167 in cash. The men left without exhibiting any weapons; Mrs. Pizzamiglia was not touched. An hour and forty minutes later, she was dead of progressive cardiovascular collapse.

The prosecuting attorney said to me, "I want these men—not just for a felony, but for felony murder. Do I have a case?"

I asked to see the coroner's findings, and I immediately reviewed the heart muscle slides. I had never seen a heart more extensively riddled with contraction band lesions than was that of Mrs. Pizzamiglia. Furthermore, her coronary arteries were open and hardly diseased.

At the trial I spent four hours on the witness stand explaining my findings. Three days later the jury delivered a verdict of felony murder. This was the first time that a person had been convicted of murder on the basis of someone having been literally "scared to death." No weapon had been used; no physical harm had been apparent.

The case was appealed, and the appeal was denied.

A tragic complication of the case was that twenty-four hours before the jury's decision, Mr. Pizzamiglia, the victim's husband, also dropped dead from a heart attack.

CONTRACTION BAND LESIONS EVADE HIGH-TECH DETECTION

Unfortunately, the damage caused by contraction band lesions is largely invisible before death. Even a modern, technically skilled cardiologist cannot detect contraction band lesions by means of coronary arteriography, the most common of today's invasive cardiac diagnostic procedures. While coronary arteriography outlines the coronary vessels by X-ray injection techniques, a catecholamine overdose is lodged deep within the heart muscle, in a place not surveyed and thus invisible.

> **Despite modern, high-tech diagnostic systems, the contraction band lesion remains a difficult and elusive problem to detect.**

When coronary arteriography fails to supply an answer, radioisotopic injections are the doctor's next step. This second technique may give further (and conflicting) information regarding the way in which the heart distributes blood. Groups of contraction band lesions are difficult to distinguish from multiple small-vessel obstructions, because both conditions manifest a slowed or halted circulatory pattern.

You can see why if you imagine a hollow drinking straw pushed through a common household sponge. The straw represents your blood vessels and the sponge represents your heart muscle tissue. Stretch or squeeze the sponge and it would be impossible to blow through the straw. This is what can happen to your heart muscle when you have contraction band lesions. Stuff peas into the straw and you also could not blow through it. This illustrates what happens when you have blocked blood vessels. Both conditions can look the same on all present-day high-tech imaging equipment. In contraction band lesions, slowed or halted circulation may be the result of the

Healthy blood vessels plus a healthy heart equals good circulation.

Blocked blood vessels and/or a damaged heart equals poor circulation.

compression and collapse of tiny vessels adjacent to the dead or dying heart muscle. In a coronary blockage, the slowed or halted circulation is the result of an actual obstruction.

In a third and even more confusing scenario, you may have either condition and still display adequate circulation patterns. So finding contraction band lesions before death remains an unsolved diagnostic challenge.

These attacks of recurrent small areas of ruptured muscle fibers can go unnoticed for years. Slowly, repeatedly, and imperceptibly, the heart muscle becomes depleted and vulnerable—even in those who have inherited a robust heart because of "good" genes. ("Having good genes" is a way of saying that the person has octogenarian parents or grandparents without a history of cardiovascular disease.) Environmental stresses and pressures can easily overwhelm inherited resistance. Detection and treatment of Hot Reacting is one of the most powerful weapons we have to ward off such damage.

YOUR BODY CAN LEARN TO HAVE HIGH BLOOD PRESSURE

Human physiology is an immensely complex system responding faithfully to the signals it receives. It acts reluctantly at first to signals that are new or misdirected according to established patterns; but once it decides to react, the body responds with a constellation of change. All systems are on full throttle. Everything is thrown at the problem as thousands of chemical and electrical adjustments take place. In turn, each adjustment sets into motion its own new pattern for physiological need and fulfillment.

> **The brain can teach the body to develop permanent high blood pressure. Ninety percent of high blood pressure cases have no other explanation.**

Naturally, one of the adjustments that concerns me most is high blood pressure. As blood pressure continues to rise repeatedly and to stay high over days, weeks, and months, pressure sensors in the blood vessels (called *baroreceptors*) gradually become set at those higher levels. The body thus assumes that high blood pressure is the optimal level rather than just the short-term emergency level.

As this occurs, millions of the small "controller" blood vessels (arterioles) are squeezed down like the nozzles on minute garden hoses. For this to happen, these small arterioles must thicken (hypertrophy) their muscular walls; and that action causes increased resistance as the heart must work harder to pump blood to all parts of the body. The resultant strain on the heart immediately affects its main pumping chamber (the left ventricle), causing it to thicken in an attempt to compensate for the added workload.

As we have seen, the added pressure also impacts and damages the delicate linings of the arteries (endothelium), accelerating the process of atherosclerosis in critical parts of the body. Arteries serving the kidneys, brain, and heart will become narrower, and subsequently the functioning of these vital organs will be impaired. That impairment leads to a sluggish blood flow throughout the organs, and this in turn sets the stage for other clots and blockages. If all of that weren't enough, the weaker parts of the arterial walls also may distend, balloon, or rupture, dramatically increasing the risk of future stroke or heart attack.[6]

Another example of our remarkable powers of adaptation concerns the way in which the human body holds on to salt and water in periods of stress. I've mentioned before that your body reacts to stress and loss of control in the same way that your ancestors reacted to long-term deprivation; and this ability to conserve fluids and minerals was an essential survival tool. So when you are put in a work or social situation in which you have lots of stress and little control over outcome, your body also will begin retaining these two vital substances, even though salt and water are probably plentiful in your environment. As a result, many people experience weight gain, puffy eyes, swollen hands and feet, and other outward symptoms when under stress.

In a more complex way, this kind of salt and water retention has even been used to explain the tendency toward high blood pressure that is often seen in African Americans. Those Africans brought to America in the holds of slave ships experienced an extreme physical and emotional loss of control; one physiological reaction to this was the retention of salt and water. Those people who were physiologically more efficient at this adaptation were the ones who survived to pass on that ability to their offspring. A possible explanation for this is that a high-salt diet coupled with unremitting social and economic pressures can quickly trigger that retention mechanism in modern African Americans.[7]

Recently I consulted with a corporation that had observed a startling rise in employee blood pressure levels. After my initial visit I learned that eighteen months earlier, the corporation had announced a cutback of 750 jobs. For eighteen months *every* employee had worried about whether or not he or she would be one of the 750. A review of the employee medical records revealed that the incidence of high blood pressure levels was three times higher than those recorded before the announcement.

In another example, I studied a brokerage house where 84 percent of the high-performance employees were either Hot Reactors or already had permanent high blood pressure. The analysis was easy. Ten years ago stockbrokers watched market cycles evolve over a period of several months or years. Now these same people must manage huge sums of money as stocks rise and fall by computer-driven programs on a minute-to-minute basis. And when external events, such as the war in the Persian Gulf, dramatically impact the market, the brokers have even less control over outcome. They feel as if a saber-toothed tiger were around every corner, and their bodies react by learning to maintain high blood pressure.

It's as if the brain says, "Look, Charlie, I'm tired of this up-and-down stuff; let's set it up permanently."

STRESS INCREASES CHOLESTEROL

In stressful circumstances, cholesterol production also can rise. Years ago Friedman, Rosenman and Carroll reported that during the period from January 1 to April 15, the cholesterol levels of test subjects who were also Certified Public Accountants rose as much as 100 points over their normal levels.[8]

And in a study of medical students who feared they had flunked

40

an examination, we recorded comparable rises in cholesterol levels after just thirty minutes from the time of stress.

Some of the most interesting data regarding stress and cholesterol involves navy pilots. As a consultant to the war colleges of the National Defense University, I have observed differences in the cholesterol levels of three types of pilots, all of whom regularly ate the same active-duty diet. Transport pilots (incidently, the oldest members of the study) had the lowest levels, land-based fighter pilots had the next highest levels, and pilots assigned to aircraft carriers registered the highest levels of blood cholesterol.[9] The results are hardly surprising. Carrier pilots must land an aircraft (while it's still going 130 miles per hour) on a bobbing, four-acre airfield, with the hope that a hook will catch a big steel wire on the plane's underbelly. Faced with these daily challenges, the brain perceives danger, triggers the alarm and vigilance reactions, and signals the production and release of high-energy fats for a nonphysical struggle. Again, moment-to-moment control over outcome is the basic issue.

STRESS ACCELERATES THE FORMATION OF BLOOD CLOTS

The augmented blood clotting that accompanies stress also increases the bed for fatty infiltration seen in atherosclerosis, or hardening of the arteries, that progressively clogs the arteries of the heart and other organs. The combination of a snowballing blood clot that breaks loose and rolls through arteries narrowed by atherosclerosis spells disaster. The clot can lodge and block the blood supply to an organ (an embolism), which then becomes starved for oxygen. The resulting damage can cause a stroke, heart attack, kidney failure, or some other life-threatening situation.

OTHER PHYSIOLOGICAL DANGERS OF STRESS

The cardiovascular system is only one of many critical systems that have been molded by our ancestral past and that are at risk in our present surroundings. While heart disease remains the number-one health problem in the industrialized world, there are many other stress-linked disorders.

Thirty years ago, when I was in medical training, few professional medical studies dealt with the relationships among the brain, stress, and malfunctioning bodies. Since that time medical and behavioral journals have published tens of thousands of articles on the subject. In just the past decade, more than eight thousand articles seriously evaluated the negative and the positive relationships among the nervous system, environment, and health.

A new branch of science with the tongue-twisting name of *psychoneuroimmunology* focuses on the biochemical links among the mind, stress, and immune-system functions.

Scientists investigating the biochemistry of the brain have identified more than ten thousand power-packed chemicals called *neuropeptide hormones*. In time of need, the brain responds by figuratively writing a prescription for any or all of these chemicals.

> **Monitoring blood pressure levels or even levels of catecholamines in the bloodstream will not reveal where other organ damage is taking place.**
>
> **The cutting edge of medical research is now studying the effects of catecholamines on the nerve endings (*synapses*) where the sympathetic nervous system connects with blood vessels, heart muscle, and organs.**

We did not all inherit identical bodies. We do not all live in the same environment. Nor do we all have the same amount of resistance to stress. Each body has feedback systems that compensate for deviations in normal functioning. While an individual may have a cardiovascular system that can deal successfully with stress, he or she may experience dysfunction in some other organ system. For example, the immune system frequently is adversely affected by stress, resulting in allergies, arthritis, colds, or some other form of infectious disease. Many investigators believe that cancer cells appear in the circulatory system ten or more times during the average person's lifetime; whether or not they become problematic seems to depend on how alert that individual's immune system is to these invaders.

In one experiment, laboratory workers were exploring the reactions of mice to various cancer viruses. They found that one group of mice developed deadly cancers much faster than did their genetically identical siblings, which were being tested in the adjoining room. The researchers were stumped until they monitored the environmental conditions of both rooms and learned that the air-conditioning vent was much louder in the room with the more vulnerable mice. They repeated the experiment and demonstrated that constant noise was definitely a factor in increasing vulnerability to cancer in mice.[10]

The rate of death has been found to be much higher among widows and widowers in the first six months following the death of the spouse. While heart attacks are often responsible, deaths from all causes are increased in this population.

In 1975 a group of Australian scientists measured the number and activity of T immune cells and B immune cells in recently bereaved men and women. At two weeks and at six weeks following the deaths of their spouses, blood samples were taken from twenty-six widows and widowers. As in acceptable experimental practices, the researchers also took samples from a control group of hospital employees matched for age, sex, and race. The tests showed a significant drop in the immune function among the bereaved at six weeks, but no change in the blood taken from the control group.[11]

Blood samples also were studied from men whose wives were dying of breast cancer. Samples were taken before the death of the women and for two months after. Early blood samples showed no changes in the number of white blood cells (the germ killers) or in any other blood chemistry. The samples taken shortly after the women's deaths, however, revealed sluggishness in the men's immune systems. While immature white cells normally change into mature killer cells, in these men white cells did not mature as often or as quickly as they had prior to their wives' deaths. In time, their immune systems gradually returned to normal; but for a while, the men were in a highly vulnerable state.[12] We all know of cases, particularly involving elderly people, in which the death of one person is quickly followed by the death of the spouse.

Recent research into the mind/body connection also confirms that the reverse is true: Being able to avoid stress helps build resistance to disease. To test this statement, experimenters injected a group of mice with tumor cells. The mice were then divided into three groups. The first group was placed in regular cages; the second group was placed in electrified cages and provided a means of escape; and the third group was placed in electrified cages with no escape from shock. Members of the last group had no way of controlling what was happening to them. Those in the first group that were not shocked and those in the second group that could avoid the shock grew tumors at about the same rate. In the third group, however, the tumors grew significantly more rapidly. The investigators concluded that the rate of tumor growth correlated inversely with each mouse's ability to control the shock.[13]

I recently heard an intriguing case history from a friend and colleague, Dr. Lofty Basta, who is Professor of Medicine and Chief of Clinical Cardiology at the University of South Florida (Tampa General Hospital). Dr. Basta's story vividly illustrates the powerful connection between the brain and the heart. I call it "the case of the mother-in-law with the knockout punch." The patient was a thirty-two-year-old woman who began passing out every time her mother-in-law came to visit. Dr. Basta assumed that the young woman had developed a peculiar psychologically induced hyperventilation. He reasoned that her resultant rapid, deep breathing could then cause her to become faint from the lack of carbon dioxide in the blood. He decided to admit the woman to the hospital and monitor her under controlled conditions.

As predicted, when the mother-in-law appeared at the young woman's bedside, the patient passed out. The monitors, however, showed that rather than a lack of carbon dioxide, the patient's heart had suddenly slowed. The electrocardiogram revealed that the heart muscle lacked adequate blood flow to function properly with this particular distress. Under such circumstances, insufficient blood flow caused the young woman to faint.

Basta's concern was that despite her age and the absence of coronary risk factors, the patient might have a coronary blockage. Heart catheterization studies revealed that her coronary arteries were open and normal. While conducting the catheterization, which is done with the patient awake, Basta casually discussed the incident with the mother-in-law. Immediately the patient's right coronary artery went into spasm, shutting down the flow of blood feeding the atrio-ventricular node (the main electrical connection center for the heart). This led to a repeated demonstration of both the severe heart slowing associated with the patient's "mother-in-law syncope" and fainting. Dr. Basta's treatment then focused on controlling the spasms. He prescribed medication, counseling, and behavioral interventions, which were ultimately successful in helping the patient control her own problem.

THE UP SIDE OF STRESS

Despite my emphasis on the physical dangers of stress, I don't want to leave you with the simplistic notion that all stress is bad. Challenge is very often pleasant and, when successfully met, the spice of life. Without such stimulation, we would stagnate in an existence that was bland and perpetually tranquil. At ISM, we call this good stress NICE: easily remembered as New, Interesting, and Challenging Experiences.

NICE stress even causes distinctive, positive changes within our physiology. Successful completion of a task after thoughtful preparation; surviving a thrilling ride at an amusement park; excelling in friendly competition—all of these stressful experiences can be summed up with one key word: *winning*.

Winning—or the feeling of accomplishment and success—is the outward manifestation of good stress. As a coroner once told me, "I've never been called to a racetrack and asked to examine a body that was clutching a winning ticket."

Physiologically, winning spurs the release of adrenaline, endorphins, and sex hormones. When kept at moderate levels, these stimulants function as the brain's feel-good or chemical reward system. We can even measure substantial decreases in potentially harmful cortisol levels when animals move from a passive to a dominant situation.

Of all of these hormones, endorphin seems to be the most powerful, with approximately 250 times the strength of morphine. When you laugh, when you feel you are in control, when you have won—at all of these times your brain prescribes higher levels of endorphins (as well as other chemicals associated with feelings of well-being). In addition, the muscles of your body send positive messages back to the brain. You are not gripping the steering wheel of your car; you are not grinding your teeth. Both the chemical and the physical relaxation messages then put you in a comfortable, productive, and creative frame of mind.

So when I talk about lightening the load of stress, I'm not consigning my patients to the rocking chair! Instead, I'm trying to help them shift the balance of their lives, so that positive stress far outweighs the negative.

CHAPTER 3

ALL THAT ASSAULTS US
STRESS AND THE ENVIRONMENT

Once when I was a boy, I stopped in my mother's kitchen and mar-veled at the tiny weight that regulated the steam within the pressure cooker that sat on her stove. The weight wobbled inside a safety gauge perched on the cooker's lid, and I wondered how such a small device could control such power. Today as I visit busy corporate environments and see frantic managers and workers laboring under intense pressures, I think about the destruction building up behind their "safety valves." When the valve becomes stuck, the price for modern progress can include clogged or ballooning arteries, damaged and disintegrating heart muscle tissue, headaches, backaches, suscep-tibility to infection, and more.

GEOGRAPHY, POLITICS, AND HEART DISEASE

Nowhere have I found the evidence of the impact of environmental stress on health as compelling as in my experiences in Finland. In 1975 Dr. Penti Halonen, Medical Director of the Paavo Nurmi Foun-dation and Chairman of The First Department of Medicine at the University of Helsinki, invited me and eleven other international car-diovascular specialists to his country. Our purpose was to assess the medical research and explore the reasons why Finnish people had the highest incidence of sudden death and coronary heart disease in the world. Little did I know that this unique scientific retreat would turn into a biannual, international conference on the latest findings and greatest challenges in cardiovascular medicine.

Some readers will recognize the name of Paavo Nurmi, an Olympic athlete known around the world as the "Flying Finn." Nurmi and the foundation named in his honor represent the complex link between physical and geopolitical environment and the social identity and health of the Finnish nation. In many ways Nurmi is the personification of what could be called a Finnish identity.

Finland had long been a battle pawn between hostile neighbors. In 1809, after the Treaty of Fredrikshamm, the territory was ceded to Russia by Sweden. During the Bolshevik Revolution of 1917, the Soviets were too preoccupied with internal affairs to be concerned about 3.5 million rebellious Finns; and so the Finns took the opportunity to declare themselves to be a free and independent nation.

The first international flag-bearer of this new nation was Paavo Nurmi, an Olympic gold medalist whose career in competitive running extended from 1918 to 1932. At the end of this career Nurmi returned home to a nation that wished to bestow its love and gratitude on a larger-than-life hero. His personal friend and physician, Dr. Penti Halonen, told me of how everyone had encouraged Nurmi to run for political office; to head banks and investment and insurance companies; to start businesses; and to become a visible and dynamic public figure and role model.

Yet he was totally unsuited to any of those roles. Paavo Nurmi was a remarkably shy, modest, and retiring individual who had shunned the public throughout his career—escaping from the press, secluding himself in hotels, and surfacing only when it was absolutely necessary for competitive races. Instead of public exposure, Nurmi wanted to be a coach and perhaps to inspire other young, gifted Finnish athletes to achieve their potential. Such was not to be his fate, for he felt that it was his patriotic responsibility to accept whatever task the Finnish people requested.

Naturally, he was a remarkably fit individual who could run for miles without showing any pain or fatigue. He never smoked; his cholesterol was always normal; he never had any evidence of high blood pressure; and certainly his weight was ideal. Nurmi had *none* of the classic cardiovascular risk factors; and yet in his early fifties, he began to develop progressive, extensive atherosclerosis—which ultimately led to his long-term disability and death.

Subsequently, in love and honor of the man, the Paavo Nurmi Foundation was created from both private and public funds and charged with the mission of understanding the dilemma posed by both Nurmi's illogical disease and death and the epidemic of heart disease in the Finnish nation.

After our first conference in 1975, Urho Kekkonen, then president of Finland, held a banquet for the visiting scientists. At its conclusion, he asked each of us to discuss why we believed that Finland led the world in sudden deaths and coronary heart disease. The president asked me to go first. Unexpectedly, he locked me into an inescapable one-on-one conversation that lasted five hours.

At two o'clock in the morning President Kekkonen leaned over and asked, "Now, Dr. Eliot, please tell me why it is that Finland has such a terrible health problem."

Despite the hour, the hospitality, and Finnish vodka, I attempted to be diplomatic. The president pressed forward.

He said, "Don't be diplomatic. Be yourself!"

Kekkonen was a large, imposing man; in the 1932 Olympics, he had won the bronze medal, running slightly behind his friend Paavo Nurmi.

He pressed me again and, this time, emphasized his request by pounding his fist on my knee. I blurted out what I had recently read in a book on Europe: "Finland has been to war thirty-nine times in the last two hundred years, and it has lost every war, and that's a trend!"

Kekkonen burst out laughing, and our discussions went on for another few hours.

All of the original twelve participants (and all those who have followed) went to Finland with one hope: that if we could identify the links among stress, environment, and heart disease there, our findings would have relevance throughout the industrialized world.

Most heart problems in Finland were centered in an eastern area called North Korelia. There the classic risk factors were quite high, and it was reasonable to presume that the coronary and sudden deaths were the result of a high incidence of cigarette smoking as well as a diet high in fat, cholesterol, and salt. Studies in North Korelia made it clear that the Finns did not have a "lethal gene"—that is, they did not have unique inherited vulnerability and weakness to coronary disease. Whenever Finns emigrated to other countries their coronary and sudden death statistics rapidly became similar to those of their adopted cultures. In fact, those emigrating to the United States and Sweden lived substantially longer than did their brothers and cousins who remained in Finland.

Another significant fact began to emerge from the research. The farther a Finn lived from the Soviet border, the less likely he or she was to drop dead. Some scientists concluded that this was because the water nearest the Soviet border had relatively lower mineral deposits (it was soft water), while water in other parts of the country had high mineral deposits (hard water).

I wasn't impressed with such an explanation, and so I looked to some of the region's recent geopolitical history. At the start of World War II, a free Finland remained steadfastly neutral; however, in 1941 the Soviets launched the 100 Days War, an unsuccessful attempt to retake Finland, which they felt was their territory. One million Soviets died in the failed attempt. As a result of this war, the Finns rejected a pact with the Allies, choosing instead to protect themselves against their old enemy, the Soviet Union, and to join the Axis powers. Throughout the conflict, Finland distanced itself from the Nazi regime; but in 1944, at the war's conclusion (in what was perceived as an act of revenge), the Soviets announced that the Finns were a threat to the integrity of the USSR's western border. Consequently they abruptly proclaimed eight days during which time all Finns living in a "restricted zone" were to move back fifty miles to what is now the present eastern border of Finland. The Soviets further announced that all property and people remaining behind would become part of the Soviet empire. In short, the territory was simply seized. The war-weary Allies were eager to conclude hostilities in the Pacific; so in essence, the world community ignored this action.

The results were catastrophic for more than 600,000 human beings. One-sixth of the Finnish population moved bag and baggage to spots behind the line of demarcation. Disenfranchised from land and property, they were forced to work for others wherever they could, changing their identities from free landowners to low-status servants virtually overnight. I felt that this significant cultural upheaval had been lost in the highly focused risk factor assessments being conducted in the North Korelia region, and so I decided to look at the border myself.

With the help and hospitality of my hosts, I was escorted along an extensive portion of the eastern border where it was easy to look through barbed wire barriers and see Soviet tanks, machine-gun nests, German shepherds, and microwave devices. It resembled a negative greeting card message. That is, if the Soviets cared enough, they could send the *very worst*! All along the border, my translators relayed responses filled with fear, uncertainty, and doubt. This was a living laboratory filled with all of the struggle and defeat—all of the invisible entrapment experiments I had observed in my medical research into stress, sudden death, and coronary heart disease.

I'll never forget one specific Finnish couple who had been dislocated by the Soviet occupation. They told me of how they frequently worked their way through the barbed wire, mines, and guard dogs to visit the eastern side of the line.

I asked with some shock and amazement, "Why would you take such a risk?"

They answered, "Because it is our land; and we like to go back and sit on it to remember the way that it was. It will always be our land, not Russia's."

When I heard this response, I could only think of the research findings on submissive tree shrews. The Finns suffered from a similar entrapment dilemma—what Western politicians have termed "Finlandization." The reality was that the Finns were free to do anything that they wanted to do—as long as the Soviets agreed. The hearts of the Finns were in the West, and their bondage was in the East.

In the past decade, Finland has made some progress in the control of sudden death and coronary heart disease; now it is no longer first among countries of the industrialized world. Part of this decline is due to the remarkable efforts of Finnish physicians and health educators in targeting the recognized risk factors. In my view, part of the decline is also the result of the tenacious and skillful management of their complex geopolitical situation. The success of expanding Finnish capitalism and the recent political and economic demise of communism have helped return and reinforce the Finns' national identity, control, and self-esteem. Finland has become a major door to commerce for its previously avowed blood enemy.

STRESS: A NEW KIND OF EPIDEMIC

Until the end of World War II, the greatest environmental public health concerns throughout the world had been tuberculosis, syphilis, measles, smallpox, polio, and malaria. These, and all infectious diseases, lead to epidemics; and epidemics lead to mass death. The words *antibiotic* and *vaccine* were still relatively unknown at the time. The goal of public health physicians was to prevent infectious disease by promoting proper sewage disposal, safe water supplies, management of rodents and insects, and quarantines. Their efforts led to a vast increase in educational materials about the control of the environment.

Today we realize that the impact of the environment—including social environment—on public health includes a great deal more than infectious disease. Modern disease-busters who study these relationships are called *epidemiologists;* and they focus on social, cultural, and workplace factors that influence the length and quality of our lives. Their findings have given us remarkable new insights into the risk factor process at work.

THE HEALTH VALUE OF COMMUNITY

Epidemiologists have conducted a number of studies comparing Japanese Americans living both on the U.S. mainland and in Hawaii with their age–health status counterparts living in Japan. Much of this interest was aroused because the highly productive Japanese had the lowest rate of sudden death and coronary heart disease in the industrialized world.

Dr. S. Leonard Syme, of the University of California, Berkeley, found that Japanese families emigrating to Hawaii had higher rates of coronary heart disease than did those family members remaining behind in Japan. The heart disease rates of other family members who decided to settle in California were even higher. Japan, as we know, is highly industrialized, and the people there are exposed to air pollution and other problems of overpopulation not normally seen in the Hawaiian islands. In Japan, cigarette consumption is very high, and the Japanese abuse of salt, especially in soy sauce, is legendary. Yet despite these negative factors, the Japanese in Japan have less heart disease than those who have emigrated to the United States. One early investigative theme was that the Japanese had a hereditary resistance to heart disease, but the studies by Syme and others disproved this theory.

Another possible answer was sought in the culture and diet of the test groups. The Japanese diet, despite its high salt content, emphasizes rice, fish, and fresh vegetables; while the traditional high-fat American diet relies heavily on red meat, sugar, and white bread. However, the heart attack rates among Japanese-Americans continued to increase—even among those who chose to continue the traditional low-fat diet of their forefathers. Even more puzzling, one group of Japanese-Americans residing in California retained the same low level of coronary heart disease found in Japan. It was Syme and his colleague, M. G. Marmot, who concluded that this study group, unlike most other Japanese-Americans residing in California, had worked actively to avoid what they saw as "western ways." These people lived in totally Japanese neighborhoods, socialized only with other Japanese-Americans who also had avoided acculturation, spoke Japanese among themselves, and maintained their Japanese customs and beliefs. The researchers concluded that this remarkable sense of community and social support—a cultural cohesiveness—was the main factor separating this group from other westernized Japanese-Americans (whose levels of coronary heart disease matched the rest of American society).[1]

The value of cultural cohesiveness was also reported in the Italian-American town of Roseto, Pennsylvania. When first studied in the early 1960s, the residents of this small town had only one-half of the number of heart attacks as did residents of neighboring communities. The level of classic risk factors was comparable, but the residents of Roseto were primarily a tightly knit Italian-American group where the old-world Italian traditions were highly prized. These included such things as deep-rooted religious convictions and respect for the elderly. According to the researchers, everyone knew his or her place in the culture of the community. Everyone felt secure in an identity mandated by Italian tradition.

Over a period of twenty years, American cultural values and social mobility slowly replaced those values that the residents of Roseto had brought from Italy. Gradually the number of heart attacks in the community increased to a level equal to that recorded in the surrounding towns of Nazareth and Bangor, Pennsylvania.[2]

> **Ethnic or cultural cohesion offers the individual long-lasting support.**

Cultural cohesion can be found everywhere. People feel more comfortable and less stressed when they can predict what is expected of them and what they can anticipate.

THE FUD FACTOR AND HIGH BLOOD PRESSURE

The significant clue to the importance of cultural cohesiveness as it relates to stress is what I referred to earlier as the FUD factor. When individuals exist in a continual atmosphere of fear, uncertainty, and doubt, they respond with high blood pressure. Statistics show that this is particularly true of males.

> **Fear, uncertainty, and doubt (the FUD factor)—together with perceived lack of control—are primary predictors of high blood pressure and destructive levels of stress.**

A classic illustration of this is the Heart Study Program conducted in Bogalusa, Louisiana.[3] For many years high blood pressure was thought to be a problem that was primarily inherited, and much of the evidence for this conclusion came from the fact that high blood pressure was related to ethnic and racial groupings. Specifically, medical investigations have found very high levels of blood pressure in the African-American community; and as I indicated in the last chapter, many scientists cite the susceptibility created by the conditions under which Africans were brought to America. However, there is strong evidence that (as was also true in the case of African slaves) physical adaptation works in concert with emotional and/or psychological deprivation. In the Bogalusa Heart Study, Dr. Daniel D. Savage analyzed population research conducted by the Centers for Disease Control and concluded that high blood pressure is color blind. His findings suggest that when researchers found permanent high blood pressure in young males living in the ghetto—some as young as age *six*—this condition was not a product of their race. Rather Savage found that the best way of predicting raised blood pressure was *not* race. Better predictors were the number of police calls and fire alarms heard by children in ghettolike settings. Children living under cultural and communal stress were most liable to develop high blood pressure at earlier ages. It was not just the African-American children who were vulnerable, but children of all ethnic backgrounds who were living under these conditions.

Fear, uncertainty, and doubt—the FUD factor—kept the children in a state of sustained vigilance. Their environmental circumstances overwhelmed any resistance they may or may not have inherited. Social scientists and demographers have discovered that in crowded city neighborhoods of mixed race and class, the incidence of *all* illnesses, including high blood pressure, parallels the crime rate. Middle-class individuals living in high-crime areas have the same level of high blood pressure as do their more impoverished neighbors. Vigilance and the fear of violence, rather than income level or genetics, are at fault. The tensions of ghetto life can literally overwhelm a person's genetic or constitutional resistance to any disorder.

Of course, fear, uncertainty, and doubt are not confined to the inner cities. The conditions that can trigger long-term stress chemicals may exist in any dysfunctional home, workplace, or interpersonal relationship. We live in a very competitive society, and competition can be both challenging and stressful. Many of us struggle daily with fears about our chances for success, about our individual and collective futures. Uncertainty is built into our modern way of life.

PRESSURE-COOKER OCCUPATIONS

One study of how stress is associated with occupational uncertainty began with the observation that bus drivers employed by the city of San Francisco were experiencing unusually high rates of high blood pressure, illness, and absenteeism. Dr. S. Leonard Syme and his research colleagues began by analyzing each driver's working environment. They discovered first that bus timetables had been established by simply dividing the number of needed routes by the number of available buses. Actual driving time had not been a part of the calculations! A driver may have been expected to cover a specific distance in three minutes when the actual driving time was twenty. Aside from these impossible tasks, the drivers' rest periods were often scheduled in remote areas on the city's boundaries, so the drivers were isolated from their co-workers during these periods. There was no opportunity to chat with fellow drivers or to discuss common problems. Chronically fatigued and tense, many drivers felt as if the passengers were interfering with their impossible schedules—and this in turn led to more delays and altercations with passengers. Veteran drivers had three times the incidence of high blood pressure as did new applicants of comparable age. Moreover, they developed a pattern of getting together after work to drink and commiserate before returning home late at night. These social patterns, Syme concluded, contributed to another disturbing statistic among the drivers—an abnormally high divorce rate.

To illustrate the fact that the bus timetables were unrealistic, researchers blocked several city streets one Sunday morning and hired a professional race car driver to take a Ferrari through a specific bus route. The Ferrari failed to meet the schedule. As a result, company officials sought the drivers' help, and the drivers themselves came up with the solution. Instead of the published timetables, passengers would be told that when they waited at designated pickup points, a bus would arrive every fifteen minutes. It was predicted that the system would result in more satisfied customers and less-stressful workdays for the drivers.[4]

Another study compared the levels of job-related stress between telephone operators working with and without computer terminals. Operators on computer terminals can be statistically monitored throughout the workday. For example, if management determines that an incoming call should take fifteen seconds and an operator spends twenty or thirty seconds on that call, the operator's terminal will record this fact automatically. Performance ratings are often based on these numbers. Moreover, all operators are constantly reminded that they are in the service business and that they always should be polite and helpful to customers. Reflecting this built-in double bind, researchers found that 21 percent of the operators using computer terminals reported having had episodes of chest pain, while only 9 percent of the operators not using terminals reported similar pains.[5]

I observed a comparable reaction to stress at one of the nation's major financial corporations. During the period between the stock market collapse of October 19, 1987, and January 1, 1988, nine of its corporate managers had suffered sudden cardiac death. In the five years before 1987, there had been only two such deaths. The months following "the crash" also brought dramatic increases in psychiatric problems, suicides, episodes of violence, and divorces among the company's key personnel.

When I interviewed workers within the company, they told me of stresses concerning not only the loss of client confidence but also their own personal loss of confidence in the very stock market that was the source of their livelihoods. As commission incomes dwindled, these brokers felt that they had lost control of their own destinies. Self-esteem disappeared overnight, and to make matters worse, the company was forced to cut staff drastically. Again I saw managers who were forced to make decisions that affected the lives of people who had been colleagues and friends. Like the managers at Cape Canaveral, these people suffered severe physical problems. Those who kept their jobs and were given the task of firing others were often the ones who suffered the most. In addition, dramatic cuts in pay contributed to the downward spiral of self-doubt and poor self-confidence. These managers were in an identity crisis. The changes in their self-perceptions made them vulnerable to both physical and emotional distress.

> **Loss of identity, control, and self-esteem can create the chemistry and physiology for sudden death.**

Sudden cardiac deaths of this nature also increased when farmers of rural America faced the devastating drought of 1988. Following land foreclosures and loan cancellations, many lost farms that had been in their families for generations. The life of a farmer may look bucolic and serene as you speed by in a car, but it rarely is. Many once-successful farmers have been experiencing occupational stress unknown since the dust-bowl days.[6] These stresses are all a part of what economists call a *rolling recession*, an economic crisis that moves from one industry to another, affecting different communities and different professions at different times.

Any farmer, stockbroker, or space engineer who has experienced a dramatic change in his or her self-esteem will also experience increased levels of stress. The precise cause of the stress is not as significant as is the individual's negative perception of that change. For example, I know of one young healthy South Dakota farmer who, after inspecting his dying crops, went home and dropped dead in the shower. He was a twenty-seven-year-old father of two. This man, of healthy background (his parents and grandparents were still living), could not take the stress associated with watching his months-long efforts, his life savings, and his future hopes dry up and blow away. His overstrained body simply caved in.

YOUR GENDER MAY BE HAZARDOUS TO YOUR HEALTH

Tragically, the encouraging trend of lowered heart disease rates for males in the past fifteen years is less impressive for women. Dr. Barbara Packard of the National Heart, Lung and Blood Institute and a member of the American Heart Association's Women and Heart Disease Task Force states: "The average American woman can expect to live a third of her life at high risk for heart disease. One in nine women between the ages of 45 and 64 already has coronary heart disease, as does one in three over 65. As opposed to a one in ten chance of dying of breast cancer, for example, a woman's risk of dying of heart disease is one in two."[7]

Women get heart disease later in life than do men, but it's usually more severe. To begin with, women generally have physiologically smaller coronary arteries than do men. Moreover, women are twice as likely as men to die within the first few weeks following a heart attack. Finally, women do only half as well as men in recovering from bypass surgery. A Cedars-Sinai medical study by Dr. Steven S. Kahn and his colleagues revealed that 4.6 percent of the 482 women receiving bypass surgery from 1982 to 1987 died, compared to only 2.6 percent of the 1,800 men operated on during the same period. Kahn concluded that the women were much sicker by the time they received surgery because their early symptoms had been minimized, either by the women themselves or by their physicians.[8]

The common myth that heart disease is a "man's disease" prevails because research dollars have focused on men who have had heart attacks in their prime midlife earning years. Public campaigns for quitting smoking, lowering blood pressure, cutting down on fats, and getting more exercise also tend to be geared toward this group of high-producing males.

Several large-scale studies are now underway at major medical centers to counteract the kind of medical bias that persists in treating women's heart disease. The following example of this bias was cited in a recent medical publication:

Thirteen male internists from a leading research institution reviewed videotapes of two actors portraying patients complaining of heart pain. Both were supposedly smokers who had stressful jobs—but one was male and the other female. Two-thirds of the doctors recommended that the man undergo further evaluation; only a third suggested the same for the woman. Even more shocking, all 13 doctors recommended that the man stop smoking; *none* made such a recommendation for the woman. However, two doctors did recommend that the woman see a psychiatrist.[9]

At ISM, our research has led us to look beyond the conventional risk factors that put women at risk for heart disease.

Women face intense social and personal pressures to be competent and caring. We conclude these pressures can be hazardous to health.

Ninety percent of the women we see voice a recurring theme: "External demands are beyond my control."

The long-term Framingham Heart Study found that women from forty-five to sixty-four years of age with competitive, striving personalities had twice as much heart disease as did other women. Health problems were highest in those women who had at least three children *and* low-paying positions in an unsupportive work environment. A difficult boss, few promotion opportunities, and excessive responsibility without authority all increased the likelihood of heart disease. Women with better-paying professional or self-employment positions (usually those with more control) did not demonstrate excess risk.[10]

In our society, self-esteem is often identified with work. When a caregiver working at home, for example, exists without the challenge and structure of external reinforcements, the result can be a highly stressful situation that fuels isolation and self-destructive habits. Researchers Pearline, Menaghan, and Mullen found that depression was often the result of "role disenchantment" when women perceived that they were maintaining a job at home without the advantages of promotion or social status. The researchers concluded that "success" as a wife and mother is elusive in a repetitive, isolated environment, and this can result in low self-esteem and a lack of self-worth.[11]

These examples illustrate the kinds of stress women experience when faced with a loss of control and/or low self-esteem. Unlike most men, however, many women face the added stress of dual identities— the social pressure to "act like a lady, think like a man, and work like a dog."

A study done by Dr. Marianne Frankenhauser at a Volvo automobile plant in Sweden measured catecholamine levels of men and women through their workday and home life. For all the men in the study, the stress hormone readings increased in the morning and decreased in the evening. But the women showed decreased stress hormones while at work and *increased* levels on the homefront![12]

Statistically, well-paid positions at work appear to *protect* women from increased risk of heart disease; however, the dual responsibilities of breadwinner and caregiver are causing many women to overload their circuits and be at increased risk of stress-related illness. In spite of increased sensitivity of men to the need to share responsibilities, women are still primarily responsible for household tasks, discipline of children, and taking care of aging parents.

A CHANGE IN BEHAVIOR CAN BRING THE SOLUTION

The search for the positive solutions to environmental stress has been my concern since those early days with the young aerospace engineers and managers I saw dying in Florida.

Now I focus my efforts on both *predicting* and *preventing* similar deaths—finding disorders before they become disasters.

When patients come to the Institute of Stress Medicine, environmental stresses are a crucial part of our evaluation. I'd like to tell you about two cases where changing the balance between stresses and strengths resulted in dramatic improvements in physical health.

CASE PROFILE: ROB DEMMING

Rob Demming had every reason to value his life, but when he first came to our institute, he was a *super* Hot Reactor. During tests of mental stress, his blood pressure rose to over 300! A major worry was that he had hypertrophy of the left ventricle—that is, that the main pumping chamber of his heart had become thick because of the high resistance against which it had to pump. This is a very dangerous sign, which often leads to stroke, heart attack, heart failure, and many other complications.

To make matters even more difficult, Rob was totally against taking any medicines. He had tried them; he hated the side effects. Because his physical condition was serious, we described the risks of avoiding medications, but Rob was adamant. He said that he couldn't function with them, and he asked us to do the best we could to teach him how to reduce his blood pressure without them. In his own words, he wanted "nothing to do with those damn medicines." He'd die first. So we tested him, and we taught him.

Our last visit was two-and-a-half years later. Rob's blood pressure was normal, and he had become a Cool Reactor. Furthermore, the echocardiogram demonstrated that his thickened heart wall had completely returned to normal. Rob had lost 50 pounds and was now a bouncing 185. His cholesterol had slid from 301 milligrams per deciliter (mg/dl) to 201 (mg/dl). The treadmill test demonstrated that he had 25 percent more work capacity.

All this was good news, but the one thing that had really impressed him and continued to motivate him was that his sales commission income had more than doubled in this same period!

Our initial evaluation had determined that Rob was carrying two heavy invisible weights in his knapsack. The first major stress was a secret Rob had held since childhood—he was plagued with dyslexia, a learning disability. Amid the disarray of his office and the confusion of his staff, he had become a top performer in sales—one of the top 5 percent in his company. And yet, all the while, he could not read *a single word*. Imagine the constant vigilance it required to conceal this fact!

Rob's second major stress was that his wife was undergoing extensive treatment for cancer. He had been able to control almost every other thing in his life, but he couldn't prevent her cancer. He didn't know how to deal with his powerful feelings. In particular, he didn't know how much time to spend at work and how much time to spend at home with his wife. No matter how much time he spent with her, to him it never seemed enough.

Rob was performing a high-wire balancing act with guilt on one side and an inability to read on the other. He was making it, but he was paying a tremendous physiologic and emotional price. He valued his wife and marriage, and he valued his work and his clients.

We put a plan together. First, we found an expert on dyslexia at a nearby university who began teaching Rob how to read. He would never be even "average," but he would be able. He valued that. To further his professional control and reduce the office chaos, we suggested that he develop a partnership with a colleague who understood his reading disability and who could function as the office manager. The partnership was a great success. Rob taught his partner how to sell, and she ran the office admirably. They both profited. Their abilities differed; their values were identical.

We also suggested that he seek individual counseling to help him cope during whatever time his wife had left. Rob valued spending supportive, guilt-free time with his wife. With the counselor's help he could focus on what she needed and not on how helpless he felt.

As Rob's knapsack became lighter, he was able to value his own life and health. Only then could he begin to lose weight, exercise regularly, eat properly, learn to relax, and generally take better care of himself.

Don't misunderstand. Rob did not make a total and sudden about-face. He and his wife still face the terrible uncertainty of her illness. Rob did, however, learn to read, to take care of his health, and to handle destructive habits. He has converted his major stresses into strengths, and he continues to improve his life and health.

CASE PROFILE: FLORENCE WASHINGTON

Florence was a bright, gracious nurse in her early fifties who knew about the institute from the lectures I had given to her nursing colleagues, and so when Florence was told that she was developing high blood pressure, she consulted us. She suspected that the stress load at work probably contributed to her blood pressure elevation. After a thorough medical evaluation, we assessed her life's strengths and stresses.

During the preceding three years, she told us, her life had become much more difficult. It was marked with periods of perceived struggle followed by defeats. Florence used those words to describe her present circumstances. She knew, and others affirmed, that she was an extremely capable and effective obstetrical nurse. For almost thirty years, she had enjoyed her work with her patients and their newborn babies. She was proud of the fact that she was now assisting mothers who had been the babies she had delivered years ago. Over the years she had developed a positive and ongoing relationship with several of these families.

Lately medical and bureaucratic restrictions had conflicted with her professional and personal view of her duties as an obstetrical nurse. She no longer felt that her work was fulfilling—and yet, she needed to work. She felt psychologically trapped in an unsympathetic bureaucratic world. Improvement in the conditions at her rapidly changing, growing hospital was unlikely.

Some kind of change was imperative, and she knew it.

To help lower Florence's blood pressure, it was clear that, as her physician, I would need to help her find ways out of her daily struggle/defeat style of living. Evaluation confirmed a need for both medication and teaching. I sat down with her. We quietly and methodically assessed her situation:

- She related well to people.
- Her training and personal inclinations made her a well-organized person.
- She had great ability to attend to and follow through on details.

I asked myself, "How can this woman transfer her skills to another career in a productive and rewarding way?"

I then asked Florence what she would like to do more than anything else. She paused for a moment and answered, "Travel." She smiled and added, "You can't raise children and deliver babies when you are away traveling."

Here was a woman with a desire to travel, great people skills, and a yen for managing detail. These were the very traits I appreciated in my own travel agent! I raised the question, "What would stop you, Florence, from being a travel agent?"

After completing a night course at a local college, Florence took a part-time job in a travel agency. She contacted some of the mothers and grandmothers she had known through the hospital and told them what she was doing. When she asked if they would like to use her services, they responded favorably, and her client list grew. As she became more pleased with her success, her blood pressure lowered. The travel agency was also pleased and so her self-esteem rose. Within six months Florence felt she had established herself well enough to move away from the hospital into a full-time travel agent position.

Soon she realized that with only a modest investment she could open her own agency. Life was no longer one emotional defeat after another. Changes in her physiological life paralleled each event in

Florence's successful professional life. Steadily and surely, I reduced her medications until she no longer needed any at all.

Unfortunately, traditional medicine often has ignored the relationship between a patient's stress and his or her environment. The next chapter focuses on how I propose to change that model.

CHAPTER 4

THE NEW STRESS MEDICINE

CHANGING DIAGNOSIS AND TREATMENT

In January 1989, I was asked to examine Ferdinand Marcos, former president of the Philippines. Specifically, the court wanted to know if his body and his heart could withstand the mental stress of arraignment in New York City's Federal Court.

I arrived at the patient's hospital bed in Honolulu with an engineer and the crated Cardiac Performance Laboratory (CPL) testing system I had developed at the Institute of Stress Medicine. However, as I later reported during my official testimony in New York, the FBI had already inadvertently run a mental stress test on the former president when they first placed him in custody in November 1988.

At that time, the authorities escorted Mr. Marcos from his Honolulu compound and put him in an official car bound for local FBI headquarters. For several weeks prior to this journey, his doctors had been monitoring potentially fatal heart rhythms on a portable electrocardiogram (EKG) device. En route that day, their fears materialized. Marcos's heart rhythms suddenly became a chaotic pattern called *ventricular tachycardia*. Fortunately, the chaos ceased spontaneously.

As a political leader who had been forced from office, Marcos's identity had been suddenly and unceremoniously stripped away. Personally, he had experienced an extreme loss of control and self-esteem, accompanied by an Olympic-size dose of the FUD factor.

This kind of reaction could befall any of us should we lose our jobs, our homes, or our loved ones.

We wired up Mr. Marcos and began our test. Within minutes, CPL measurements revealed a remarkable rise in Marcos's total systemic resistance and a collapse of his cardiac output.

Later, when the court asked, "Dr. Eliot, is he [Marcos] faking it?" I replied, "Your Honor, if he is, he is faking impending death better than anyone I have ever studied."

At the time I examined him, Marcos was a seventy-one-year-old man, dying from end-stage complications of uncontrolled hypertension. As I later discovered, his medical history dramatically portrays the need to identify and control Hot Reacting as early as possible.

Medical records revealed that Marcos's blood pressure had been out of control since his early forties. From the very first, his career was filled with long-term vigilance, struggle, defeat, fear, uncertainty, and doubt. According to his personal physicians, Drs. Zagala and Ramos, he was a Hot Reactor from day one. Over the years, excessive amounts of cortisol and adrenaline had damaged his heart muscle tissue and steadily softened his resistance to disease. The process is very much like the structurally fatiguing effects 25,000 takeoffs and landings can have on the body of a 747 aircraft. Such prolonged abuse can have disastrous results on a plane: Mechanical latches may weaken and a cargo door may fall off.

Marcos's coronary arteries were clean. But two biopsies of his heart demonstrated that extensive tiny bites of heart muscle had been removed by contraction band lesions and that the muscle had been replaced by patches of scar tissue. The contraction bands had weakened his heart and ultimately caused it to fail. In addition, frequent surges of blood pressure had destroyed the arteries to his kidneys. And yet throughout his life, Marcos had rejected medicines to control these medical effects of Hot Reacting because he felt crippled by the unpleasant side effects that often accompany such drugs.

Many people are surprised to learn that in 1984, after one failed attempt, Marcos underwent a successful kidney transplant. For the last ten years of his life he was determined to prevent the public, and especially his many enemies, from discovering his vulnerable physical condition—and this too increased his vigilance. Proper maintenance could have prevented the particular health scenario Marcos experienced. Preliminary weaknesses could have been detected and sensible measures could have been taken, had the patient permitted his doctors to do so. Because of the unpleasant side effects of early antihypertensive drugs, Marcos was unwilling to accept treatment. Today we can find the precise mechanisms of high blood pressure and select an appropriate medication. The result can be few or no side effects. Many Hot Reactors controlled in this manner continue to live full and vigorous lives. This could have been the case with Ferdinand Marcos; instead, shortly after our meeting, the former president was dead.

NOT ALL CARGO DOORS FLY OFF OLD AIRCRAFT

Not everyone faced with mental stress dies of SCD, develops progressive heart failure or kidney failure, or experiences brain damage from chronic high blood pressure. What makes the difference? Why are some of us more sensitive to catecholamines than are others? The answer, in part, lies in the steady structural weakening caused by cortisol excesses brought about by long-term feelings of struggle and defeat. This, depending on inherited factors and the amounts of adrenaline involved, can lower resistance.

Is it necessary to wait until these "adrenaline junkies" simply drop dead? Must therapy be withheld until such individuals develop acute heart or kidney failure? Can we select blood samples at regular intervals and compare a person's blood adrenaline (catecholamine) levels with his or her daily activities?

Dr. Joel Dimsdale did just that.[1] He rigged up a tiny pump that could be worn on the body and which, at a very slow, steady rate, would withdraw a blood sample into a test tube. During each sampling, subjects wrote down what they had been doing. The results clearly revealed that catecholamine levels increase dramatically during certain stressful activities. Highest levels were especially evident during public speaking or visits to the dentist! However, people rarely drop dead in the dentist's chair. (They may feel like it, but they don't.) This is because only some of us have been softened up for the final blow. Monitoring levels of adrenaline and other cate-

68

cholamines remains a difficult and expensive procedure at this time, and as such it is *not* a practical clue to the identification of Hot Reactors.

USING BLOOD PRESSURE TO MEASURE STRESS

At the time of my work at Cape Canaveral (1968–1976), the question of how to measure the effects of stressful changes on the heart and blood vessels was still unanswered. I could see the tragic end results of stress, but I needed to identify overreactive people and prevent stress-linked health disasters *before* they occurred. My efforts involved two avenues of research: the use of blood pressure readings and the use of standardized fitness testing.

Our first approach was to measure the blood pressure response to standard daily stressors. Portable blood pressure measuring devices had just become available, and we used this new technology to check and record blood pressure levels as a person went about his or her regular activities.

Blood pressure measurements taken over a twenty-four-hour period have proven to be highly valuable. Those readings taken during work periods correlate particularly well as predictors of future cardiovascular disasters, including enlargement of the heart, permanent high blood pressure, heart attacks, stroke, and sudden cardiac death (SCD).[2]

By contrast, as mentioned earlier, blood pressure recorded in the doctor's office has been shown to correlate very poorly, if at all, when compared with measurements taken during times of routine daily stress.[3] This is because blood pressure taken in the doctor's office reflects only your level of comfort or apprehension at that specific time and under those unique circumstances. It is *not* an indicator of the actual daily stresses you face in the real world. Generally, if you are comfortable with your doctor, your blood pressure readings will be low; and if you are uncomfortable, they will be high.

For me, one of the most relaxing times of my day may be going to my own personal physician. I can read a magazine in the waiting room and then lie on the examining table waiting my turn. I'm not frightened, nor am I worried about the equipment or the procedures to come. This is a time when my blood pressure is probably going to be at its lowest. However, my doctor will find it more helpful to know how I react when I'm in the heat of battle (that's when I personally go ballistic)—or how I react when I leave the office and drive home during rush hour. It is during these potentially Hot Reacting times that more lesions may be bitten out of my heart muscle tissue, or more chinks may be etched out of a vascular wall as my blood surges through my body.

On the other hand, going to the doctor for a routine physical sends some people right up the wall. Often, it's simple fear and apprehension that the doctor might find something wrong. This individual probably hates taking medications and has a deep distrust of the entire medical establishment. The visit itself may come only after months and years of prodding from an employer and/or concerned family members. We call this the "White Coat Syndrome"; such people may exhibit abnormally high at-rest blood pressure readings, but only in the doctor's office. Unfortunately, physicians faced with such high readings often prescribe something to bring the pressure down— and the unsuspecting patients spend their average day unnecessarily overmedicated.

> **Blood pressure recorded in the doctor's office is *not* an indicator of your blood pressure's actual response to the "real world."**

How can you interpret the numbers when it comes to your own blood pressure readings? As you would suspect, normal blood pressure varies according to age, heredity, and health. However, I consider that a mean (average) blood pressure reading of 107 mmHg or below is in the safe range. Here's how to find your mean blood pressure:

$$\text{MEAN BLOOD PRESSURE} = \frac{\text{systolic blood pressure} - \text{diastolic blood pressure}}{3} + \text{diastolic blood pressure}$$

As an example: If the blood pressure is 120/75, then the mean blood pressure would be:

$$\frac{120 \text{ minus } 75}{3} + 75 = 90 \text{ mmHg}$$

The World Health Organization's criteria for high blood pressure is 140/90, which gives a mean blood pressure of 107 mmHg.

If the mean blood pressure is below 107 mmHg, the best procedure is: "If it ain't broke, don't fix it."

If the mean blood pressure is between 107 and 117 mmHg, I suggest weight control, reduction of caffeine and alcohol, discontinuance of cigarettes, lowering salt consumption, and initiating an exercise program. This normalizes blood pressure in about 80 percent of patients. Anything above 117 mmHg mean blood pressure calls for a thorough investigation.

Generally we have found that among individuals (average age 42.3 years) registering a mean blood pressure of 127 mmHg and above, 38% already have disease in place. Our data shows that 8 percent of people with blood pressure between 117 and 127 mmHg already have disease in place. Any mean blood pressure over 117 mmHg should initiate an immediate search for the cause and correction.[4]

Many studies regarding problem blood pressure levels have looked not to the absolute values of blood pressure but to the changes—patterns of peaks and valleys—of numerous blood pressure readings. However, we have found that while a rapid rate of blood pressure elevation can cause significant wear and tear on the blood vessels, *the most important predictor of blood pressure-related cardiac inci-*

dents will be the absolute level of pressure to which you rise. This is because the highest level obtained during a testing situation will most likely reflect the mean level that you will maintain during periods of stress throughout your day. In other words, this high level most clearly reflects your risk level.

THE LIMITS OF FITNESS TESTING

Blood pressure rises during both emotional and physical stress, yet the bodily reactions associated with these two stresses are dramatically different. To understand fully each reaction, let's compare what happens to the body's blood supply to a large muscle when that muscle undergoes physical versus mental stress.

During aerobic physical stress, small blood vessels open up like millions of small nozzles on millions of tiny garden hoses. This action supplies the muscles with needed oxygen and nutrients. By contrast, mental stress will cause these same blood vessels to clamp down. And let me repeat—in today's world, physical stress is less common than is mental stress. Moreover, physical stress is usually more easily controlled and predictable; mental stress is most often sudden and unexpected and it may become chronic.

Standard physical stress tests, such as the treadmill EKG, are useful for revealing the presence of advanced blockage of coronary blood vessels and for assessing the extent of any existing heart damage. The treadmill EKG test also helps determine safe levels of physical exercise for either a healthy or a recovering individual. However, all physical stress tests fall short as *predictors* of cardiac risk.

Why? Because these tests can remain negative until there is a major structural change in the heart. The early signs of the physiological impact of mental stress go undetected. These signs include early coronary vessel obstruction, functional abnormalities, and the damage caused by surges in adrenaline and catecholamines.

Our early efforts at preventing heart disease told us that we needed to detect the forerunners of the obstructive processes early in the game. Only in that way could we teach the patient to manage his or her individual reactions to stress. And should a patient later require treatment, we could begin it in earlier "functional" or "reactive"

72

stages, before the body had made permanent, undesirable structural adaptations—and well before the onset of complications in other systems of the body. This is why the sophisticated measurement of blood pressure became our primary tool for evaluating risk.

SPACE-AGE TECHNOLOGY APPLIED TO STRESS MEASUREMENT

Modern technological developments now permit measurement of the heart's moment-to-moment pumping action, its pumping volume, and the resistance to flow in the blood vessels against which it must pump. These three heart measurements, once difficult and dangerous to obtain, are now readily accessible with equipment we have helped to develop and that we utilize in our institute.

The technology actually came from the space program. It was designed to show medical supervisors the spectrum of critical cardiovascular changes astronauts experience as they move freely about in the new, gravity-free environment of space. Needles and catheters (tubes) were obviously impractical and had the added risk of causing infection or bleeding. The advent of microchip technology, improved computer software, and advanced electronic design made it possible to increase the accuracy of our system. With this new testing strategy we had the critical centerpiece for a diagnostic system to identify the early stages of heart disease here on earth. Our version for highly stressed earthlings allows us to measure cardiovascular events while subjects face controlled, low-challenge, standardized mental stressors that ultimately mimic real-world events quite accurately and ultimately predict real-world physiological responses.

Computer software is the key to our equipment, and it has evolved after twenty years of work in this field. We also have devised a unique electrical filtration system that compensates for the hodgepodge of conflicting signals which can produce static in any testing situation. This electrical "noise" is everywhere in our environment; it can include microwaves, radio waves, and electrical impulses from normal maintenance systems within any modern building. Unless we compensate for this, the electrical feedback produced can impair the cleanliness of the electrical waves emitted by the body. In addition, we have developed our own scales for charting electrical responses. One is for people who are walking and reasonably well, while the other is for those who are critically ill.[5]

All of these tests have been statistically verified in clinical settings other than our own. They have undergone the rigorous peer review procedures of testing and retesting that establish any new technique as a bona fide tool in the arsenal of medicine. Independent researchers have compared our techniques to traditional methods (including catheterization, in which a tube is placed directly into the patient's arteries) and found us to be accurate 90 percent of the time. Each step has been carefully recorded as part of my over three hundred published research papers and seven books. We know that our procedures work!

Occasionally we run into doctors who are resistant to our program—not because they challenge our basic principles, but simply because they are unfamiliar with the literature on our techniques. Unlike more traditional procedures, such as echocardiography or invasive techniques, our methods are not taught routinely in medical school.

Frankly, I think it's good that doctors are cautious. However, our data and that of others indicate that we are on the right track. As a result, our system of stress detection by physiologic measurement is now being used by an increasing number of major medical groups throughout North America.

HOW THE NEW STRESS TEST WORKS

We can now road test the heart under conditions of mental stress by challenging a person to a series of mild stressors. The new Cardiac Performance Lab (CPL) developed at the Institute of Stress Medicine consists of three stages: the mental arithmetic challenge, the competitive video game, and the cold pressor test.

During the mental arithmetic challenge, the patient is placed in an isolated environment; seated in a comfortable but alert position; and attached to recording electrodes. A televised, nonthreatening guide then tells the patient to: "Subtract sevens serially from 777, going as fast as possible. That is, 777, 770, 763, and so on. Keep going. You have three minutes. Don't make any mistakes."

Then, while in the same isolated environment, the patient is challenged to improve his or her performance at a competitive video game, Breakout, by Atari. We have been asked many times why we continue to use this older video program. We use it because this particular game has been statistically standardized in numerous testing situations. We can graph mathematically how such a competitive situation should affect individuals of a certain age, sex, health, and so on.

As the subject's skill improves, the game becomes more difficult, more competitive, and thus more stressful. In potential Hot Reactors, it is a perfect tool for raising blood pressure to its highest level.

The final stage consists of the cold pressor test. It is a classic, standardized test of the body's physiological responses to a physical stress—in this case, extreme cold. Studies by Dr. Ancel Keys at the University of Minnesota cite more than twenty-three years' experience with the test, reporting that it is the best single predictor of cardiovascular catastrophes.[6]

In the procedure, the subject is asked (again, through recorded instructions) to immerse his or her hand in a bucket of ice water and to try to hold this position for sixty seconds. After that time, they are told to withdraw the hand from the water, to avoid unnecessary discomfort. The higher the blood pressure rises, the more likely the person is to have a premature cardiovascular catastrophe. These catastrophes could include heart attack, stroke, or high blood pressure and its complications.

During the standardized testing period, all instructions are prerecorded and the operator is not visible. This is important, because we all respond emotionally and physiologically to the style and appearance of the person testing us. You can imagine the difference if a male technician reminds Patient A of his best friend, while he reminds Patient B of his strict father. In our experience, when the subject can see and interact with a technician, the results are too variable to have clinical meaning and scientific predictability.

If the subject's mean blood pressure rises inappropriately and/or abruptly (above 107 mmHg) during any of the three tests, then he or she is definitely a Hot Reactor. This is true even if his or her *resting blood pressure* is normal. Such a person is at increased risk for the myriad of stress-linked problems.

Our studies of several thousand subjects (average age 45.8 years) have shown that about one in five (17 percent) of those individuals previously identified as being apparently healthy actually is physiologically hyperresponsive to our standardized mental stressors. Some of these Hot Reactors actually display higher blood pressure during mental stress challenges than they do during physical treadmill testing; and this incidence rises with age.

WHAT KIND OF HIGH BLOOD PRESSURE DO YOU HAVE?

As the testing proceeds, automatic recorders monitor blood pressure, the electrocardiogram, and heart rate. Simultaneously, the system measures the amount of blood pumped by the heart during each heartbeat.

A computer records all data and rapidly calculates the resistance in the blood vessels against which the heart must pump.

From moment to moment, we rapidly track seventeen physiologic measurements. This information tells us precisely what is causing the patient's blood pressure to rise. We can then assess the three key functions of the autonomic nervous system as it governs the heart.

1. *Cardiac output* (the contribution to blood pressure from pumping blood) is increased by what we call a *beta challenge*. The best inducements for this are the mental arithmetic and the time-reaction tasks posed by the video game.
2. *Total systemic resistance* (the rise in pressure when small regulatory blood vessels clamp down) is called forth by an *alpha challenge*. It is best brought about by either the cold pressor test, a hand-grip test, or weight lifting with strain.
3. The elevation of *both cardiac output and total systemic resistance*.

Armed with this information, we can prescribe behavioral interventions and/or medications that can either reduce the pumping volume of the heart, or lower the resistance caused by the clamping action of the vessels, or both. It is therefore possible to select appropriate medications specific to the underlying physiology of each in-

WHAT IS A HOT REACTOR?

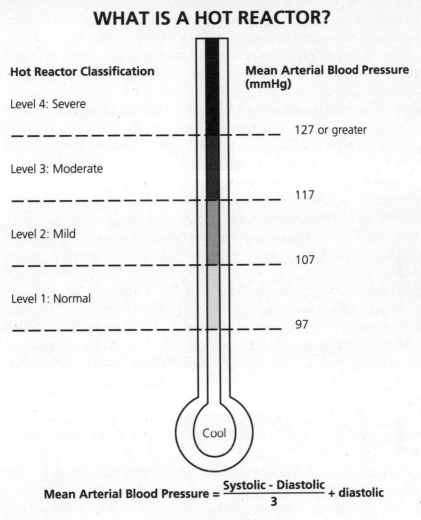

Hot Reactor Classification

Mean Arterial Blood Pressure (mmHg)

Level 4: Severe

— — — — — — — — — — — — — 127 or greater

Level 3: Moderate

— — — — — — — — — — — — — 117

Level 2: Mild

— — — — — — — — — — — — — 107

Level 1: Normal

— — — — — — — — — — — — — 97

Cool

$$\text{Mean Arterial Blood Pressure} = \frac{\text{Systolic - Diastolic}}{3} + \text{diastolic}$$

©1989 Institute of Stress Medicine, Inc.

dividual that will control real-world blood pressure. We are accurate six out of seven times—an accuracy much greater than when only cuff blood pressure measurements are used!

DETECTING A DEADLY PATTERN

Over the past eight years we have also been able to identify a potentially fatal physiologic pattern usually associated with severe coronary blockage. The pattern begins with a marked increase in total systemic resistance, the clamping down of the blood vessels against which the heart must pump. Coupled with this rise in pressure and resistance is a measurable reduction in cardiac output, a faltering of the heart's ability to pump blood.

Contrast this with pattern #3, described earlier, where cardiac output increases despite simultaneous increases in systemic resistance. Here we have a fourth pattern of high blood pressure: The elevation of total systemic resistance together with lowered cardiac output.

I liken this pattern to the long-term consequences of driving the car at full speed with the brakes on. After enough of that abuse, the motor will eventually overheat, sputter, and die. It occurs at a very late stage of Hot Reacting or hypertension, and it is the harbinger of sudden death. This was the pattern displayed by former president Marcos.

We first saw this pattern in Bill, a fifty-three-year-old executive who was also a world traveler. He had been sent to the Institute because his physician was not satisfied by his response to his blood pressure medication. He was in a hurry to leave from the moment he arrived. Once we determined that Bill's heart was faltering in its ability to pump blood, we asked him to stay on for more tests or return for further evaluation.

He replied, "I can't fit it into my schedule. I don't have the time."

Two months later Bill was found dead at his desk. Denial can be fatal.

We continued to study this phenomenon during a comprehensive testing program for managers and executives in a large national corporation. Among those supposedly healthy, top-level executives, we found eight who fit Bill's potentially fatal Hot Reactor profile. Six developed major cardiovascular catastrophes within eight months of our initial contact. Now whenever we find a pattern like Bill's, we immediately warn the individual and begin rigorous diagnostic and interventional approaches. This is true whether or not they have had chest pain or *any* other symptom of heart disease.

Our first step is the standardized heart catheterization procedure. In most cases like Bill's, we find a critical lesion—that is, a blockage of one or more of the heart's major blood vessels that could critically impair circulation. Patients with these blockages may benefit from techniques such as angioplasty (which dilates the blocked area) or bypass surgery. Laser therapy has begun to show some promise in such cases, but it is a research procedure at this time.

Once the coronary circulation has improved in these patients, we continue to teach them the prevention and behavioral techniques covered in later chapters of this book. Only in this way can they avoid recurrence of the factors that caused coronary obstruction in the first place.

GOING PORTABLE

Until recently, the management of high blood pressure was like a guessing game in which doctors had to evaluate whether or not levels observed during an office visit truly reflected a patient's blood pressure. Then came the twenty-four-hour ambulatory monitoring device, a procedure that, while better than guessing, still had many drawbacks. First, it was bulky and cumbersome, placing some patients at actual risk of developing a hernia. Second, the pump activated to inflate the blood pressure cuff at fifteen-minute intervals, and each time the cuff deflated it made bizarre and embarrassing noises. Third, the device was still considered experimental and, therefore, not reimbursable; and fourth, twenty-four hours is a long time to lug around a clumsy, noisy piece of equipment.

Because of some spectacular advances in technology, we've been able to perfect the Portable Stress Lab (PSL) and thus take our own testing procedures into the field. Weighing only twenty-five pounds, the PSL can be placed in a doctor's office, a corporate or factory setting, or an educational facility. In a simple thirty-minute adaptation of our clinical procedures, we can measure stress blood pressure physiology as it is found in real life and while people are running at full tilt. Best of all, the equipment provides test results comparable to newer twenty-four-hour blood pressure monitoring devices. (With a reliability factor of .86.)

Evidence gathered with the PSL not only identifies peak daily blood pressure and Hot Reactors; it also places them in various priorities or categories of risk and concern. It tells us who needs to undergo full testing in the Cardiac Performance Lab. In medical meetings and corporate settings, Hot Reactor screening results help us to decide whether it would be best to handle clients in an individual or a group training session. That is to say, we decide whether to treat or to teach.

THE ART OF TREATING HIGH BLOOD PRESSURE

Thirty years ago, as a cardiology fellow doing rotations through the hypertension clinic, I observed that people would walk in feeling fine, sit in the office to take their medications, stand up, and collapse. (Not exactly a confidence builder for those awaiting treatment!) The empathy and frustration I felt prompted me to compose the following poem:

> Whilst treating hypertension our patients oft complain
> The treatment we apply to them increases stress and strain.
> We concentrate our attention on their pressures diastolic
> With a disregard for comfort they consider diabolic.
> But would we not join this chorus of derision
> With blocked bowels, impotence, and blurring of the
>   vision?

It's better today, but there is still much room for improvement.

During the early 1980s, my colleagues and I reviewed the criteria used by Nebraska physicians for instituting antihypertensive treatment in more than five thousand patients. We discovered that doctors dreaded the entire process. This is because high blood pressure patients often feel worse, not better, after taking medication. The side effects of such drugs can be devastating: the most common include lethargy, dizziness, nausea, and sexual impotence. Many times a friendly, supportive patient-doctor relationship can turn sour as (in the patient's mind) the doctor's prescriptions merely make him or her sick.

Worse still, the medications prescribed may not even control the blood pressure successfully—even when both doctor and patient think they do.

In our most recent examination of this effect, we studied 140 patients taking accepted medications for chronic hypertension. According to resting blood pressure measurements obtained in their physicians' offices, all of the patients were being controlled adequately. Our study asked two questions:

1. Were their blood pressure levels really controlled in the course of the patients' daily activities?
2. Did the medication normalize all components of the hypertension? That is to say, if the cardiac output had been too high, was it lowered by the medication? If the systemic resistance was high, was it lowered? If they both were high, were both lowered? Was this done without triggering any other potential complications or unpleasant side effects?

Only twenty of the 140 subjects tested affirmatively! This means that six out of seven individuals thought to have blood pressures normalized by medication did not.

Today sixty million Americans have known hypertension, and it is estimated that another 20 million are in the early stages. Tragically, the current treatment for this condition has not produced the expected dramatic reductions in the incidence of sudden death, myocardial infarction, stroke, or other complications of this condition. This disparity between effort and results may be partially explained by the usual approach to medication.

The commonest forms of treatment today are drugs called beta blockers and diuretics. Beta blockers lower blood pressure by reducing the heart's pumping capacity—sometimes by as much as 50 percent. (This in itself can make you feel terrible!) At the same time, beta blockers can actually increase the resistance against which the heart has to pump by causing the blood vessels to clamp down. (That's why people on beta blockers often have decreased tolerance for cold.)

Now suppose you try to supply the heart muscle with blood in a situation of mental stress (which, by the way, will further reduce the size of your blood vessels). Can your heart meet the new demand? As I've described, this is like trying to gun your car up a hill with the brakes on.

In addition, diuretics not only further constrict the walls of the arteries, but they deplete fluids from the body. This increases the viscosity of the blood—like molasses in January instead of a mountain stream in July. It is a lot harder to pump molasses than water. In addition, diuretics often increase triglyceride and cholesterol levels, and make the clotting elements of the blood more sticky and cohesive—not a good idea if you're trying to prevent blood clots and atherosclerosis. They can also remove potassium and magnesium from the body, potentially destabilizing the activity of the heart.

These effects are one reason doctors are now beginning to worry about the so-called J-curve. That is, the lower they make the blood pressure, particularly using these most commonly prescribed medicines, the more likely are heart attacks, sudden death, stroke, and other dangerous outcomes.[7]

To make the picture more complex, these cautions apply only in cases of high blood pressure where the main pumping chamber of the heart (the left ventricle) is normal and where the main problem is vasoconstriction. When the heart already has had blocked coronary vessels—as in the typical heart attack—the left ventricle is weakened and small doses of beta blockers can lower the heart's demand for oxygen, thereby significantly increasing life expectancy.

For hypertensive adults over 40, 85 percent of whom have high blood pressure with vasoconstriction, my drugs of choice are the so-called calcium channel blockers and (for more resistant cases) ACE inhibitors. These open the blood vessels and improve the circulation to the heart—without affecting its pumping capacity to any significant degree.[8]

These complexities explain why choosing the correct medication is so difficult when the physician knows only the at-rest blood pressure taken in the office. The result is often a time-consuming, complication-ridden, trial-and-error procedure that is frustrating to both doctor and patient.

But with the newer evaluation systems I have been describing, we are able to customize blood pressure treatment. Once we know precisely what is causing the elevation in pressure, we can select the physiologically correct medication six out of seven times (as compared to the rate of one out of seven we discovered in our study). This often reduces the amount of medication needed, and it also reduces the likelihood of side effects. The result: important savings in time, money, and—most important of all—improvement in health and quality of life.

SHAPE—A COMPREHENSIVE MEDICAL PLAN FOR STRESS CONTROL—THE BASIS FOR THIS BOOK

Over a fifteen-year period, we consolidated our program of comprehensive diagnosis with a unique plan of action called SHAPE (Stress, Health, and Physical Evaluation). Originally this program was developed as a management tool for those individuals we identified as Hot Reactors in our stress measurement/screening programs. Over the years, we found that many so-called Cool Reactors have also benefited from the SHAPE evaluation, instruction, and follow-up services.

The key to the program is a mind/body connection that focuses on teaching a patient to improve his or her health from all angles: physical, psychological, and behavioral. Our goal is to help each participant make immediate, manageable, long-term lifestyle changes that will improve his or her health.

DAY ONE

On the first day at the institute, every patient—from the plumber with migraines to the prima donna with performance anxiety—undergoes a comprehensive medical evaluation. This evaluation includes:

- a complete medical history
- a complete medical examination
- an EKG treadmill test
- the Physiological Stress Test Evaluation
- a blood lipid profile
- a percentage of body fat evaluation
- a fitness analysis
- nutritional analysis
- a behavioral interview

83

Throughout the assessment we encourage patients to explore the stressful attitudes, behaviors, and lifestyle situations that produce invisible weights in their daily lives. A complete psychophysiologic profile is created through psychological interviews, self-assessment tests (including our own tool, the Quality of Life Index, which helps to identify how individuals perceive their level of control over their lives), and other objective medical measurements. By the end of the first day, the clinic staff has gathered enough information to create for each patient a set of customized health prescriptions for promoting both the quality and length of life.

DAY TWO

Self-knowledge is the first step toward real change; and so on the second day of the SHAPE program, a staff physician presents an individually tailored prescription to each patient during a one-and-a-half- to two-hour individualized instruction period. Our ultimate goal for this session is to teach every patient how he or she may convert damaging physiological or personal responses to stress into healthy, productive strengths. Each session is recorded on an audiocassette, to provide an immediate, permanent review and motivational tool. The patient learns about the mechanisms by which stress and other heart risk factors have influenced, caused, or affected his or her life, blood, chemistry, metabolism, and physiology.

THE DAYS THAT FOLLOW

After these initial diagnostic and teaching phases, a physician or a nurse calls the patient once a month (or as needed) in order to provide support and follow-up evaluation. If necessary, return visits to the clinic are scheduled.

Thus the SHAPE program consists of five steps:

Step 1.   Determine the stresses and strengths inherent with their present lifestyle as well as their state of health.

Step 2.   Measure their physiological response to stress.

Step 3. Teach ways in which they can gain control of their lives, increase their quality, and control their physiologic reactions to stress.

Step 4. Retest to determine if these efforts have lasting benefits.

Step 5. Adjust and reinforce needed changes.

The tremendous amount of data and experience from this comprehensive program has now been condensed to its key elements for you in this book.

HOW TO BEGIN YOUR OWN SCREENING PROCESS

Even if you don't have access to one of the clinics associated with the Institute of Stress Medicine, you can still initiate the screening process we utilize; and you can still begin the stress control techniques I will detail later in this book.

Start by obtaining one of the new digital blood pressure units now on the market. These give you a direct numerical read-out of your diastolic and systolic blood pressure. Personally, I have seen good results with the digital units distributed by both Omron and Sunbeam; I'm certain there are other good ones available. The important thing is to take the blood pressure device of your choice to your physician's office and ask to have it calibrated with his or her professional device (sphygmomanometer). Then your home readings can be accurately compared with your doctor's.

First, designate a period of a week or ten days during which you will establish your range of blood pressure during your everyday activities. On alternate days during this period, take and record your blood pressure a number of times during the day. It's important to do this at your workplace, and also to do it whenever you know that you are going into or coming out of periods of routine and extreme stress. The more measurements the better. Then calculate your mean blood pressure by using the formula on page 71. Pay particular attention to peak mean blood pressure readings and where they occur in your daily routine.

You can also give yourself the cold pressor test. To do so, get a bowl of ice water and set a timer not to exceed sixty seconds. Take your blood pressure immediately before and immediately after you immerse your hand in the water. Remove your hand before the sixty seconds elapse if it becomes too uncomfortable. Record these readings in your blood pressure log. *If you have, or suspect you have, heart disease, DO NOT conduct this test without the supervision of a physician.*

You can even replicate the mental arithmetic test and the computer-video stress test, again recording blood pressure before and after each one.

Your results will not be as accurate as those obtained with our equipment, but they can be valuable reference points as you read the rest of this book. In addition, your blood pressure log can provide important baseline data for your own physician.

Let me repeat two key markers for the interpretation of mean blood pressure readings:

107 mmHg or below: You are probably in the physiologically safe range.

107 mmHg or above: Contact your physician for a program of blood pressure regulation.

In general, low blood pressure is a strong indicator of good cardiovascular health. The exception to this rule is when low pressure is accompanied by other symptoms, such as light-headedness or fainting when standing.

HOW THE PRINCIPLES OF THE SHAPE PROGRAM CAN TEACH YOU TO CONTROL STRESS

When I identify a blatant or subtle Hot Reactor, the most important task is to teach that individual how he or she may become a Cool Reactor when handling stress. Because much of the stress we all face today comes from how we handle our hectic environment, the easiest and most logical solution seems to be to slow down, or to take it easy. Like much good advice, this is easier said than done. Few people can actually drop out of their current lives and move to a serene, Utopian environment. More realistically, we are going to continue to face overcrowding, fear, layoffs, financial crises, deadlines, illness, and other pressures.

Therefore, the only way to begin a plan of stress control is to deal with the individual's *perception* of a stressful situation rather than with the actual situation or threat itself. We cannot control others; we can only control our reactions to them. Actually, there is much evidence that our unique perceptions and coping strategies are the primary catalyst for stress-linked disorders within our bodies.

> **When you can't change the world, you can learn to change your response to it.**

In our clinical setting, we found that a variety of psychological techniques proved effective in changing the way individuals perceive stressful events. The most successful techniques for us have been initial coaching, relaxation techniques, behavior modification and cognitive therapy, and organized follow-up.

INITIAL COACHING

For behavioral change to be effective, it must be a positive, personal, and progressive process. We have found that behavioral change usually requires initial coaching by health professionals, such as a physician, nurse, fitness expert, nutritionist, or psychologist. Input from these professionals can go a long way toward motivating the individual to learn about and take an active part in his or her lifestyle changes. In this book, I've tried to give you the essence of our coaching program between two covers.

Naturally some people with severe emotional disturbances need referral for special clinical help. However, the majority of our patients need only to know the right path and be given a little encouraging push.

RELAXATION TECHNIQUES

It's surprising how few people know how to relax. Even recreation turns into a competitive blood sport. For these individuals, we have found that simple coping strategies, such as biofeedback (learning to recognize the way parts of your body can become tense in times of stress), meditation exercises, and regular physical exercise can improve dramatically the body's blood chemistry and physiology. For example, Dr. Dean Ornish has recently reported that blockage of blood vessels can be opened with a combination of stress management, group therapy, relaxation techniques, and aggressive reduction of dietary fat.[9] Often these techniques are plain common sense. If, for example, you can recognize that every time you drive in heavy traffic you grip the steering wheel until your knuckles turn white, simply focusing on the conscious releasing of your grip can be a momentous step toward handling stress and reducing the muscle tension leading to backaches and headaches. The first step to fixing a problem is knowing what it is.

BEHAVIOR MODIFICATION AND COGNITIVE THERAPY

These are fancy words for learning to break bad habits and replacing them with more constructive ones.

Initially, we advocate attacking only a couple of key habits at a time. It's not necessary (and rarely successful over the long haul) for you to turn your entire daily routine upside down. Significant improvement can be made by removing just one or two of your heavy, invisible mental burdens from your knapsack. Start with a small one—and, after a few successful steps, it's much easier to tackle your heavier invisible weights.

ORGANIZED FOLLOW-UP

For successful change to occur, support must be provided in a wide range of areas that affect a person's health and life. If, for example, you have set a goal of a specific stress-reduction exercise, you will find more success if you can integrate this into several different parts of your regular routine. Change requires organized and long-term encouragement! Few of us can sustain motivation alone, so we suggest follow-up through professional contact or group reinforcement. I'm often amused at how intelligent people belittle the group dynamics of some of the popular weight-reduction clubs. The truth is that group songs, chants, and encouragement—as silly as they may appear—can keep many people very highly motivated toward success. There is nothing like group support with friendly peer pressure. At the very least, make yourself a list of goals and check it weekly.

LIVE LONGER, EARN MORE

One study utilizing our methods involved a group of top-performing insurance sales professionals who had all been initiated into a prestigious peer group called the Million Dollar Round Table (MDRT).[10] We began by taking our Portable Stress Laboratories to one of their annual meetings, where we tested a random group of 132 volunteers, all of whom identified themselves as being healthy. Each had completed a thorough medical checkup within two months prior to testing. None was on medication. Of the 132 screened, we found that 39 percent were Hot Reactors. This is more than twice the national average of 17 percent! An additional 25 percent had high blood pressure—and were not aware of it. Only about one-third of the group could be classified as Cool Reactors.

For the next four months, we worked closely with a sample of these Hot Reacting insurance super-salespeople. First they came to our institute for our comprehensive SHAPE program. One month after this initial contact, we surveyed their progress through thirty-minute telephone interviews. Sixty days after the initial contact, we reconvened the group for a two-day teaching seminar to reemphasize specific techniques for the control and reduction of stress. Ninety days into our experiment, each member discussed his or her progress in a thirty-minute telephone conversation with psychologist Layne Longfellow. The experiment was concluded after four months with a final one-day seminar, after which all participants were retested.

What occurred during those four months surprised and encouraged us. Independently from our study, these insurance men and women (from all parts of the country) began to bond and to form their own individual support groups. This kind of networking sustained personal motivation and, we think, impacted remarkably on the end results.

At the time of retesting:

- 77 percent of the Hot Reactors had "cooled down," and an additional 23 percent had become "lukewarm"
- scores for strengths on our Quality of Life Index increased 31 percent
- scores on our Struggle Index decreased 39 percent
- resting blood pressure levels went down
- average serum cholesterol levels declined
- average body weight went down 5.5 pounds

Weight, blood pressure, and cholesterol levels all decreased. Moreover, psychological tests revealed that the participants were less angry, less depressed, and much less anxious. Most had also initiated regular exercise programs.

What we found to be of most interest was that our group of test subjects then reported that they had changed their work habits. They went from an average of seventy hours per week devoted to work to an average of fifty hours per week. The discussion also pointed to parallel improvements in their marriages and in their relationships with their children and others.

When this news got back to corporate headquarters, the alarm went off and our phones started ringing. Had we turned their prize-winning salespeople into laid-back corporate hippies? Psychological tests revealed that our Million Dollar Round Table winners remained extroverted, but the question persisted, "What about their productivity?"

This was the easiest element of all to track in our study. Because all participants were paid almost exclusively by commission, it was easy to record the following year's incomes and compare those figures to the incomes of other Million Dollar Round Table winners who had not participated in our program.

In the year following initiation of the pilot program, income in the control (nonparticipating) group of insurance professionals averaged an increase of 11 percent. For that same time period, *the test group reported increases of from 25 percent to over 200 percent in their annual commission incomes*. Two years later most of the group had sustained their original improvements, and a number had further gains. Only a few reported no gain.

> **You can become productive *without* being self-destructive.**

After our test study, both the insurance CEOs and their sales stars were enthusiastic. Improved income, improved performance, higher morale, *and* better health are that "quadruple win" we all seek.

A NEW GOAL FOR MEDICINE

Early in my career I sometimes felt that while we physicians were saving lives, the quality of those lives was decreasing. Like midnight heroes we would rush to a patient's bedside, drag him or her off to the critical care unit, insert a heart catheter at the eleventh hour, and keep the patient alive. Many times after such an event, I felt that we had merely prolonged death—not improved life; and I worried about why this wasn't satisfying to me. Finally I came to realize that hospitals and doctors were spending lots of time and money keeping people alive—and precious little determining why they got sick in the first place.

My first reaction to this insight was to blame myself. Maybe you're just getting chicken, I thought. I worried that having been a critically ill patient myself had taken away my chutzpah. After all, my entire education and experience had taught me that this was the way things operated; but the more I examined my feelings, the more I realized that fear was not the culprit. I still wanted challenge; I was still willing to take risks. I realized that my new goals had become trying to find the ways that disease develops, detecting disorders before disasters, and teaching people to change.

Now I believe that physicians need to use medicine to empower

91

patients—we must teach them to take control of their own lives and whenever possible to literally become their *own* physicians. You can't think away a blocked artery; you can't just diet your way out of progressive heart disease. We need high-tech medicine, but we need it blended with "high touch." For *most* people, early detection and aggressive prevention can delay disease and add years of healthful, high-quality life.

> **Life-threatening overreaction to stress is neither innate nor inevitable. We were not born with this trait. We have learned it. We can *unlearn* it.**

Now let me help you assess the way in which you handle stress.

PART II

FROM STRESS TO STRENGTH

CHAPTER 5

THE QUALITY OF LIFE INDEX

A PERSONAL ASSESSMENT TOOL

The Quality of Life Index (QLI) was developed as a diagnostic and motivational tool for helping my patients evaluate their individual balance of stresses and strengths and then to make the appropriate adjustments. Each of the items on the index represents issues my findings (as well as those of others) have shown will distinguish whether or not a specific lifestyle is high in stress. When the QLI is taken in good faith, it can provide remarkable insight into your individual stresses and strengths; and this knowledge can be the basis for your plan of stress control.

The QLI consists of forty categories that require you to evaluate and then rank, on a scale of 1 to 9, your perceptions of activities and situations within your environment. It's important to remember that this is a unique, individual, and personal tool to help you quickly gain insight—a stimulus for helping you categorize your own specific life circumstances. As such, there are neither right nor wrong answers, and it is not designed for you to compare yourself with anyone else.

These forty items will help you to identify the invisible, stressful weights you carry with you throughout your life wherever you go. When you know what they are and where they are, you can do something about them. You will also identify the parts of your life that already are helping you to lighten your load so that they can be strengthened.

INSTRUCTIONS

The following index asks you to evaluate your current perceptions of your life, family, work, and community. After reading each category statement, circle the number that most accurately reflects either your attitude or action.

Number 1 represents the most stressful response, and number 9 represents the least stressful response. Mark only one response per item. If a particular question does not pertain to you mark it NA (not applicable). If you feel neutral about the category, circle the number 5.

The results will be most accurate if you answer quickly and honestly with the first gut-level response that comes to mind.

Many self-assessment tests are filled with tangential questions that are designed to corral a problem into a particular interpretation. The QLI is *not* such a test! It asks you to respond quickly and honestly for your own information. Of the thousands of people we have tested in this manner, we have reached a greater than 90 percent accuracy, as assessed by personal interviews.

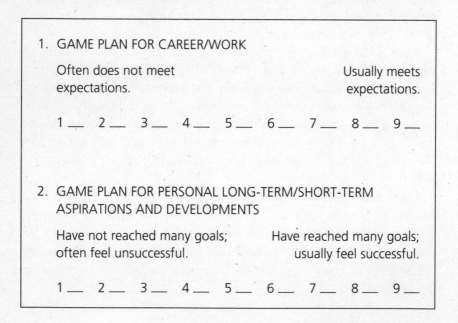

1. GAME PLAN FOR CAREER/WORK

   Often does not meet
   expectations.

   Usually meets
   expectations.

   1 __ 2 __ 3 __ 4 __ 5 __ 6 __ 7 __ 8 __ 9 __

2. GAME PLAN FOR PERSONAL LONG-TERM/SHORT-TERM ASPIRATIONS AND DEVELOPMENTS

   Have not reached many goals;
   often feel unsuccessful.

   Have reached many goals;
   usually feel successful.

   1 __ 2 __ 3 __ 4 __ 5 __ 6 __ 7 __ 8 __ 9 __

3. HEALTH

Often ill.   Usually well.

1 __   2 __   3 __   4 __   5 __   6 __   7 __   8 __   9 __

4. PRIMARY RELATIONSHIP
(spouse, companion, significant other)

Not going well.   Going well.

1 __   2 __   3 __   4 __   5 __   6 __   7 __   8 __   9 __

5. TIME SPENT WITH MY PRIMARY RELATIONSHIP
(away from home, alone, and nonbusiness)

Rare.   Frequent.
(less than one per year)   (six or more per year)

1 __   2 __   3 __   4 __   5 __   6 __   7 __   8 __   9 __

6. RELATIONSHIP(S) WITH CHILD(REN)

Unrewarding.   Rewarding.

1 __   2 __   3 __   4 __   5 __   6 __   7 __   8 __   9 __

7. RELATIONSHIP(S) WITH PARENTS

Unrewarding.   Rewarding.

1 __   2 __   3 __   4 __   5 __   6 __   7 __   8 __   9 __

8. RELATIONSHIPS AT WORK
(with co-workers, boss, others)

Fraught with discord.   Usually harmonious.

1 __   2 __   3 __   4 __   5 __   6 __   7 __   8 __   9 __

9. SOCIAL RELATIONSHIPS WITH FRIENDS, NEIGHBORS, GROUPS,
AND OTHERS

Nonexistent.   Strong.
I feel distant.   I feel close.

1 __   2 __   3 __   4 __   5 __   6 __   7 __   8 __   9 __

10. RELIGIOUS AND SPIRITUAL SUPPORT

Not relevant.   Essential.

1 __   2 __   3 __   4 __   5 __   6 __   7 __   8 __   9 __

11. SOURCE OF APPROVAL/VALIDATION

External—   Internal—
people pleaser.   self-assured.

1 __   2 __   3 __   4 __   5 __   6 __   7 __   8 __   9 __

12. PETS

Problematic.   Either satisfying or
                                         I don't need them.

1 __   2 __   3 __   4 __   5 __   6 __   7 __   8 __   9 __

13. HOBBIES/OUTSIDE INTERESTS

Unsatisfactory or   Satisfactory.
nonexistent.

1 __   2 __   3 __   4 __   5 __   6 __   7 __   8 __   9 __

14. TIME MANAGEMENT/CIRCUIT OVERLOAD

Never enough hours   Time well paced.
in the day.

1 __   2 __   3 __   4 __   5 __   6 __   7 __   8 __   9 __

15. NEIGHBORHOOD

Unpleasant and dangerous.   Comfortable and safe.

1 __   2 __   3 __   4 __   5 __   6 __   7 __   8 __   9 __

16. THE TELEPHONE

Often hampers   Not a problem.
my effectiveness.

1 __   2 __   3 __   4 __   5 __   6 __   7 __   8 __   9 __

17. COMMUTING/BUSINESS TRAVEL

Burdensome.   Reasonably pleasant.

1 __   2 __   3 __   4 __   5 __   6 __   7 __   8 __   9 __

18. PHYSICAL WORK ENVIRONMENT

Noisy, hazardous,   Safe and pleasant.
a nightmare.

1 __ 2 __ 3 __ 4 __ 5 __ 6 __ 7 __ 8 __ 9 __

19. FINANCES

Out of control.   Manageable.

1 __ 2 __ 3 __ 4 __ 5 __ 6 __ 7 __ 8 __ 9 __

20. MAJOR LIFE CRISES IN PAST SIX MONTHS

One or more devastating crises.   Smooth sailing.

1 __ 2 __ 3 __ 4 __ 5 __ 6 __ 7 __ 8 __ 9 __

21. RELAXATION/MEDITATION

Not helpful.   Beneficial.

1 __ 2 __ 3 __ 4 __ 5 __ 6 __ 7 __ 8 __ 9 __

22. CAREER/JOB MATCH

Mismatch.   Good match.

1 __ 2 __ 3 __ 4 __ 5 __ 6 __ 7 __ 8 __ 9 __

23. HUMOR/PLAY/FUN

Who has time?   The staff of life.

1 __ 2 __ 3 __ 4 __ 5 __ 6 __ 7 __ 8 __ 9 __

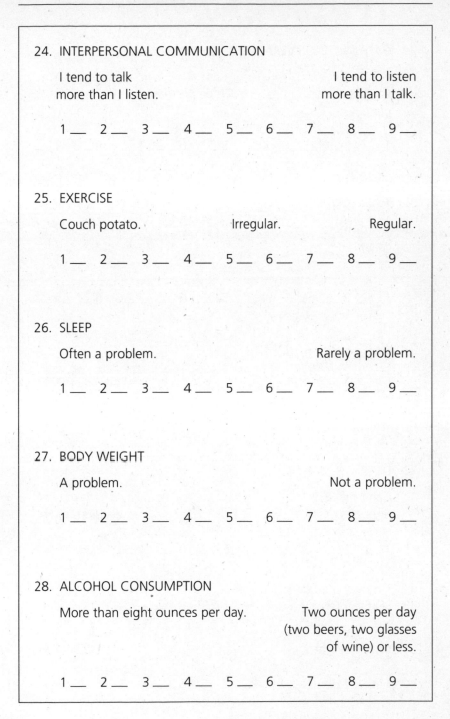

24. INTERPERSONAL COMMUNICATION

I tend to talk   I tend to listen
more than I listen.   more than I talk.

1 __   2 __   3 __   4 __   5 __   6 __   7 __   8 __   9 __

25. EXERCISE

Couch potato.   Irregular.   Regular.

1 __   2 __   3 __   4 __   5 __   6 __   7 __   8 __   9 __

26. SLEEP

Often a problem.   Rarely a problem.

1 __   2 __   3 __   4 __   5 __   6 __   7 __   8 __   9 __

27. BODY WEIGHT

A problem.   Not a problem.

1 __   2 __   3 __   4 __   5 __   6 __   7 __   8 __   9 __

28. ALCOHOL CONSUMPTION

More than eight ounces per day.   Two ounces per day
                                        (two beers, two glasses
                                          of wine) or less.

1 __   2 __   3 __   4 __   5 __   6 __   7 __   8 __   9 __

29. CAFFEINATED BEVERAGES
(coffee, tea, cola)

More than five   Three per day.   None.
per day.

1 __ 2 __ 3 __ 4 __ 5 __ 6 __ 7 __ 8 __ 9 __

30. TOBACCO

Ten or more   Never smoked or
cigarettes   have not smoked for
per day.   three or more years.

1 __ 2 __ 3 __ 4 __ 5 __ 6 __ 7 __ 8 __ 9 __

31. DEGREE OF CONTROL

I am invisibly entrapped.   I have adequate options.

1 __ 2 __ 3 __ 4 __ 5 __ 6 __ 7 __ 8 __ 9 __

32. DECISION-MAKING

Can't make   Make most
decisions easily.   decisions easily.

1 __ 2 __ 3 __ 4 __ 5 __ 6 __ 7 __ 8 __ 9 __

33. PERFECTIONISM

Things should always   I do the best
be done right.   that I can.

1 __ 2 __ 3 __ 4 __ 5 __ 6 __ 7 __ 8 __ 9 __

34. TENDENCY TOWARD OPTIMISM/PESSIMISM

Whatever can go   Most things
wrong, will.   work out.

1 __ 2 __ 3 __ 4 __ 5 __ 6 __ 7 __ 8 __ 9 __

35. FEELINGS OF GUILT AND/OR SHAME

Frequently.   Infrequently.

1 __ 2 __ 3 __ 4 __ 5 __ 6 __ 7 __ 8 __ 9 __

36. ASSERTIVENESS

I rarely say   I usually say
what I think.   what I think.

1 __ 2 __ 3 __ 4 __ 5 __ 6 __ 7 __ 8 __ 9 __

37. ADAPTABILITY/FLEXIBILITY—PERSONAL/PROFESSIONAL

It's hard to change   It's easy to change
a plan.   a plan.

1 __ 2 __ 3 __ 4 __ 5 __ 6 __ 7 __ 8 __ 9 __

38. ANGER

I am often angry.   I take most things
                                         in stride.

1 __ 2 __ 3 __ 4 __ 5 __ 6 __ 7 __ 8 __ 9 __

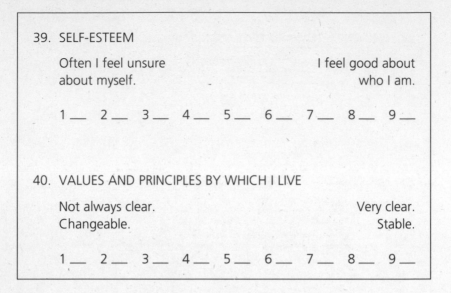

39. SELF-ESTEEM

Often I feel unsure   I feel good about
about myself.   who I am.

1 __   2 __   3 __   4 __   5 __   6 __   7 __   8 __   9 __

40. VALUES AND PRINCIPLES BY WHICH I LIVE

Not always clear.   Very clear.
Changeable.   Stable.

1 __   2 __   3 __   4 __   5 __   6 __   7 __   8 __   9 __

PRELIMINARY INTERPRETATION

When you have responded to the list of 40 categories and feel that the scores represent your current perception of life, transfer the scores to the graph provided on page 105.

1. For each category, place a dot on the grid indicating the number (from 1 to 9) that you chose. Note that there is a separate line for NAs.

2. Now draw a line connecting the dots. You will probably see a zigzag pattern like the one shown on the completed graph on page 146.

3. Next, compute an average score by adding all your scores and dividing the total by the number of categories that you completed. Do not count the categories you marked NA.

4. Now draw a straight line across the Quality of Life grid at the point of the average of your scores. For example, if your average is 6, draw a straight line from one 6 to the other.

This average is useful in two ways. First, the dots above the average line represent your strengths and your perception of the degree of your strengths. The scores below the average line represent your

QUALITY OF LIFE INDEX
Summary Report

Name

Date

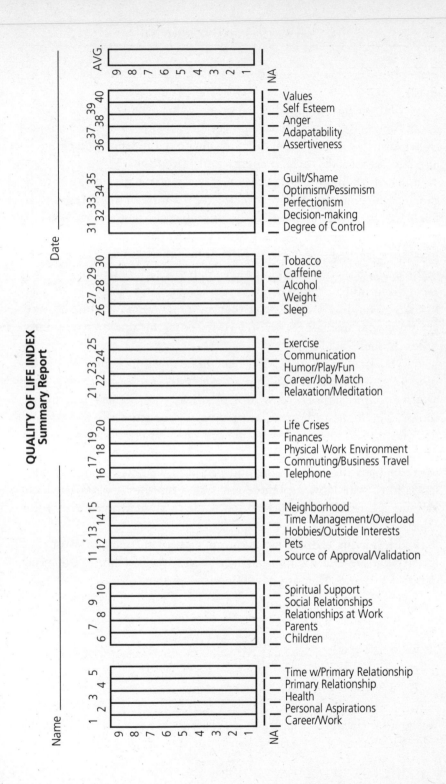

AVG.

Values
Self Esteem
Anger
Adapatability
Assertiveness

Guilt/Shame
Optimism/Pessimism
Perfectionism
Decision-making
Degree of Control

Tobacco
Caffeine
Alcohol
Weight
Sleep

Exercise
Communication
Humor/Play/Fun
Career/Job Match
Relaxation/Meditation

Life Crises
Finances
Physical Work Environment
Commuting/Business Travel
Telephone

Neighborhood
Time Management/Overload
Hobbies/Outside Interests
Pets
Source of Approval/Validation

Spiritual Support
Social Relationships
Relationships at Work
Parents
Children

Time w/Primary Relationship
Primary Relationship
Health
Personal Aspirations
Career/Work

perception of the types and degrees of stress and struggle you currently face.

Second, we have found that the average line usually correlates with energy level. Respondents whose average is below 5 are often experiencing a low energy state such as burnout or depression. Higher averages often indicate high energy and optimism.

A word of caution: If all of your scores are high (in the 8 to 9 range), you may need to reevaluate the candor of your responses. Such scores usually turn out to be unrealistic. To consistently score 8s or 9s is to live in a Utopian world that does not exist. You also may have learned to deny pain or to internalize your stress by never complaining. Such a lifestyle pattern can be very destructive as unrecognized and unresolved stress merely builds in intensity. If you know you tend to be more stoic than others, you may obtain a more accurate assessment by lowering your scores by one or two points on each question.

As you examine your profile, remember this important point: *The numerical scores are not as significant as the position of the scores relative to one another.* Now look again at your highest and lowest scores. The highest identifies areas where your strengths and coping abilities can be found. These skills can cushion more negative areas of stress. The lowest scores need your greatest attention; they indicate areas of your life—the visible and invisible weights—that are most stressful to you. However, these areas also represent points at which change is possible and where opportunities abound to lighten your load.

The following chapter will explore each of the categories on the Quality of Life Index in more depth. Then we will return to the more detailed interpretation of your individual profile.

CHAPTER 6

IDENTIFYING YOUR STRESSES AND STRENGTHS

AN ITEM-BY-ITEM ANALYSIS OF THE QLI

1. GAME PLAN FOR CAREER/WORK

Your professional game plan probably dominates many of your waking hours. At any given time you may be satisfied with your career progress, or you may feel that you are either slipping behind or not advancing fast enough.

This continuing self-assessment is important because in our work-oriented society, much of your identity derives from how you choose to make a living. Consequently, anyone who is unemployed, whose career does not meet his or her expectations, or who suddenly retires is under a great deal of stress. When the aerospace engineers and technicians were fired from Cape Canaveral, their career plans vanished; but more important, their self-esteem plummeted as their stress levels rose.

Whether you are a production-line manager for Chrysler, a financial planner at Merrill Lynch, a star quarterback, or a homemaker, your sense of identity is often synonymous with the assigned status of your job title. Therefore, your stress level rises whenever your job undergoes a drastic change. If a surgeon injures his hand, he becomes a nonoperating surgeon. When the price of oil drops, a degree in exploratory geology can become useless overnight. The fact that your family has farmed for generations is no guarantee that you will be able to make a living on the farm.

"If it were considered desirable to destroy a human being, the only thing necessary would be to give his work a climate of uselessness."

—Fyodor Dostoevsky

It is important to prepare yourself for change so that you do not become an endangered species in an ever-changing world. Look ahead and ask yourself: When this service or product is outdated, what is the next generation likely to need? How can my talents be utilized for these new opportunities? Success is intoxicating. Your perceptions can become dulled by the deceptive security of your current profession. But an important rule is to keep yourself as *complete* as possible so that if the world should change, as it undoubtedly will, you will not become a dinosaur. Adaptability is the key.

2. GAME PLAN FOR PERSONAL LONG-TERM AND SHORT-TERM ASPIRATIONS AND DEVELOPMENTS

Self-esteem should never be tied to any single facet of your life. Rather it is best to balance your identity portfolio just as you would your financial portfolio. A sense of fulfillment follows when you develop as many of your talents as possible. Unused talent is stressful. Developed talent prepares us for change and new opportunities.

Individuals may be successful in their professional lives and have great voids in their personal lives. Talents and abilities that are not utilized in their business activities may be crying out for expression.

Many of our patients have also discovered to their regret that spouses and children cannot be kept on hold indefinitely. Some are caught up in a dual-career married-with-children sweepstake that leaves them constantly exhausted. They are always living behind their expectations and beyond their income. Others, however, seem to juggle an amazing number of activities and obligations and to thrive on the challenge. Their stress balance is still tipped toward the NICE end of the scale—new, interesting, and challenging experiences.

This is why only you can evaluate your personal game plan. Only you can identify where the imbalances lie, and what long-term goals may be losing out to short-term pressures. Our role is to point out to our patients the cost of neglecting these concerns and to urge them to take their personal development as seriously as they take their careers.

3. HEALTH

Tinsley Harrison, M.D., is a revered academic clinician/physician and former chairman of the Department of Medicine, University of Alabama College of Medicine. He often told his students that, in his experience, people who had chest pain *for no apparent medical reason* were likely to develop heart disease in the future. Whereas those who felt healthy usually remained healthy! As unscientific as this sounds, one cannot turn away from the lifetime of clinical acumen and experience backing Dr. Harrison's observation.

There are many factors at work here. First, self-fulfilling prophecy. That is, if you see yourself as healthy, under control, and dealing with life well, you probably are not carrying a dangerous load of stress. Second, our bodies are an amazing feedback system; when we feel that "all systems are go," we are usually right. Granted, medical screening is now turning up previously undetectable problems—such as breast and cervical cancer, prostate and colon cancer—before they produce symptoms. Nevertheless, if you feel well, if you are not a "denier," and if your doctor says you are well, there is a very strong likelihood that you will remain well for quite some time.

Mental attitude and health are intrinsically linked. There are people in sustained states of anxiety and vigilance who dedicate their lives to awaiting a disaster. As John Barrymore's epitaph asserts, "I told you I was sick." Worrying about becoming ill can actually help to precipitate illness. As Dr. Harrison taught, it sets in motion the wrong kind of self-fulfilling prophecy.

Regular medical checkups can be a great source of comfort because, if you feel okay and the doctor confirms it, your personal biofeedback system is reinforced. Furthermore, early detection and redirection can prevent problems from becoming worse.

So ask yourself whether the instruments on your mental dashboard say "everything is okay" or "check engine." If your "check engine" light is blinking on and off, perhaps you require not only a thorough medical evaluation but some other kind of individual help to reduce anxieties, ruminations, or unnecessary concerns about potential or existing health problems.

If you have a weak plank in your health platform, such as high blood pressure, headache, or ulcers, take whatever action you can to support and buttress it. One of my favorite professors once said—with tongue in cheek—that the best way to live to be one hundred is to get a chronic disease and to take good care of it. That's not my recommendation, but the spirit is right. If you feel in charge of your health, you are sending the best kind of prescription to your body. If you feel you aren't, try to rewrite that prescription to be more positive and health-giving.

4. PRIMARY RELATIONSHIP

Why should a cardiologist be interested in his patients' primary relationships? If I could give you a magic pill that would reduce your risk of all forms of illness, accident, and death to one-half of what it would be for others, up to the age of seventy, and if this pill had very few side effects, would you take it? I suspect that you would. This magic medicine would be labeled the "Marriage Pill." Studies at the University of California have demonstrated that people who are married have a built-in health capsule. Don't ask me whether the marriage is good or bad. Don't ask me if such a marriage is the second or the third. The researchers simply identified whether or not their subjects were married, and they discovered significantly better health among those who were wed.[1]

> High blood pressure, high cholesterol, and cigarette smoking produce new coronary heart disease in only 14 percent during each decade up to the age of seventy. The reason the big three killers don't cause premature heart disease in us all is that there are counterbalancing forces. Marriage is one of these.

Other studies have focused on the physical value of a loving relationship. One famous study by R. M. Nerem and associates has now been duplicated by many other researchers. Originally Nerem set out to produce coronary artery disease in rabbits.[2] During the study two genetically identical sets of rabbits were kept in two different but identical rooms. Both groups were receiving diets high in fat and cholesterol, which had been designed to induce coronary heart disease. The rabbits in one room remained quite healthy, despite blood cholesterol levels equal to that of the unhealthy rabbits in the second room. The experimenters were mystified. When the explanation for the differences was uncovered, it lay in the activities of the caretaker's daughter. She often accompanied her father to the laboratory as he cleaned the cages and fed the rabbits. She had identified one room as containing her favorites, and while her father worked in both rooms, she would stay with her rabbit friends, picking them up, petting them, and showing them affection. These rabbits tended to stay more healthy.

Recall the price that the male Hamadryas baboons paid when separated from their monogamous mates. Part of the strength that comes from marriage is having a married identity. A married identity is formed by accepting oneself as a part of a couple and reacting to others in such a way that they see you as half of a bonded pair. Married individuals who perceive themselves as being single, and who act as if they were, separate themselves from this coupled identity. In doing so, they also separate themselves from some of the healthful benefits marriage can bestow on them.

Just as a primary relationship can be a strength, it can also be a great stress. One of my patients remarked, "My divorce was my heart attack. It was a powerful, painful, shocking wake-up call." The death of a spouse is a major life crisis. (See number 20, page 127).

5. TIME SPENT WITH PRIMARY RELATIONSHIP, AWAY FROM HOME, ALONE, AND NON-BUSINESS

Frequent, nonbusiness three-day weekends away can provide a powerful enhancement to coupled identity. Americans today seem to prefer this kind of vacation to the previous generation's two-week marathon holiday.

If you are very involved with your work, periodic breaks can have significant health benefits, helping you gain perspective on both projects and problems. The benefits can be even greater when you share this time with your spouse. However, such getaway time is a scarce commodity in modern households. It has been estimated that if we were to take away the time spent eating, moving, working, and settling kids, the average American couple shares less than seven minutes of quality communication per day.

This point is amply illustrated by a conversation I had with a rather uptight physician who was a patient of mine. He told me that he was planning a vacation just before beginning our SHAPE program, and so I asked, "What are you going to do?"

He replied, "I'm going to put the family in our new van and see the West Coast."

"Great!" I said. "Where are you going?"

"Well," he answered, "we're going to see San Diego, Los Angeles, Santa Barbara, Monterey, San Francisco, Portland, Seattle, and Vancouver."

"That sounds wonderful," I said. "How long have you got?"

With a determined look, he responded, "Five days."

He quickly detected the look of horror on my face and attempted to reassure me with the following explanation: "You see, we put a thick clear plastic shield between us and the back of the van to make it soundproof. The kids can mess around in the back without bothering my wife or me. We have a one-way speaker phone hooked up so that we can talk to them and they can hand-signal us. We also bought a large cooler that can hold a three-day supply of food. We have an auxiliary forty-gallon gas tank and two potty chairs that can cover any emergencies in that area. All of these preparations will cut down on stops."

I convinced him that such a trip would probably destroy his family, and I suggested that he find an alternative plan.

He and his wife took my advice. They decided to leave the children with an aunt and go off to enjoy a relaxing three-day weekend at a nearby resort.

6. RELATIONSHIP(S) WITH CHILD(REN)

Our clients are often overtly ecstatic about their children, but there are always areas where they wish they had done better. They've discovered that parenting isn't quite as joyful as they had imagined when the "little darlings" were in their bassinets. They have also discovered that their ability to control their children's destinies is far less than they had anticipated. And more than a few parents carry heavy burdens of conflict and disappointment for years.

> "Literature is mostly about having sex, and not much about having children. Life is the other way around."
>
> —David Lodge

Childrearing is one area where the clash between expectations and reality can be devastating. It is still true that a great deal of control—and hence responsibility—belongs to the parents. But significant influence comes from children's friends, teachers, cultural role models, the environment (including the security of the neighborhood), television, and peer pressure of various types. Most important, children come into the world with differing sets of genetic potentials. One need only look at siblings to see that, although there may be some physical resemblance, their behavior and life outcomes can be as different as night and day. Even with the same parents, divergent results can be expected that are not fully influenced by direction from the finest of super moms and dads.

In the case of adopted children, it is estimated by the National Association of Homes for Children that failed adoptions today range from 10 to 33 percent.[3] By failed, they mean children who get into real trouble; where there is such a degree of incompatibility that the adoption is terminated; or where the child does not develop normally.

Whether you have your own or adopted children, the challenge is always whether your expectations are realistic with regard to each child's inherited behavioral tendencies and aptitudes. If you cannot accept *who they are,* you are creating a lasting burden for yourself and for them. Perhaps the worst thing that parents can do is to assume that a child's success or failure is totally the result of parental influence in today's multifaceted world.

Interaction with our children is also far more intense today because life's choices have become much more complex, far-reaching, and uncertain. For example, it's not unusual to find children in their mid to late twenties still living at home or in college and still requiring parental support. It seems that independence has a higher price tag these days.

Bill Cosby once gave a graduation speech that he titled "Go Forth!" His theme was simple: "We love you. But remember, 'forth' is out *there* somewhere; it isn't at home."

In order to decrease our own stress as parents, we must recognize three critical factors that affect the lives of our children:

First, they need to have opportunities to express their own ideas. Often this is covered with the blanket phrase "being themselves." Being oneself may mean getting one's own way occasionally, but ultimately it consists of knowing one's strengths and weaknesses.

Second, they need adults they can look up to and admire. This mentoring and modeling is essential to mature growth and to turning weaknesses into strengths.

Both of these factors are vital elements in building healthy self-esteem.

Third, children today may need to remain closer to home longer than in earlier generations. This can give them perspective, background, courage, and even the income necessary to succeed in an extremely complex, ever-changing society.

7. RELATIONSHIP(S) WITH PARENTS

What type of relationship do you have with your parents? Do you often feel you are still the child? Are you a peer? Or has there been a role reversal because your parents, owing to finances or illness, have become your dependents?

Relationships with parents are ever-changing. If you are lucky, you may finally feel as though your parents have become your friends. A new source of strength and enrichment has entered your life. As your parents bask in your accomplishments, you revel in the fact they have finally evolved into human beings. (In fact, you and they have probably made a consistent, conscientious effort to arrive at this place.) If they then become adoring grandparents to your children, this further enhances your sense of connectedness, bonding, and mutual support.

However, a growing number of our patients have two sets of children—the younger ones and the older ones. This dual parenthood is one of the great weights and stresses in their knapsacks. Some of the most stressed are trying to arrange extended care for ill parents with inadequate (or no) insurance coverage. We are beginning to see some financial disasters and even bankruptcies in circumstances where children attempt to go beyond their means in serving the needs of parents while keeping their own households running. Life is a balance of giving and getting. I think you have to be a little selfish here. If you don't guard your time, aspirations, and family, your own self-esteem and health will suffer.

If your parents have become a financial or health burden and you are fortunate enough to have siblings, make sure that the burden is shared—if not on a financial, at least on a time-sharing basis. Don't underestimate the importance of emotional sharing. It is painful to see parents slipping away into different kinds of human beings than one recalls from earlier days. I sometimes urge overburdened adult children to find a home, extended-care facility, or retirement village where their parents can have new support systems, safety, and social activities. Children and parents alike need to overcome the view that these places should be called Terminal Oaks—parking lots for the unwanted and condemned.

The public perception of neglected old people is not met by the reality of many of the well-managed retirement homes that I have visited. Both my mother and my wife's father were in such a facility for quite some time. In each case they became part of a new community, made new friends, and had several years of a decent quality of life before their health deteriorated and they died. In this regard, as well as in so many others, prevention is the best form of therapy. Thinking about these situations in advance will enable you to assist your parents in making the appropriate plans. Keep in mind that developing and maintaining control and self-esteem will continue to be as important for them as it is for you.

8. RELATIONSHIPS AT WORK (WITH CO-WORKERS, BOSS, OTHERS)

When they conducted a long-term study of the worksite relationships among employees at a Volvo plant, Swedish researchers demonstrated what Gertrude Stein had already known: "A healthy group is a healthy group is a healthy group."

The data showed that when people work in an environment where they have a sense of fulfillment and accomplishment, they are more likely to remain healthy. Moreover, their productivity goes up. When our colleagues at work become a surrogate family, providing mutual support and connectedness, the positive results will spill over into all aspects of our lives.

The reverse is also true, as I saw when I was asked to evaluate stress in a national catalog sales company. The company's Medical Director told me that they had recently seen a dramatic increase in the number of employee illnesses. Absenteeism was up and visits to the corporate health center had tripled over the previous six months.

After testing employees with our Portable Stress Lab (PSL) we found the incidence of Hot Reacting to be a negligible 11 percent in all but one department—where an amazing 46 percent of the employees were Hot Reactors! Upon further investigation we learned that this was a new department set up to transform all company orders from their original paper and pencil format to a computerized system. Attempts had been made to reassure employees during the transition period. Employees had been told that job security would be guaranteed, overtime would not be required, and vacation schedules would be maintained. Despite these assurances, personnel unfamiliar with computers complained of symptoms such as: eye strain, headaches, back strain, and frequent upper-respiratory infections. The incidence of hypertension or Hot Reacting was almost three times the national average. What was the problem?

Our initial interviews indicated that some of the staff and managers

116

were doing quite well. Those managers with the least number of Hot Reacting employees would meet each morning with their staff to plan and discuss the tasks of the day. They gave frequent pats on the back and also met at the end of each day to debrief staff members and to reaffirm their sense of purpose, direction, and accomplishment.

The managers with the greater number of stressed employees generally held staff meetings only whenever there was a problem, a mistake, or a missed deadline. Even then, those sessions were often bland and nonproductive.

We suggested the development of a buddy system—pairing the good managers with the less effective managers; and for several weeks, each management team met in joint sessions with the combined staffs. Most of the poor managers began to catch on. Productivity increased over the next four months; and visits to the corporate medical facility dropped 50 percent. After the four-month trial, retesting with the Portable Stress Lab demonstrated that the level of Hot Reacting in the problem department had fallen to 22 percent! Coaching the supervisors turned out to be a more appropriate, cost-effective therapy than individual treatment for high blood pressure, Hot Reacting, and all of the other stress-related illnesses.

9. SOCIAL RELATIONSHIPS WITH FRIENDS, NEIGHBORS, GROUPS, AND OTHERS

If you wish to produce a measurable reduction in all forms of illness, accidents, and premature death (up to the age of seventy), give yourself another magic pill. Countless studies have demonstrated the healthful value of friendship. In one monumental research project, L. F. Berkman followed the health histories of seven thousand non-Japanese residents of Alameda County, California, for nine years. She gathered statistics on factors such as marital status, club membership, and attendance at religious services. Berkman found that those with the fewest social connections had mortality rates (from all causes) two to three times higher than those individuals who maintained high levels of social connectedness. This was true even when such factors as age, race, cigarette smoking, and income were taken into consideration.[4]

Dr. Theresa Seeman also studied this issue when she queried patients preparing to undergo coronary angiography, a diagnostic procedure that investigates the causes of severe chest pain in patients who might have coronary artery obstructions. When comparing patients who had friends with those who did not, Seeman found significantly more coronary blockage in those who lacked regular contact with friends.[5]

Friends are not just nice; they are a necessity. These relationships can become a powerful life-support system when our own internal resources have fallen short. If you found your score in this category to be 5 or below, you may wish to reevaluate your social relationships and begin to seek out other individuals with whom you may share experiences, hobbies, and other activities.

10. RELIGIOUS AND SPIRITUAL SUPPORT

A third magic pill could be our religious or spiritual feelings. These three life ingredients—marriage, friendship, and spiritual support—appear to lower the risk of all forms of illness and accidents. Statistically, individuals with high levels of satisfaction in these three categories have one-third fewer incidents of illness, accidents, and premature death up to the age of seventy as do individuals who report none of these in their lives.

It may surprise you that it's not just the risk of heart disease that is reduced, for the magic pill of spiritual support also appears to lower the possibility of contracting cancer, infectious diseases, and connective-tissue diseases, such as arthritis. We do not fully understand why this is so; but there appears to be a very definite, measurable correlation.

Researchers Berkman and Syme asked subjects of one study if they attended a church or a synagogue on a regular basis. No attempts were made to determine how deep, strong, or important were these spiritual connections; however, follow-up revealed that those reporting weak religious attendance had mortality rates two to three times greater than those who reported strong religious affiliations.[6]

Perhaps these studies simply measure a sense of completeness or wholeness in the lives of those they questioned. Those affiliated with a religious community may have a sense that past mistakes are forgiven and that indiscretions are understood in the present. Therefore, they enter the future with a sense of optimism. Forgiveness, understanding, and hope are three very powerful means of stress reduction.

11. SOURCE OF APPROVAL/VALIDATION

Psychiatrist Heinz Kohut theorizes that we all share a lifetime need of being needed.[7] The effect of being needed and needing one another is both powerful and mutually reinforcing. There can be a negative side to being needed, however. Some people are so dependent on the approval of others that they become people pleasers. They say yes to any and all demands and at the same time suppress their own needs. This is a sure way to lose control of your life, identity, and self-esteem. People pleasers often feel like puppets on a string, literally pulled in all directions by a multitude of forces and people. Because they can't say no, their circuits get overloaded. Then they begin to glow like a house with only one fuse in the box, drained by demands from too many lights and appliances.

Fuses blow, and, similarly, people pleasers often have surprisingly mercurial tempers. This can lead to distrust and impaired relationships. They then may feel guilt and remorse and withdraw socially over the associated embarrassment.

If you are a people pleaser, know that it is an impossible role to play. Many of our clients learn to take the initiative to unburden themselves of some of the responsibilities for others that they have assumed. They also learn to take their own needs more seriously. Obviously, there is a fine balance to be struck here. But if you need to feel indispensable and stretched to the limit by other people's needs in order to feel good about yourself—you've gone too far!

12. PETS

Studies at Johns Hopkins Medical Center have indicated that those who recover from severe illnesses and who have pets appear to survive longer than those who do not. Specifically, fifty out of fifty-three people who had pets were alive after one year following their first heart attack; while only seventeen of thirty-nine patients without pets survived the year. In reviewing the medical literature, the researchers also found that several studies verified the therapeutic effects of pets to both elderly people and the infirm. When an elderly or ill person was given a puppy or kitten to hold or to stroke, measurable drops in blood pressure and heart rates occurred. Breathing rates also slowed to a more relaxed and comfortable pace.[8]

For many of us, pets provide companionship. As warm living things, pets often return the favor of our attention by being affectionate and attentive to us. I agree with Dr. Edward Ryerson who has stated that the attachment to pets can be an excellent substitute for many who need closeness. As we all know, they are often substitutes for children.

I do not recommend that you run right out and find a pet if you do not have one. Only you can decide whether a pet will become one more burdensome responsibility in your life—or an added pleasure. However, I do know that if you are a pet lover, you may live longer.

13. HOBBIES/OUTSIDE INTERESTS

Stress seems to be incompatible with happiness, and so hobbies and interests designed to make you happy help you live longer and better. Dwight Eisenhower enjoyed golf and oil painting; Winston Churchill also escaped the rigors of leadership by painting in oils—and by building brick walls. The only rule is to find a form of relaxation that is fulfilling without being frustrating—a little world where the FUD factor is absent.

My own hobby is building model railroads. This activity gives me both a sense of detachment and a feeling of constructive creativity. While a project may require some study and effort, working with the rails, miniature towns, depots, scenery, and trains relaxes me. As an added bonus, I find that when I'm relaxing in my train room, I often stumble upon solutions to problems that have been plaguing me in my professional life. Once given the opportunity to unwind, a relaxed mind frequently is set free to be more creative and more functional.

Years ago a good friend (and former Hot Reacting patient) was sitting in my basement train room watching me trying to put down some recalcitrant, unforgiving pieces of model railroad track.

He asked, "How do you manage to keep up with all of the things you are doing and continue to work on your railroad?"

I honestly replied, "It isn't easy."

His response was "You've helped me; let me offer you a suggestion. Why don't you hire somebody to do your hobby?"

We both laughed, but later I thought about the suggestion; and in a few weeks, I located an excellent person to do just that. Sometimes my train companion worked with me; sometimes he worked without me. I was able to provide all the tools and supplies; he was able to supply all of the time I didn't have. Together we agreed on what would be done and how we would do it. Sometimes he thought of things that had not entered my mind; and sometimes I thought of things he had never considered. Before this time, my hobby and the goal of building a large-scale working model railway system had really just been a series of frustrating fits and spurts of attention. As a team, my partner and I have been able to build and run a railroad that neither of us could have accomplished alone.

14. TIME MANAGEMENT/CIRCUIT OVERLOAD

Mahatma Gandhi said, "There is more to life than just increasing its speed."

Are you running your life, or is your life running you? Are you constantly caught up in deadlines and dilemmas? Does living require a Herculean effort? When you look at your desk, is it a pile of incomplete tasks? Has corporate life become a series of endless, seemingly meaningless meetings? Is life a game of "catch-up"?

Too many simultaneous life events are physically harmful and the pathway to burnout. For this reason, time management has been of substantial benefit to a large number of patients at the Institute of Stress Medicine. We have steadily added more time-management techniques to our therapeutic approach. Specifically, we have found that using a day planner is very productive. By systematically planning your day, you can follow your progress and see more clearly what needs to be done. Minor tasks need no longer dominate or overshadow major ones. A few minutes of planning can control hours of chaos.

A planned day allows you to schedule stress-reducing breaks and rest periods—and to save time for family, friends, personal development, and hobbies. Simply obtaining this level of control over your life also reduces stress.

Successful time management is based upon knowing what's important to you. Therefore, it is based on your values. They will help you to start and to set priorities—the first step in time management. See Chapter 10 for more suggestions about getting time under control.

15. NEIGHBORHOOD

Tragically, living in the center of a major city has become synonymous with feelings of fear, uncertainty, and doubt (the FUD factor). This trio of troubles changes physiology and metabolism. Researchers have found that the conditions existing in neighborhoods can even determine whether or not a person has high blood pressure. As we learned previously, one sad complication of the FUD factor is that it contributes to the development of high blood pressure in the very young. The calm, quiet, and comfort that a controlled neighborhood can offer is more than just the "American Dream"—it is a means for extending your life.

16. THE TELEPHONE

The telephone symbolizes the best and worst of our modern industrialized society. It's now possible to pick up a telephone in the middle of the Sahara Desert and "reach out and touch someone" halfway around the globe. You can even place a phone call when flying forty-thousand feet above the ground. For many of my stressed patients, this technical breakthrough is the number-one irritant in their busy lives. It always surprises me when, after having described the telephone as a major stressor, a patient will very likely say, "I even have a phone in my car."

A phone call can interrupt. It can be an invasion of privacy and personal schedules. It can cause uncertainty or force an immediate response to a question that might otherwise be better left for later consideration. It can hound you when you would rather be reading, or thinking, or simply relaxing.

You need to learn to control the telephone rather than allowing it to control you. Think of ways your telephone use can be better managed and thus less stressful. What about the revolutionary idea of *not* having a phone in every room? Or *not* carrying a portable phone with you when you walk out into your backyard? Or something even more drastic—*not allowing* the phone to interrupt? If you are involved in work, study, or contemplation, and the ringing phone is causing you undue stress, get yourself an answering machine, turn off the phone bell, and simply answer your messages when you are ready. It gives you some space and time and thereby reduces your sensory overload.

All of this is very well, but what do you do in a situation where you have a job in which *the phone must be answered*? Suppose you are a stockbroker and your phone is your livelihood? Suppose the market takes a 300- or 400-point dip and you are at the other end of the phone to explain your recommendations to a platoon of unforgiving Hot Reactors? Now the phone is an instrument of torture, piling on loads of guilt, shame, and hostility. In a recent study, we found that 88 percent of the two hundred top-performing brokers in a major financial planning firm tested as Hot Reactors. All were multimillionaires, but they were living a reactive life and were headed for major health problems. But what really interested me was the 12 percent who were *Cool Reactors*. If only we could understand how they stayed cool under this pressure, we might have some additional clues for controlling Hot Reacting.

If the phone is your livelihood, it is important to have a substitute and to take relaxation breaks away from the battlefield—just as athletes are rotated in competitive games. Build this into your job description. In reactive uninterrupted telephone answering, you feel you have no choice and no control. Knowing that there is a break ahead is an important part of pacing yourself. If you find you are becoming ill more frequently, having more upper respiratory infections, or if your blood pressure is climbing, this is an early indicator of circuit overload from telephone tyranny.

It is also important for a reactive person to avoid caffeine during work breaks. Your body is pumping plenty of adrenaline already! Instead, try taking a walk, visiting with someone you like, or learning a relaxation technique. The key to the telephone is to stay cool and be proactive whenever you can, so that you can shut off your alarm and vigilance reactions from time to time.

17. COMMUTING/BUSINESS TRAVEL

Your perception of commuting is the primary key to whether or not you find it stressful. If you travel by bus or train and you consider the ride an opportunity to read, relax, or reflect, this experience can be a very positive one. If you perceive commuting as a tiresome and frustrating nuisance, it can be the source of physiological distress. Moreover, the very act of complaining about the turbulent hours of commuting can multiply your stress. Tonic or toxic—the traveler decides.

Commuting by automobile presents a greater challenge, for sitting behind the wheel when traffic grinds to a halt is certainly not a rewarding experience. Under these conditions, your pleasant home in a remote area can be a source of great stress when the long drive home makes you miserable and crabby. Ask yourself if you can stop thinking of your car as a frustrating "waiting room on wheels." For example, can you relieve your stress by turning your car into a place for dictating letters, listening to tapes, making phone calls, reviewing the day, or planning for tomorrow?

Business travel today can be a stressful blur of different climates, time zones, foods, and cultures. Even in seemingly passive airline travel, "jet lag" can mean an excessive buildup of cortisol, resulting in the silent disruption of your physiology, your body rhythms, and your metabolism.

You can control travel stress to some extent by scheduling enough time between transfers and allowing for periods of rest both before and after a trip. If all else fails, simply cut down on the number of times you crisscross the country or the world. Use phones or video conferences instead of flying.

18. PHYSICAL WORK ENVIRONMENT

The quality of your environment at work is as important as the quality of your environment at home—but you often have much less control over it.

Perhaps your work site is in an unsafe or highly polluted area, and you dread the passage from your bus, train, or car to the entrance. Once you get inside, what greets you?

Is your workplace itself unsafe, dirty, crowded, too hot, too cold, too dry, too humid, too noisy? All these things will influence your ability to get the job done without unnecessary wear and tear.

In some workplaces, noise is a major form of pollution that makes any attempt at concentration an exhausting struggle. Excess noise is not only annoying; it can destroy your hearing. There may also be a problem with subsonic noise. Low-frequency vibrations cannot be heard, but they can be very fatiguing. (An engineer can pick these up with a low-frequency vibration detector.)

If everyone in your department is "sick all the time," the building itself may be sick. Legionnaire's disease is only the most dramatic example. A fungus, mold, or pollen may be involved. Cigarette smoke, as well, is often carried by a poorly designed ventilation/filtration system from one part of a building to another.

Other kinds of work stress come from inadequate support facilities: broken equipment, tightly rationed supplies, antediluvian phone or computer systems.

Having a good work ethic doesn't require toughing it out in such conditions until your body sends you an unmistakable distress signal. If you are an employee, take whatever action you can on behalf of yourself and others. If you are a manager, rethink the work environment as a bottom-line issue.

19. FINANCES

Ernest Haskins wrote, "Save a little money each month, and at the end of the year, you'll be surprised at how little you have." My own financial enlightenment came from two very different sources.

Source 1: In 1962, I was doing specialized postgraduate work in cardiac research. A faculty position was offered to me at the University of Minnesota, which I hesitated to accept. Working in the same university was a Polish cardiologist of Jewish descent. During World War II he had avoided being shipped to a Nazi death camp by hiding in a Warsaw attic for *five years*. He was a brilliant physician and a human dynamo with a "low whir." I respected his opinion, and so I told him of the offer.

He congratulated me by saying, "It's a great honor."

"But," I replied, "they only offered me $10,500 a year."

He looked up with disgust and muttered, "How many steaks can you eat in a day?"

I joined the faculty.

Source 2: Another point of view was offered ten years later by my attorney. He had come to visit me as I lay in the coronary care unit.

"If you don't survive your heart attack," he said, "your family will be out on the streets. You don't have any savings or life insurance." What a great bedside manner, I thought.

After years of academic medicine, I had assumed that my company (the university) would take care of me. Not so!

At that point it became clear to me that the function of money lies somewhere between the altruistic views of my cardiologist mentor and the realistic concerns of my bedside attorney. Money provides options. With money, I could do some of the things I wanted to do; without it, I would be forced into corners not of my own choosing.

As I rested in the coronary care unit, I realized that I was trapped. I could move neither physically nor financially. I realized, too, that my medical skills could not be passed on to help my wife and two children—they would need something much more tangible. I decided that having money could provide my family with alternatives and ease my mind. I embarked on a real plan of money management; and this helped me live more peacefully. Regardless of your income, managing your finances in the most prudent manner possible can actually be a lifesaver. Money has one major value; it gives you choices. But simply piling money higher and deeper often becomes a stressful obligation in itself.

20. LIFE CRISES IN PAST SIX MONTHS

If you turn on enough home appliances at the same time, you'll blow an electric circuit. The same thing can happen with your physiology.

How do you know when one more crisis will be too much? Several years ago Drs. Holmes and Rahe tried to answer that question by developing an index for predicting the possibility of future illness from the number of existing life crises.[9] They discovered a correlation between the number of significant life changes a person experienced during the previous six to twelve months and the state of his or her health. The Holmes/Rahe list defines one hundred significant life changes, including divorce, death of a spouse, loss of a job, and problems with children.

To use the index, an individual checks off those events that have occurred during the previous year. From that selection, the reviewer attempts to predict future health. While indexes such as this can present opportunities for self-evaluation, I believe the technique has some important flaws. The major problem is that such an index fails to evaluate a person's *perception* of each crisis. In other words, was the event deemed a "plus" or a "minus"? The QLI attempts to resolve this problem.

Ultimately, a person's perception of any life event and the way in which he or she reacts to it determine its physical consequences. Thus perception determines reality. Or, as others have remarked, "Perception is reality." Devastating experiences do not disappear overnight; and the reality of a tragic event must become a part of a person's awareness. This awareness can ultimately bring about resolution; and such resolution can help the person to avoid rather than initiate physical distress.

I remember an excellent example of this kind of resolution. During the stock market decline of October 19, 1987, one of my patients (a man I'll call Irving) lost over $10 million. Most of us would agree that this was a major crisis; and Irving's reaction to it was a severe loss of self-esteem. Even though he still had a net worth of over $120 million, he could not forgive himself for what he saw as a lack of foresight. He felt that he should have known better. The day after the loss, Irving felt light-headed and some numbness, and his usually normal blood pressure rose to an alarming 259 over 140. That's when his physician referred him to our institute.

As Irving moved through our diagnostic procedures, we learned of his perspective of his financial loss. We learned also that money meant everything to Irving. *For all his life he had measured his self-worth by his net worth.* His opinion of himself was proportionate to the size of his bank account; his ego was attached to his wallet. His fiscal and emotional accounting systems had nearly killed him.

Although he had two sons, Irving had decided that they were "failures and losers"; and so his family contacts were minimal. The more I listened, the more it became clear that both of his young sons were active businessmen, self-sufficient, and financially successful beyond the levels of their peers. It was true that they hadn't yet reached the goals set by their father, but they certainly were well on the way.

After just two days at the institute, Irving was visibly calmer; and yet it was clear that he was going to need more than just money if he was going to survive. We prescribed medications to protect his heart and blood vessels temporarily; but our primary prescription was that he reevaluate his life and his values. Specifically we suggested that he begin strengthening his relationships with his sons. During the months and years of follow-up, we've seen a remarkable change. After recognizing the link between stress and bodily functions, Irving recovered with amazing speed. His Hot Reacting continues to cool steadily. He has greatly increased communications with his family, and he has established a new relationship that may lead to marriage. The connection between his wallet and his heart has lessened, as have his symptoms.

Irving's crisis appeared to be financial, but in reality it was a crisis of values and perceptions. The same is true of many patients who have come to us in times of stress. As you evaluate your own crisis events, try to step back from the surface problems and consider your innermost feelings and emotions. If you are unsuccessful in resolving

128

the crisis yourself, seek professional help so that you can go on with your life.

21. RELAXATION/MEDITATION

As important research by Herbert Benson, M.D., and Dean Ornish, M.D., has clearly demonstrated, meditation and relaxation can be important not only in reducing blood pressure and reversing arteriosclerosis, but also in enhancing the quality of your life and performance. Meditation and relaxation are strong antidotes for the fight or flight (alarm) reactions. They produce a reduction in physical levels of adrenalinelike substances and relaxation of muscle tension. The blood vessels open and the blood pressure drifts down.

When this happens, the body is at rest and the cardiovascular system is cool, but the individual's state of mental clarity and alertness is retained and heightened. This is very unlike the exhausting vigilance and hyperalertness caused by the FUD factor. This relaxed yet alert state can be attained through all scientifically based relaxation and meditation techniques. When regularly practiced, this state becomes sustained; it can change how you experience your life from the inside out.

You cannot simply tell yourself to relax. You have to learn the appropriate stepwise method to do so. Drs. Ornish and Benson have extensive experience in teaching meditation as part of a daily stress-reduction routine, and you will find their techniques in their books.[10] In addition, some of the techniques are reviewed in my first book, *Is It Worth Dying For?*

Once you have mastered these techniques, they can be put to work anywhere. They are often of greater value than a stimulating catecholamine-loaded cup of coffee during a break. Simply to be able to close ones eyes, detach, and relax can be very refreshing and allows one to return to work in a more creative and less combative frame of mind. In the longer term, the habit of meditation can clear the mind and help you to make the choices that are so important in improving your life situation.

22. CAREER/JOB MATCH

We separate this item from number 1, Game Plan for Career/Work, for a reason. You may be progressing steadily in a career you basically dislike. You may be a successful lawyer because your family insisted on your becoming "a professional," when what you've always longed to do is open your own restaurant. Or you may have enjoyed your career when you were younger, but now feel a new person emerging who no longer fits the old job description.

Too many of us brush aside such basic issues for our identity because we "don't have time to think about it" or have "too many responsibilities" to make a change. One of the opportunities we offer our clients is the chance to take seriously the long-term stress of being a fish out of water. When we learn in our six-month follow-up that such clients are making concrete plans for retraining or for transferring their skills to another field, we know we have succeeded.

23. HUMOR/PLAY/FUN

In his best-selling book *Anatomy of an Illness,* Norman Cousins described his miraculous recovery from a debilitating connective tissue disease (ankylosing spondylitis). His recovery is perhaps one of the most profound examples of the value of humor in healing. Told that all medical avenues had been exhausted, Cousins devised his own treatment of watching humorous films. He said that he substituted humor for aspirin. In time his fever and pain diminished and the disease itself dissipated. Cousins believed that laughter, hope, faith, love, cheerfulness, and other positive emotions can have therapeutic value. I believe that he was correct. Humor is an essential medication in my practice. I've been known to prescribe a Bill Cosby or Mel Brooks tape or a Pink Panther video.

Healing, in fact, can begin with the simple act of smiling. Scientists have identified a physical connection between the nerves of the facial muscles and a specific area of the brain that is capable of releasing "feel-good" chemicals. Smile now and notice the feeling of well-being that ensues. When people smile, researchers can even measure

130

declines in blood pressure similar to those recorded as people held their pets.

Laughter can stimulate the body in much the same way as physical exercise. The heart beats faster, and the lungs expand. In addition to these physical manifestations, noradrenaline and other chemicals are released into the bloodstream. Cousins called it "internal jogging." I like that. Laughter turns off the production of stress chemicals and turns on the production of endorphins, the powerful neurochemical painkillers two hundred times more powerful than morphine.

In addition, laughter is the perfect antidote for fear and anxiety. Fear is what you feel when a tiger charges; anxiety is what you feel when you think a tiger *might* charge. Neither incident is funny, but both can be relieved with humor. It's no coincidence that in most stressful situations, a clown will appear. Art Buchwald once suggested that if we were going to have a portable missile system, we should simply install it on Amtrak trains and send the schedule to the Russians. "That way, they'd never find them."

Ten years before the destruction of the Berlin Wall, I heard one of my favorite East German jokes: "Two East German border guards, Hans and Fritz, were chatting. Fritz asked, 'Hans, what would you do if the Wall fell down?' Hans answered, 'I would immediately climb the closest tree.' His friend frowned. 'Why would you do that?' Hans replied, 'I don't want to be killed in the stampede.' "

Humor can give us a feeling of control in situations that would otherwise seem uncontrollable. Complex situations can be made more understandable with comedy. When I say that having a heart attack was like having an elephant sit on my chest, I'm trying to use a light-hearted and understandable means for describing what was, in truth, the awful leadlike pressure on my thorax.

Humor provides other social benefits. Look at an audience watching a stand-up comedian and you will see a form of group stress management. People come together into a homogeneous, friendly group, smiling at strangers and sharing common insights. This kind of social interaction is another component of the "magic pill for life." Harmony with others is helpful for all physiological functions. And while no normal human being can hide all of his or her negative feelings behind a clown's mask, a person who is genuinely fun to be with will have no trouble finding other people who are supportive.

Humor can provide insights into mundane, dull, routine, and minor crises that touch everyone's life. Comedians, such as Bill Cosby, use humorous vignettes to show us how daily stresses can be turned into strengths; and yet humor is rarely acknowledged for its true social and individual value.

Humor can take many forms, from a surprise ending to a story to the unexpected way in which two opposites are put together in a rhyme. It can be physical or analytical. Sometimes it's simply seeing the funny side of the ordinary things that happen around us. Whatever the mode, this whimsical perception of life detaches a person—at least momentarily—from pressing problems and conflicts. Incongruous situations, ironies, and ludicrous circumstances give people a break. At the very least, humor provides time to detach temporarily and to acquire a more balanced perspective on life. In terms of self-talks, humor counterbalances negative thinking.

24. INTERPERSONAL COMMUNICATION

George Bernard Shaw once said, "The danger of communication is to assume that it occurred."

Inappropriate or inadequate communication is a great source of stress in our daily lives, leading to frustration, anger, and resentment. For this reason, improving your communication skills may be a primary step in reducing the stress you feel in both personal and professional relationships.

I find that the best communicators are also the best listeners. They can listen to what's in between the lines. True communication depends on this ability to understand not only what other people say, but also the nonverbal ways in which they are expressing their unique points of view.

People often change for the better when they perceive that they are being understood. Clinical experience has demonstrated this repeatedly. When I observe a Hot Reactor making advantageous lifestyle changes, I ask, "Why have you changed *now,* when it seemed so impossible for you to change in the past?" Frequently the answer is something like, "You took the time to find out who I really was, and so you earned the right to teach me."

25. EXERCISE

Exercise can lower anxiety, relieve temporary depression, and help increase a person's sense of control and self-esteem. For this reason, regular exercise is essential in any program of stress reduction. However, to be medically beneficial, this exercise must also be appropriate to the individual. Determining your current and desired level of fitness and correlating these with recommended levels of exertion is discussed thoroughly in Chapter 12.

26. SLEEP

Most of us spend a third of every day asleep. If the amount of time spent sleeping is shortened or lengthened, usually something is amiss. Overuse of caffeine or alcohol, sadness, humiliation, and unresolved personal dilemmas are but a few of the stresses that can cause sleep disturbances.

We all have daily tensions, but generally we have learned how to detach and calm ourselves when we become physically tired. Adults who did not learn this relaxation or self-soothing ability may need to be taught relaxation skills as a part of their stress-treatment program.

If you begin the night by falling asleep easily, but then awaken in a few hours, this could mean that you are anxious or unable to control unfinished mental business. In this case, you may be helped by improving your time-management and organizational skills and, thus, resolving some stress.

Early-morning awakening (when not accompanied by early retirement and a full night's sleep) may indicate depression; and in this case, personal counseling often can identify the underlying problems that are disturbing your rest. In all cases, sleep disorders can be quite disruptive and stressful. Regular exercise can help mitigate the effects of these disorders as well as improve the quality of sleep. Sleep disturbances are important warnings. If they persist, seek professional help.

133

27. BODY WEIGHT

Uncontrolled stress is often directly related to body weight in that it affects patterns of both under- and overeating. Weight problems, in turn, have profound effects on our health and on our identity in an image-conscious society. For this reason, the habits that will effectively control weight must include personal, emotional, and mental "weights" as well as dietary concerns. Chapter 11 will explore this topic in detail.

28. ALCOHOL CONSUMPTION

Several studies have established that moderate amounts of alcohol (2 ounces or less) taken on a daily basis (for those who choose to drink) may reduce the risks of coronary heart disease in some people. And yet I never recommend drinking for this reason. Our own clinical evidence is that consuming more than 2 ounces of alcohol a day actually contributes to high blood pressure and worsens Hot Reacting. Moreover, the research also is very clear that prolonged, excessive drinking (that is, more than 4 ounces a day) often leads to a variety of health complications, including cirrhosis of the liver, heart disease, and certain cancers of the digestive tract. Equally proven is that alcohol use during pregnancy jeopardizes the well-being of both mother and child.

One patient asked me if the daily maximum recommended amount of 2 ounces per day could be "saved up" for Saturday night. I had to tell him that 14 ounces of alcohol on any night is not a healthy idea. It is simply a way to get "pickled," not protected from the effects of stress.

29. CAFFEINATED BEVERAGES (COFFEE, TEA, COLA)

Caffeine is a chemical substance related to the adrenalinelike compounds, catecholamines. In many of us it potentiates alarm reactions that make the body respond as if it must fight or flee. The more caffeine you take in, the more agitated you will become. Therefore, substituting noncaffeinated beverages for caffeinated ones can help restore many mild Hot Reactors to Cool Reactor status.

In addition to the usual sources of coffee, tea, and cola, caffeine can come in some surprising packages, including cocoa, chocolate, and medications (both prescription and over-the-counter).

One recent report suggested that four cups of coffee per day (or its equivalent) are harmless. My clinical experience suggests that this is not true for everyone. People react in varying ways to caffeine— and in general, the more caffeine you consume, the more agitated you will become.

If you are a hypertensive or Hot Reactor, check your blood pressure after a few days of caffeine abstinence and then decide for yourself if caffeine is a factor for you. By the way, don't be surprised if you get a few caffeine-withdrawal headaches. These, too, may be a clue that caffeine is not for you.

30. TOBACCO

I have only one recommendation for those who smoke: *Stop!*

If you stop today, statistics confirm that you will greatly improve your current health level *and* you will prolong the length of your life. Best of all, *it's never too late and you're never too old to stop.* Most former smokers report that after stopping, they experienced significant health benefits within six months to a year. Statistically, in just three years, the risk of coronary heart disease and lung cancer in former smokers plummets to nearly the same levels seen in those who never smoked. Studies of the coronary arteries of people who have had heart attacks demonstrate dramatic differences between those who continued to smoke as compared to those who quit. Smokers develop steady, progressive blockages in their coronary arteries; formation of these obstructions often ceases or slows when an individual stops smoking.

This damage occurs partly because once nicotine enters the bloodstream, it functions in much the same way as does adrenaline. It revs the engine, compounding all of the negative physiological effects experienced during high levels of stress.

In addition, inhaled smoke (even when someone else is doing the smoking) contains over four thousand compounds, many of which have subtle, cumulative, and potentially fatal effects on the body.

The bottom line:

- If you smoke, stop. (Combine a stop-smoking seminar with use of the nicotine patch, under your doctor's supervision.)
- If you don't smoke, don't start.
- Avoid environments where passive smoke from others accumulate and campaign for smoke-free environments.

31. DEGREE OF CONTROL

When people fail to recognize options for control or feel they cannot exercise the options they have, they are invisibly entrapped. This kind of stress is most often experienced by a "people-pleaser," someone whose self-esteem is completely dependent on the opinions and validations of others. Someone else is always pulling the strings—even the strings of their own identity. They may or may not exhibit outwardly dependent or needy behavior. What is important is their internal sense of control or lack of it.

By contrast, pro-active people accept responsibility for their own actions and circumstances. They can often find options where other people don't see any opportunity for choice. And when they are up against something they truly can't influence, they may make an active choice to detach or to "go with the flow" rather than continue to struggle.

Such people make things happen, rather than simply allowing them to happen. Even in very difficult external situations, their sense of internal control gives them some protection from the negative effects of stress.

32. DECISION MAKING

Effective decision making is closely related to your sense of control, and vice versa. Indecision often stems from a failure to clarify desired outcomes on the basis of personal interests, needs, wishes, and goals. The first step toward effective decision making is knowing where you want to go. Stating the outcome clearly to yourself gives purpose and direction to all the interim decisions to be made.

The second step is reconciling the methods required to achieve the outcome with your personal value system. You also need to take into account the wishes and needs of others who will be influenced.

It is helpful to list a few important decisions and then consider how they will affect your life and those whose lives you touch. Sleep on your list and see if the picture clears. What deserves to be done? If it succeeds, will it make a significant difference? If it fails, will it make a significant difference? What is the balance of assets and liabilities?

Often the worst decisions are those we feel compelled to make in a short time frame, on impulse rather than after reflection. On the other hand, too much reflection without action may indicate perfectionism or a reluctance to take responsibility.

33. PERFECTIONISM

Perfectionism is expectation that never meets reality, and it is fueled by the fear of failure. It is comprised of guilt, defensiveness, and the fear of ridicule. Clues to this behavior are the words *should* and *have to*. Perfectionists believe and practice the adage, "If you want something done right, do it yourself." Unable to delegate even the most minor tasks, they become angry with themselves or others whenever *any* detail can't be done "just right."

Perfectionism imposes tremendous burdens. First, it frequently restricts relationships with others, since few people can meet the standards perfectionists may set for self and others. Second, because perfectionists have so much trouble delegating, their productivity is usually *limited* rather than increased. If your sense of perfectionism is beginning to cause you such stress, you need to find the balance between "well done" and "over done."

> **"The difference between 'good enough' and 'perfect' is a logarithmic increase in effort."**
>
> **—Otis Baughman, M.D.**

34. TENDENCY TOWARD OPTIMISM/PESSIMISM

C. P. Kimble, at the University of Rochester, interviewed fifty-four patients just before they were to undergo open-heart surgery. Kimble classified the patients into four groups:

Group I was classified as *being optimistic.*
Group II had *mixed feelings.*
Group III *denied their anxieties.*
Group IV was *passive and/or depressed.*

The results of the surgeries paralleled the outlooks expressed by each group. Nine of the thirteen optimistic patients improved, one died, and three were still unchanged after surgery. Of the fifteen patients with mixed feelings, only one improved; one died, eight remained unchanged, and five got worse. Of the twelve patients labeled "deniers," three improved after surgery, three remained unchanged, two became more ill, and four died. Those patients identified before their operations as being passive or depressed had the worst postoperative histories. Of fourteen individuals in this grouping, one showed improvement, one remained unchanged, one became more ill, and eleven died.[11]

This study gives dramatic support to the power of belief in health. My own experience, however, suggests that under normal circumstances, neither unqualified optimism nor pessimism is an ideal state of mind. The problem with optimists is that they will constantly try to do more than is practical or possible, failing to take advantage of the caution that can come from a touch of fear. Conversely, pessimists often miss opportunities or lack the enthusiasm necessary to overcome life's obstacles.

> **"A pessimist is an individual who, when confronted with two unpleasant alternatives, selects both."**
>
> —Oscar Wilde

My own view is that it's better to try to be a little of both—with a tilt toward optimism.

35. FEELINGS OF GUILT AND/OR SHAME

Focusing on past mistakes or bursts of anger can produce unnecessary guilt, which in turn produces stress. Life inevitably has both successes and failures; and the only thing you can change about the past is your attitude toward it. For this reason, the only practical way to control stress over past setbacks is to think of them as learning opportunities—ways in which you may reevaluate how you will act in the future.

Some of our clients have a terrible time letting go of guilt over unfinished relationships. Not having said good-bye to Pop before he died becomes a burden they carry through life. The fact is, if there was a good relation with Pop, he probably knew it. If there wasn't, he also knew that, and saying good-bye wouldn't have made much difference.

On the other hand, some guilt is real and legitimate. If a client feels guilty about behavior that violates personal commitments, social mores, or laws, our focus is on changing the guilt-producing behavior. In this case, the guilt is a valuable wake-up call.

We see this quite often in the case of extramarital affairs. There's no question that some individuals feel no sense of guilt about them whatsoever. But many affairs are initiated out of low self-esteem, depression, or professional boredom, and the affair adds guilt to an already toxic mix. Add drugs and alcohol, and self-esteem and control are thrown into a tailspin. Here, the answer is not more guilt, but finding a different solution to the basic problem.

If you're carrying a load of guilt—for whatever reason—you may need one-to-one counseling to discover its cause and resolve it. There should be no guilt or shame involved in seeking such help!

36. ASSERTIVENESS

Unassertive individuals do not express irritation over the little things of life. Rather, they carry around a knapsack full of emotional IOUs until some trivial event causes the knapsack to overflow and they blow up. We have found that many of our patients are literally stewing in their own stress chemicals. While appearing cool on the surface, these people often explode unexpectedly when confronted by a seemingly minor situation.

Unassertive people are also full of self-doubts, which become manifest as fears about themselves and uncertainties about what to do. They seem to be saying to themselves, "Why express my opinions or my needs? They can only get me into trouble." Such people often buy a temporary peace at a tremendous long-term cost to themselves and others.

Of course, it's important to learn to communicate displeasure and frustration in ways that are socially appropriate. Assertiveness is very different from hostility and aggression. Assertive people speak from their own point of view, take responsibility for their feelings, and try to help others understand why they are upset. On the other hand, aggressive people will say whatever they think—often in an abusive manner.

The two behaviors can be contrasted in the following manner:

Aggressiveness = a triple loss
• Loss #1: Leads to feelings
  of embarrassment and
  guilt.

Assertiveness = a triple win
• Win #1: Is seldom
  followed by
  embarrassment or guilt.

- Loss #2: Often makes enemies and polarizes situations.
- Loss #3: Usually results in a negative outcome.

- Win #2: Allows others to understand your point of view.
- Win #3: Is more likely to result in positive outcomes.

37. ADAPTABILITY/FLEXIBILITY—PERSONAL/PROFESSIONAL

For the person who cannot adapt, life is much like riding in an automobile with no shock absorbers—it generally produces a very painful posterior.

My favorite story about flexibility was told to me by an internationally renowned pipe organist. I had asked her to recall her most stressful professional experience.

"That's easy," she replied. "One Easter I was playing Handel's Messiah in a famous old German church. The organ was an antique, hand-pumped instrument. I was within twenty bars of completing the piece, when all of a sudden, the air went out of the pipes!

"My critics later reported the sound as 'the agonal cry of a fatally wounded bagpipe.'

"I rushed into the pump room where I found the elderly German pump operator who was responsible for hand-pumping air into the organ's pipe system. Seated stoically next to the pump he had lovingly tended over many years, he stared directly at me with his arms folded across his chest.

"I asked, 'Is it broken?'

" 'Nein,' he responded.

" 'Then why aren't you pumping?' I asked.

" 'Madam,' he announced, 'in my career, I have pumped one hundred and three Messiahs on this organ, and you have received all of the air that this piece requires.' "

Rigidity, whether it is your own or that of others, can be a most difficult situation to deal with. This is because rigidity is the antithesis of life—it blocks out choices. Today adaptability is essential for survival in our rapidly changing world.

A related quality is resilience, the emotional shock absorber that allows us to bounce out of life's unpredictable chuck holes. It helps to move past unpleasant events rather than to become mired down in them. Ruminating over missed opportunities, disappointments, and losses (real and perceived) saps our creative and problem-solving vitality. Becoming thick-skinned does not mean becoming insensitive. It simply implies that we have the ability to bounce back rather than fall back.

38. ANGER

Anger is a normal, useful emotion. However, it can be destructive unless it has a realistic basis. When anger is based on honest, realistic convictions, and is expressed assertively and respectfully, it has a greater probability of having a productive end. We can use anger to motivate ourselves to convert our stresses to strengths. But when we use anger as a weapon, we often stack the cards against ourselves.

The relationships among anger, personality, and physiology are explored by Redford Williams in his books, *The Trusting Heart* and *Anger Kills*. Williams contends that physically destructive anger, the kind that can lead to stroke and/or coronary blockage, is *anger turned inward* and that this is the most important component of the Type-A personality.[12] For example, you may become very angry with a co-worker as the two of you walk to the company parking lot. However, you may suppress this anger as you are joined by the boss and as you later get in your car and drive away. You even may hold it in as a police officer writes you a ticket for speeding. Yet the anger is still there and is still doing its damage. Moreover, rumination on anger can multiply its effects. As you rehearse and replay the details of an angry situation, you merely sustain negative emotions and their physiologic consequences.

Through our work with Hot Reactors, however, I have come to believe that anger is only the tip of the iceberg. It is often a simple expression of a more complex problem. When we explore anger with our clients, we look at *where anger comes from*—not only where or to what extent it is exploded or suppressed. Anger emanates or dissolves according to our perceptions. If anger is a consequence of an event, we must first ask how a person *perceives* that event. I have

142

observed that anger often is caused by one (or a combination of) the following behaviors and circumstances:

Perfectionism. Unrealistic expectations insure that no situation and no person is ever "enough."

Unassertiveness. Unexpressed annoyances do not go away. They can grow into volcanoes, or they can wreak havoc underground in the body.

Circuit Overload. Like electrical systems, people who take on more than they can handle are likely to blow a fuse.

Aggressiveness. Aggressive personalities want what they want, when they want it. All decisions are made from their own point of view. Because the feelings or perceptions of others are of little or no consequence, aggressive, angry individuals polarize viewpoints and instigate anger in others.

Loss of Control. For all of us, loss of control leads to fear; and this, in turn, often leads to anger and frustration.

Denial. If there is one personality characteristic common to all Hot Reactors it may be denial. These individuals feel no pain. In their struggles to cope with a situation, they deny rather than allow themselves to feel defeated. During treadmill testing, they usually report feeling significantly *less* discomfort than Cool Reactors at every stage of exertion. Furthermore, they express the belief that discomfort and struggle are part of a *normal* state of mind. They rarely recognize the symptoms of their own fears, uncertainties, and doubts.

Depression. Psychoanalysts often characterize depression as anger turned inward. But might it not also be true that anger is depression turned outward? For example, patients often become *less* angry and *less* irritable when treated with antidepressant medications. Depression is always about loss—and it is, by itself, a symptom of underlying problems. In troubled times, it may even be a "logical" response. In any case, we have learned to look for it in chronically angry people.

Obviously, these are not the only ways that people become angry—but they are common ways. What's important is that we recognize anger not in isolation but as one component of behavior. Changing a number of the factors contributing to anger may reduce stress and anger far more effectively than trying to deal with the anger head-on.

39. SELF-ESTEEM

Psychologists often remind me that self-esteem is a difficult topic to understand; and yet it is clear to me that a lack of self-esteem is a very stressful life circumstance. It is often associated with poor decision making, guilt, people pleasing, and feelings of invisible entrapment—which in turn further reinforce low self-esteem.

I define self-esteem as a sense of well-being and a positive view of yourself in your world. It is not at all the kind of preoccupation with self that we call narcissism, which is usually based on insecurity. Rather, it reflects a clear understanding of who you are and how your identity is expressed in what you do.

In the course of a lifetime, self-esteem can take severe blows from external events. The loss of a job or a spouse, criticism from the boss, even the failure of a child at school or work, may provoke feelings of failure and personal abandonment. Taking personal action to convert such stresses to strengths is the best way to recover lost self-esteem.

40. VALUES AND PRINCIPLES BY WHICH YOU LIVE

The final item on the Quality of Life Index is the most important. Developing and honoring your personal value system is the foundation for taking control of your life. When your values are unclear, or when they are constantly changing, you cannot have a firm sense of direction or even know when you have arrived. Values are the compass, the navigational system, and the beacon to guide your decision making and give order to your priorities.

In the chapters that follow, you will see the central role values play in our stress reduction program. It may seem that a vast distance separates the physical concerns that opened this book—concerns like sudden-death syndrome, stress-band lesions, and catecholamine overload—from the intangible world of values. But the relationship is concrete and real, and I hope to show it to you in action.

CHAPTER 7

FROM EVALUATION TO ACTION

RESPONDING TO THE QLI

It is easier to interpret your own QLI if you compare it to a model grid. I've constructed such a model from a hypothetical patient I will call John. John is the forty-six-year-old manager of a large industrial plant. After completing the QLI, his score grid was as follows:

Fortunately, few people have as many problems as does our hypothetical John. You can review his QLI test results with the following steps.

1. Glance at the completed grid.

Note the remarkable configuration of peaks and valleys. This is John's life at a glance.

2. Look next at the average.

In John's case, the sum of his scores was 190. Divide this total by the number of completed categories that received a score (in this case, 38), omitting the NAs. John's average overall score then becomes 5.0. A line drawn through this score represents his approximate energy level. In John's case, 5 is an average energy level. In general, the lower the energy score, the higher the stress load, and vice versa. Low energy averages may also reflect poor health and perhaps an element of depression. High averages tend to indicate low stress loads and high energy and optimism. All 8s and 9s, however, usually indicate the person is a denier or trying to beat the test.

In conducting the remainder of the evaluation with our clients, we *de*-emphasize the actual numbers on the grid. It is the *relative differences* between peaks and valleys that count. What really matters is

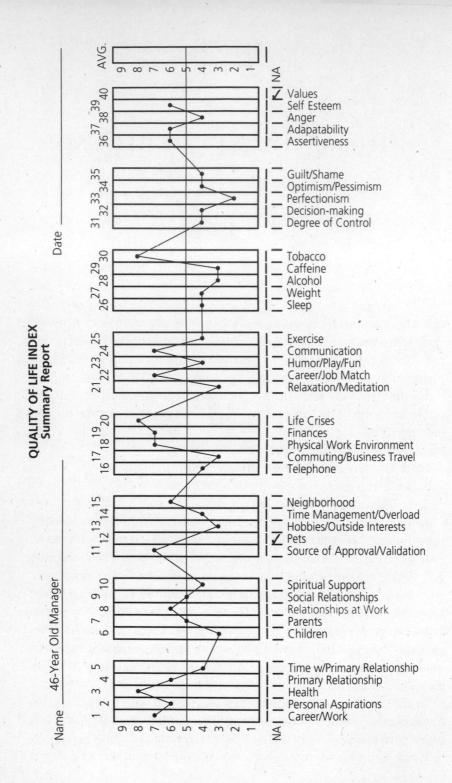

QUALITY OF LIFE INDEX
Summary Report

Name ____ 46-Year Old Manager

Date ____

AVG.

9 8 7 6 5 4 3 2 1 NA

40 39 38 37 36
— Values ✓
— Self Esteem
— Anger
— Adapatability
— Assertiveness

35 34 33 32 31
— Guilt/Shame
— Optimism/Pessimism
— Perfectionism
— Decision-making
— Degree of Control

30 29 28 27 26
— Tobacco
— Caffeine
— Alcohol
— Weight
— Sleep

25 24 23 22 21
— Exercise
— Communication
— Humor/Play/Fun
— Career/Job Match
— Relaxation/Meditation

20 19 18 17 16
— Life Crises
— Finances
— Physical Work Environment
— Commuting/Business Travel
— Telephone

15 14 13 12 11
— Neighborhood
— Time Management/Overload
— Hobbies/Outside Interests
— Pets ✓
— Source of Approval/Validation

10 9 8 7 6
— Spiritual Support
— Social Relationships
— Relationships at Work
— Parents
— Children

5 4 3 2 1
— Time w/Primary Relationship
— Primary Relationship
— Health
— Personal Aspirations
— Career/Work

9 8 7 6 5 4 3 2 1 NA

the person's impression of what is going well and what is not going well.

3. Identify the strengths.

John is strongest in the following: career/work, personal aspirations, health, primary relationship, dealings with co-workers, source of approval/validation, neighborhood comfort, work environment, finances, no recent life crises, career match, communication, no tobacco use, assertiveness, adaptability, and self-esteem.

4. Identify the stresses.

John experiences stress with the following: telephone, time with primary relationship, children, spiritual support, hobbies, time management/circuit overload, commuting/business travel, relaxation/meditation, humor/play, exercise, sleep, weight, alcohol, caffeine, control, decision making, perfectionism, optimism/pessimism, guilt/shame, and anger.

5. Identify the primary strengths and stresses.

To some extent, this will necessarily be a subjective judgment. But we have found that certain factors are so important that they almost always take a primary position as either a stress or strength. (See the chart on page 148.) Others can be either primary or secondary. Still others are usually secondary: that is, they tend to develop out of primary stresses.

"Secondary" does not necessarily mean such stresses are not serious. Excessive alcohol use, for example, can produce personal and health disasters, and it may have to be addressed before any other significant changes can be made. But it almost always occurs in conjunction with other primary stresses. These are sometimes less obvious, but they are absolutely crucial in finding long-term solutions.

Perfectionism, unassertive behavior, and values are among these less obvious primary stresses or strengths. If one of these is a stress, it is a primary contributor to other conditions. For example, reducing perfectionism can help reduce time-management problems, which in turn may have caused anger and poor performance, accompanied by guilt and shame. It's a domino effect, beginning with a primary stress that sets the chain reaction in motion again and again.

Obviously, time-management problems, anger, and guilt do not cause perfectionism. It is the reverse. Perfectionists have trouble delegating, take on too much, and then get tired and angry. They feel especially angry when they or others don't do as they "should." This may result in relationship problems, as well. Thus, identifying the primary stress helps with the secondary stresses. It is unproductive to try to address most secondary stresses without dealing with the primary ones.

Stresses and Strengths

Primary

game plan for career/work   spiritual support
personal aspirations   perfectionism
primary relationship   assertiveness
children   self-esteem
social relationships   values

Primary or Secondary

health   physical work environment
relationship with parents   finances
neighborhood   life crises

Secondary

time alone with primary   exercise
   relationship   sleep
work relationships   body weight
validation by others   alcohol
pets   caffeine
hobbies   tobacco
time management   degree of control
telephone   decision making
commuting/business travel   optimism/pessimism
relaxation/meditation   guilt/shame
career/job match   adaptability/flexibility
humor/play/fun   anger
interpersonal communication

Returning to John, we find his primary strengths are:

- career/work
- health
- primary relationship
- self-esteem

His primary stresses are:

- children
- lack of spiritual support
- perfectionism

In reviewing John's chart, I added values as a primary stress. Note that John scored both pets and values as "not applicable." It's understandable to score pets as not applicable. But values are our life navigational system. They are necessary to establish priorities. John may in fact have strong values that he has not identified to himself. But unless he does identify them, he cannot use them to reduce his load of stress.

Lacking clear values, John is at the mercy of his perfectionism. Everything has to be done just right. John probably feels he has no time for anything. He can't maintain an exercise program or a hobby. His children have drifted off into their own problems. He overeats in response to his primary stress and "handles" the rest of the push and pain with caffeine and booze.

6. Prepare a plan of action.

Luckily for John, his primary strengths offer him excellent support for change. He has a strong marriage, which can only get better as he gains control of his stresses. His wife's load will be lightened along with his. And he has no immediate career or financial worries that might prevent his focusing on long-term issues.

My prescription for John might include:

- Involve his wife in evaluating his test results. He might ask her to take the test for herself, then again as if she were in his shoes. He might also take the test for her. As they compare their results, they will identify the main issues in many of their stresses and build on their already good relationship.

- Make clarification of values a central part of their discussions. This may include seeking additional spiritual support in their lives.
- Begin to address John's perfectionism through suggested reading or through professional counseling.
- Suggest that John enroll in a value-based time-management course.
- Determine whether the children's problems have gone beyond parental insight and/or management. If so, seek professional help for them.
- Suggest that John take a daily walk with his wife, but delay a more formal weight-control program until other stresses have been brought under control.
- Encourage John to plan regular three-day weekends away with his wife, leaving the children with a relative or trusted babysitter.

If John and his wife continue to use each other as sounding boards, they will come up with many ideas for reducing such stresses as commuting and telephone use. As John becomes less burdened, he will find it easier to reduce his intake of alcohol and caffeine, and he will undoubtedly sleep better as a result. He will also be much more likely to undertake a successful exercise and weight-loss program.

GETTING READY TO CHANGE

Mark Twain said, "Habits are habits. You can't throw them out the window. You have to coax them downstairs one step at a time."

And so it is that stress can become a habit. Coaxing it out of the front door of our lives is a step-by-step process involving good common sense and positive personal change. A primary goal of my current clinical and corporate activities is to encourage people to use such a process for converting stressful habits into beneficial habits—doing something good for themselves. By reading this book, you have taken the first step.

Once you have defined your stresses, your next step is to find ways of reducing them; but as the saying goes, that's easier said than done. Like it or not, in some circumstances you may have little or no control. For example, a small child in the ghetto hears the scream of police sirens and sees fire trucks rush past his home. He is bombarded by repeated episodes of stress that are not under his control. As a result, his small body is riddled with surges of blood pressure that can permanently reset at an abnormally high level. Progressive architectural changes will then take place in his cardiovascular system, and premature hypertension and heart disease will be his destiny.

By contrast, many of us *can* control much of our personal lives— we merely choose to live with our stressors and suffer the physical consequences. A better plan is to transform this stressful energy into strength before suffering a physical overload.

The following diagram represents a model for behavioral change that is designed to help you transform one stress at a time into a strength.

YOUR VALUE-BASED PLAN

Change involves learning to do what does not come naturally! It requires information and insight—which it has been the goal of this book to provide. But change also requires action, something that can come only from you.

Plans for change work best when you want to change. If you don't, then nothing will happen, no matter how much you know. As my wife, Phyllis, often remarks, "Feelings become facts." You need to establish a mind-set in the direction you wish change to occur. In accomplishing this, your values are your best allies. Chapter 8 will help you explore these powerful motivators.

YOUR SELF-TALKS THAT LEAD TO NEW BEHAVIOR

Self-talk is the moment-to-moment voice in your head that determines your response to any given circumstance. It also tells you what you can and cannot do—much more frequently than any external voice. Yet most of us are unaware of this constant companion.

Chapter 9 will demonstrate the power of self-talk and show how

CONVERTING STRESSES INTO STRENGTHS

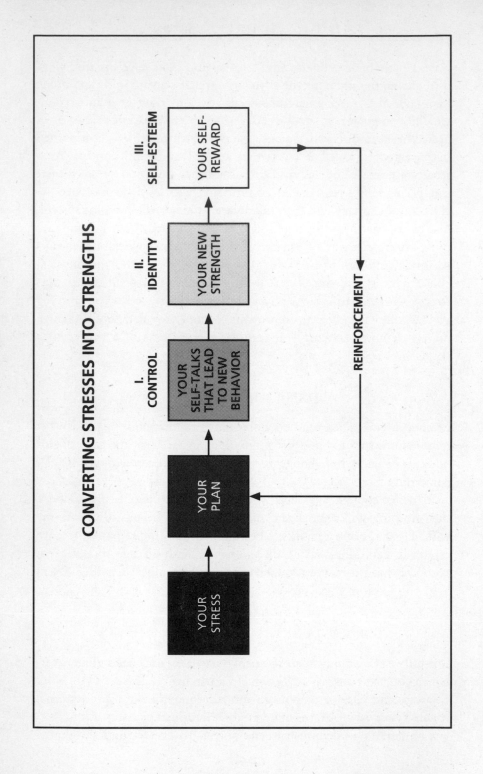

you can make it a conscious tool for change. It's not always as simple as transforming an internal "I can't" into an internal "I can," but changing your perceptions can put you back in control of your life.

I like to repeat to clients a story I heard about Willie Nelson. It seems that Willie rarely had an opportunity to enjoy his favorite pastime, golf; and so he built a course on his family ranch. Once during a game a friend asked, "Hey, Willie, what's par on this course?"

Willie answered, "Any damned thing I want it to be. For example, par on this here hole is forty-seven. And I birdied the sucker yesterday!" When you can't change the world, you can change the way you see it.

As you talk yourself through your new behaviors, slow down and observe the yeses and nos you say to yourself. By defining and appreciating your own successes, you can reinforce every step you take.

YOUR NEW STRENGTH

Your identity is your description of yourself. As you make new choices and change your behavior, you will also be changing your identity. This is one reason change is so difficult; our desire to do something new may not fit with our old self-description.

But if you keep talking yourself through your new behavior, it will start to feel like "you." Your new strength will become part of your identity. For example, you become "a person who takes a walk every day" rather than "a couch potato." And since you are likely to meet other walkers, they will further reinforce your new identity as they recognize you. Once this identity shift is made, you will find it takes far less effort to maintain your changed behavior.

YOUR SELF-REWARD

Psychologists and psychiatrists tell us that self-reward systems are more complicated than merely feeding ourselves M&M candies after doing the "right" thing.

Surprisingly, the best kinds of rewards are neither money nor material objects. Once the basic needs of shelter, food, and clothing have been met, material rewards carry little impact. The rewards that have the greatest impact in sustaining positive behaviors are those that are *personal and social.* "Personal" implies something totally distinctive to your needs and perceptions, while "social" involves the needs and perceptions of others.

Social rewards may be as simple and as powerful as a colleague saying, "I like the cool-headed way you handled Mr. Jones." In that case, the reward must come from someone whose opinions you respect, and it must be linked with something specific you have done.

When we convert a stress into a strength and unburden ourselves of a chronic mental complication, other rewards can ensue. For example, if you stop being angry and start being assertive, you may find that others listen to your point of view without rancor or defensiveness. You have a better chance of influencing the situation.

Enjoying an achieved goal reinforces your success and enhances your self-esteem. You can use this system over and over again to achieve new goals as soon as you formulate them. Each challenge successfully met will motivate and prepare you for the next. When a subsequent success occurs, replay it in your mind. Notice how it feels. Now you are becoming the accomplished captain of your own life. Even if your next voyage through stress is a little longer, or a little more difficult, you will have learned how to guide your ship with greater skill.

CHAPTER 8

VALUES

A FUNDAMENTAL STEP IN THE
SOLUTION TO STRESS

The personal values acquired throughout your life are your greatest strength. Conversely, if your values are out of sync with your lifestyle, this fact alone can be the source of your greatest stress. An individual value may be as simple as the responsibility you feel for a pet, or it may be as complex as your spiritual convictions.

I define a value as anything with intrinsic worth, utility, or importance to you. Values are what you personally rate highly—what you prize, what you esteem. I'm not concerned here with value judgment, a term describing the attributions of good, evil, beautiful, or ugly to values that are to be sought or rejected. The purpose of this book is to teach, not preach.

Because values define the direction and the boundaries of your life, a firm understanding of your own values allows you to set priorities and to manage time effectively. That's how decisions are made. Values provide the push and pull that can allow you to convert stresses into strengths. They help you bond with or feel alienated from others. They let you know where sand can be released from your knapsack.

VALUES SHAPE HISTORY

In my talks, I like to use two illustrations from twentieth-century history to dramatize the significance of a clearly defined value system.

First, I recall the life example of Mahatma Gandhi, who defeated the British in India through his campaigns of nonviolent civil dis-obedience. Armed with a law degree obtained in England, Gandhi took over leadership of his country without firing a shot and led his people in their struggle for independence. He was arrested and im-prisoned again and again, but the colonial authorities always released him. He founded his campaign on a basic respect for life, coining the term *satyagraha* to describe a "force which is born of truth and love or non-violence." Even when his followers were fired upon, he con-demned any form of violence in response.

Gandhi accomplished his goals not only through his moral pres-tige, but through his thorough knowledge of British law and culture. He once told a British viceroy, "By resisting an agelong tyranny, I have shown the ultimate sovereignty of British justice." This appeal to the shared value of justice proved in the end more powerful than the entire might of the British Empire.

Here is my second example: At the end of World War II, a Soviet soldier committed a crime in occupied Berlin. He was court-martialed by a military review board consisting of a Soviet officer, an American officer, and a British officer. Using values based on the Anglo-Saxon legal system, the Briton and the American interrogated the soldier via an interpreter. As the questioning proceeded, the Soviet officer became conspicuously annoyed and indignant. He suddenly ap-proached the soldier, grabbed him by the collar, and demanded, "Did you do it?"

The soldier became pale and began to sweat. The officer repeated the question as his grip became tighter. Grudgingly the soldier said, *"Da."*

Upon hearing the Russian word for yes, the officer pulled out his service revolver, placed it to the soldier's head, pulled the trigger, and executed the man on the spot. The stunned American and English officers looked on in horror and shock.[1] And yet the Soviet officer was functioning according to his values and his authority as pre-scribed in the Soviet military code of behavior.

These two illustrations are 180 degrees opposed. Imagine, for ex-ample, what would have happened if Gandhi had been dealing with that Soviet inquisitor instead of with the British government in co-lonial India.

VALUES AND SELF-ESTEEM

Failing to live up to the values and expectations of others may result in feelings of guilt, while not living up to your own values may result in feelings of shame. Rather than stewing in the stresses caused by guilt and shame, cherish that precious part of your personality called the self. Closely monitor both the external standards you accept and the internal standards you place upon yourself, and work always for a balance between what you can and what you cannot change. All of us know only too well how our spirits can be crushed; but we also know that they can be resurrected. Therefore, value your right to prevent others from trampling all over your self-esteem. The best way to accomplish this goal is to have a clear understanding of your own values, goals, beliefs, and principles.

> **Values provide emotional boundaries and help you avoid fear, uncertainty, and doubt. Without boundaries, a person can feel completely vulnerable.**

Sometimes what may appear to be a value can be carried to such an extreme that it actually becomes a detriment. For example, psychologists have identified individuals who value doing *everything* correctly at *all times*. These extreme perfectionists develop a mind-set in which nothing can ever be quite good enough. They seem unable to recognize when their circuits are becoming overloaded, and the result can be constant stress and lowered self-esteem.

Our research has shown that those who can learn to say no and do their best—*perfect or not*—have actually embraced an attitude that is more realistic and healthful.

DEFINING YOUR OWN VALUES

Clarifying basic values is not a modern dilemma. Benjamin Franklin faced it over two centuries ago. At the age of thirty-two, he seemed to be running in circles. As an initial step toward gaining control of his life, he compiled a list of twelve long-range goals that were in keeping with his basic values and beliefs. The first five were as follows:

1. Be a better father.
2. Be a better husband.
3. Be financially independent.
4. Improve my mind.
5. Be temperate.

These values became the pathways and boundaries of his life. Franklin probably derived some of them from the writings of the ancient Greeks. I believe these core values can fit modern times as well.

But how can you identify your own values? One method is through a series of simple self-evaluations. The following tests can help you examine your beliefs and clarify your values.[2]

THE ADJECTIVE TEST

The purpose of the Adjective Test is to list words and phrases that define your current behavior.

Step 1.   List at least ten adjectives that describe how you would like to be perceived. (For example, wise, compassionate, studious, or friendly.)

Step 2.   Ask a friend to list at least ten adjectives that he or she thinks describe you.

Step 3.   Imagine a list of at least ten adjectives that an enemy or adversary would use to describe you.

Step 4.   Chart the three lists of adjectives into columns.

Step 5.   As you analyze the columns, do you see any similarities? Any contradictions?

Step 6.   Can you identify adjectives you *wish* were associated with you but are missing from the columns?

Step 7.   Are there some negative adjectives you'd rather be rid of?

Such an exercise helps you ask yourself, "Who am I now? Who do I wish to become?" Once you commit such an analysis to paper, you can begin to think about it objectively. Incongruities are areas

158

of discord that lead to stress. Only by clarifying your current identity can you consciously begin to make rational commitments to change. As you adjust and correct any disharmonies, you steadily develop the new identity you seek—and you lower your internal stress.

THE ACCOMPLISHMENT TEST

Step 1.   Think about the achievements in your life, and list those that have given you the greatest sense of personal satisfaction.

Step 2.   Now identify the five achievements that have given you the greatest sense of personal satisfaction, and rank them in descending order.

A Life Worth Living

Something and someone to love.
Something to learn and to do.
Something to look forward to.

THE OBITUARY TEST

As with the others, this test is designed to expand your thinking about your values and to help you determine what will make your life seem more worth living.

Step 1.   List what you would like to have accomplished by the end of your lifetime.

Step 2.   List the items you would like your local newspaper to include in your obituary.

Step 3.   What would your friends, your spouse, your enemies, or your boss add to your obituary?

Step 4.   In a nutshell, how do you want to be perceived and remembered?

THE CHECKBOOK TEST

This test will help you answer the question "Do I put my money where my mouth is?" or "Am I spending my money for what *I* value?"

Step 1.   Open your checkbook.
Step 2.   Categorize your expenditures: for example, house, car, food, clothes, entertainment, education, charity, health.
Step 3.   Observe where your money is going. Note the number of times you expend dollars in each category. Is your money helping to move you toward your goals? Are optional expenditures keeping you off course?

It isn't the money that you *make,* but the way you are spending it that can add financial stress. Your values will help you put financial direction into your life.

SETTING LONG-TERM GOALS

Becalmed is a term sailors use for being adrift without wind. Sometimes you can feel becalmed when you are living your life without direction or goals. Imagine yourself in six months, a year, five years, or ten years. Many successful individuals use this sort of mental visualization exercise to set long-term goals. They imagine themselves where they would like to be, and then they go about taking short, practical steps to get there. They see themselves at a destination before they arrive; for them, reaching a goal is not a random experience.

> **If you can't conceive it, it's unlikely you will achieve it.**

The process of career visualization, in particular, is not daydreaming—it is preplanning. Similarly, to reach a less stressful life you need to conceive, plan, and then rehearse each change necessary to lower your stress level a notch or two. Keep in mind that when NASA's space engineers planned for man's trip to the moon, they actually first plotted the course from the moon *back* to earth, not the other way around.

Every successful individual I've ever seen at the institute was a person who had viable, livable dreams. Margaret Thatcher is said to have imagined herself as Prime Minister when she was only twelve years old. The CEOs of many Fortune 500 companies aimed for the top from the moment they joined their organization. Entrepreneurs must also have this ability to see a complex future and devise methods for coping with it and profiting from it. The same can be said of anyone who feels fulfilled in his or her life pursuit.

> **"No wind blows in favor of the ship without direction."**
> **—Hans Selye**

You can reinforce your values by allowing yourself to visualize the options that may be available to you in hypothetical situations. Ask yourself the following: "Knowing my values, what would I do if this situation were to develop? If I followed this action, what would be the result? How would I have to respond? Does a specific action make sense? Could I defend my action to myself or to others?"

You can use your Quality of Life Index to clarify your values and goals further. For each item, you must ask whether this category represents a value of importance and significance to you at this time.[3] When you find one that does, ask the following questions:

1. Would I openly affirm or defend this value?
2. Is it one of my top five or six priorities?
3. Will it have an impact on my future goals?
4. Did I choose this value because I believe in it or because I feel I should believe in it?
5. Am I willing to work out a game plan for achieving this value?
6. Is this a realistic goal for me?
7. Will this goal become an active priority in my future?

161

The more you are able to answer in the affirmative, the closer you will be to matching your goals to your values.

Your final step is to rank each value-based goal according to its ease of accomplishment. Even though you have some very important long-term goals, it's wise to start with the one that is doable in the short term. Or construct a game plan for that distant goal that will give you many easily achieved interim goals to aim for.

Interim goals are useful whether your value-based goal is to improve your marriage, to change your career, or to lose thirty pounds to improve your health. Establish a maximum of twelve goals; six is much better. Constantly reinforcing your sense of progress is the key to maintaining the motivation to move ahead.

Another key to motivation is your internal self-talks, which we will explore in the following chapter.

CHAPTER 9

THE POWER OF PERCEPTION

TAMING YOUR SELF-TALK

A few years ago, musical performer Bobby McFerrin introduced an overnight hit based on a simple, positive state of mind: "Don't Worry, Be Happy." He took a particularly stressful situation, such as not having enough money for the rent, and came up with a ubiquitous solution to all stress. Imagine the reaction if his song had espoused the opposite state of mind: "Try Worry, Be Crabby." "Be happy" feelings may not pay the rent, but they may save your health and even your life. "Try Worry, Be Crabby" won't pay the rent either; however, it *will* definitely reduce your options, prolong stress, and perhaps even shorten your days.

Most of our feelings of struggle and defeat come from the self-talk that streams through our minds from minute to minute. The problem is that many of us aren't even aware of this internal dialogue—much less that we are in charge of its content.

At the Institute of Stress Medicine, we devised The Struggle Index to get a sense of our clients' self-talk. How many of the items on the test match your feelings?

THE STRUGGLE INDEX

Indicate how strongly you agree with each of the following statements:

4 = All of the time
3 = Often
2 = Sometimes
1 = Never

___ I am regularly exhausted by daily demands at work and home.
___ My stress is caused by outside forces beyond my control.
___ I am trapped by circumstances that I just have to live with.
___ No matter how hard I work to stay on top of my schedule, I never feel caught up.
___ I have financial obligations that I cannot meet.
___ I dislike my work but cannot take the risk of a career change.
___ I'm dissatisfied with my personal relationships.
___ I feel responsible for the happiness of people around me.
___ I am embarrassed to ask for help.
___ I do not know what I want out of life.
___ I am disappointed that I have not achieved what I had hoped for.
___ No matter how much external success I have, I feel empty inside.
___ If the people around me were more competent, I would be happier.
___ Many people have let me down in the past.
___ I "stew" in my anger rather than express it.
___ I become enraged and resentful when I am hurt.
___ I can't take criticism.
___ I am afraid I'll lose my job (home, finances, etc.).
___ I do not see the value of expressing sadness or grief.
___ I do not trust that things will work out.
_____ Total number of points.

SCORING:

80–70 Life has become one crisis and struggle after another.
69–50 Your options are often clouded and you feel trapped.
49–30 You have an awareness that your life is in your hands.
29–20 You are your own best ally with a high degree of control, self-esteem, and identity.

THE ABC'S OF STRESS

The road from worry to happiness is not as simple as Bobby Mc-Ferrin made it sound; but his suggestion to chant away your problems is related to some longstanding theories about modifying your behavior.

Rational-Emotive Therapy (RET), a procedure developed by Dr. Albert Ellis, involves focusing on what you say to yourself when you are under stress.[1] The goal of RET is to move these thoughts from the negative to the positive.

Learning to change your responses under stress begins with the recognition that when you are presented with a dilemma, your thinking process consists of three phases, which can be either positive or negative.

For example, when an executive assistant makes an error, such as scheduling the wrong airline flight for the boss, his thoughts may progress as follows:

Step A:　　*Activating Event.* Here the problem is recognized. "He said he had to be in Albuquerque by noon, and I've got him on a flight arriving at 2 P.M."

Step B:　　*Belief or Perception.* This step is the interpretation of Step A based on prior learning and belief systems. Usually this step is expressed as an internal conversation called a *self-talk.* "Oh no, the boss will fire me!"

Step C:　　*Consequence.* Stress enters the picture, as the assistant imagines losing his job. He breaks out into a cold sweat, his heart races, his blood pressure goes through the roof.

What most often happens to us in similar situations is that we focus on Step A, the problem, and Step C, the physiologic or emotional response. Step B, our internalized discussion—the self-talk—is usually ignored or blended into one of the other steps. Yet Step B is the most critical because it establishes our frame of mind and accelerates our reaction into mental and physical stress. Notice that in this example, the assistant's Step B was a distinctly *negative* expression. Psychologists often refer to this kind of response as irrational self-talk; chances are, the boss will not fire the assistant over one small error. Step B is where you can gain control.

Other experts believe that the self-talk response (Step B) also determines the personality. Henry Murray of Yale University has remarked, "A personality is a full Congress of orators and pressure groups of children, demagogues, communists, isolationists, warmongers, mugwumps, grafters, log-rollers, lobbyists, Caesars and Christs, Machiavels and Judases, Tories and Promethean revolutionists."[2] It's our self-talk that puts one or another of these characters in charge.

In such a chorus, the self-talk can pass by too quickly to be noticed, only to be automatically repressed and forgotten. These self-talks are the *imagined consequences* of mistakes, problems, and conflicts. They reflect the fear, uncertainty, and doubt that eventually bring on stress. This leads to a crucial conclusion: Stress is not necessarily a result of having failed in a task. Rather it results from our mental review of feared consequences that have the potential for greater disaster. It may also result from falling short of expectations that were irrational, unrealistic, or impossible to fulfill in the first place.

This is how stress is internally generated—through wasteful ruminations and self-recriminations. Often negative self-talk will lead to a fourth step in the stress process: inaction. In our example, the assistant can become so "stressed" that he is unable to move on into creative problem-solving. He doesn't check on alternate travel routes. He doesn't find out if the boss really has to be there by noon. He stops answering the phone and leaves early—for the local bar.

THE PHYSICAL NATURE OF SELF-TALK

Physiologically, self-talk can be compared to a tape-recorded message that constantly replays in your brain. Evidence from the work of Canadian neurosurgeon Wilder Penfield has shown that when certain parts of the brain are touched with the point of a tiny pin-like instrument, past experiences and the emotional reactions to them are reexperienced.[3] Self-talk can operate just like that instrument; it keeps us locked into the emotions already etched into our brains. We may be reacting only to what is in our minds, and not to the reality we face.

Unlike our nervous assistant, we've all met people who weather disasters and still maintain a positive outlook on life. How do they do it? Don't they realize what they're up against? The truth is that positive mental tapes—not easy lives—make people positive, while negative mental tapes can make people negative in the midst of good fortune. And, tragically, self-critical mental tapes can make a hard life harder by causing a person to be inhibited or to react in inappropriate ways.

> **Negative self-talks are hazardous to your health. Positive self-talks are extremely powerful and can act as prescriptions for healthy change.**

How you talk to yourself is a very personal thing—based on the way you look at yourself, other people, and your environment. By "environment," I mean more than just a good ecological outlook! I use it to encompass your attitude toward your car as you kick the tire that has just gone flat. It may be your attitude toward a new computer you feel is beyond your understanding or toward the family that just moved in next door.

Your automatic reaction to any of life's situations is composed of numerous negative and positive self-talks. Negative self-talks are responsible for most of the internal stress that people experience. This negative chatter, although seldom accurately recalled, may nag at you over and over again. In addition, these phrases silently imperil your health. Conversely, positive self-talk contributes to your well-being and to your total health.

Both types of self-talk began in your early relationships with family and friends as they reacted to you and to your responses. Self-talks are also formed by your perceptions of how relatives, friends, teachers, clergy, coaches, and others in authority reacted to you. Self-talks build on your feelings of failure, success, worthiness, or rebellion. They may even reflect a belief that a detached or passive reaction is the best way to solve problems. Regardless of the form they take now, both negative and positive self-talks are *learned* responses, having their origins in:

- your outlook on life, best defined as your values and philosophy
- your past and present interactions with others
- your perception of yourself
- your choice of response to your environment

These learned responses are very powerful. They do not merely shape your reactions to events; they often shape the reality to which you're reacting. In any occurrence, you actively select information from your environment, often changing what you perceive to coincide with past experiences. In other words, we make sense of the "unknown" by relating it to the "known."

Over the years, I have noticed a relationship between the kind of self-talk a person reports and his or her predisposition to subsequent health problems. Self-talk becomes the self-fulfilling prophecy. Saying, "I can't do it" or "I always get the worst end of the deal" can contribute to failure or "bad luck." I advocate *choosing change* by saying, "I can do that" or "You win some, you lose some." Success rarely comes to the individual who feels that success cannot be achieved.

I want to emphasize that positive self-talk is not the same as platitudes or moralisms. For example, positive self-talk is not merely remembering to recite twelve times each morning, "Every day, in every way, I'm getting better and better." On the contrary, the most useful self-talks are solid, reality-based perceptions. They give you a way to negotiate successfully the shoals and rapids of the real world. They increase your well-being and sense of control and directly affect your physiology. And they can be learned and practiced in any circumstances.

RECOGNIZING DEPRESSION

About 15 percent or more of Americans suffer from the effects of clinical depression at some time or times in their lives. They do so to varying degrees. The real question is whether or not you are immobilized by it. If you experience depression, it is usually because you have a feeling of loss.[4] However, change and disappointment are two other recognized causes.[5]

Depression can include an orchestration of different moods and emotional tones. These can range from feeling "sad, tearful, unhappy, and discouraged" to "irritability, hostility, feelings of emptiness, apathy [and] lack of motivation." It is not surprising that anxiety is intertwined in this fabric or that it is very difficult to experience pleasure, humor, or happiness in a depressed state.[6]

Depressed people often feel that everything is wrong and they blame themselves, feeling they are incapable of doing anything right. It is an easy trip to guilt, unworthiness, and pessimism. Unfortunately, this can become a self-fulfilling prophecy. If you have unrelenting cycles of negative thinking and mood associated with sleeplessness and early awakening, it is important that you seek clinical help. Depression of this type implies that you carry a burden which you cannot manage alone.

COGNITIVE THERAPY—THE PSYCHOLOGICAL USE OF POSITIVE SELF-TALK

At the Institute of Stress Medicine, our counselors draw on a systematic, intellectual approach to problem solving called cognitive therapy. These methods are especially useful for normal, generally healthy people—the ones I call the Walking Worried Well. I advocate cognitive therapy because it represents a kind of do-it-yourself adaptation of the same techniques professional psychologists, psychiatrists, and therapists use to instigate change in more troubled patients.[7]

Changing your self-talks is not as easy as just changing your words. It involves becoming aware of what you say *when you are under stress.* Dr. Albert Ellis's interpretation of this need to think positive thoughts at the time of a stressful event is particularly useful.

According to Ellis: "Rational-Emotive Therapy's unique essence . . . is a Socratic-type dialogue through which the client is calmly, logically, forcefully taught that he'd better stop telling himself nonsense, accept reality, desist from condemning himself and others, and actively persist at making himself as happy as he can be in a world that is far from ideal."[8]

> "People will be just about as happy as they will allow themselves to be."
>
> —Abraham Lincoln

Ellis also writes:

"RET . . . shows the individual that whenever he upsets himself at point C (the emotional consequences), it is not (as he almost always thinks is the case) because of what is happening to him at point A (the activating event). Rather it is because of his own irrational and invalidated supposition at point B (his belief system). More precisely, when a person feels terribly depressed at point C, it is not because he has been rejected by someone or has lost a job at point A, but because he is convincing himself, at point B, of both a rational and an irrational hypothesis."[9]

Such a process is illustrated by a patient I will call Mr. Johnson. This forty-three-year-old accountant sought our services in the early 1970s, and I remember him especially because he was a perfect example of a person who almost killed himself because of misunderstood information at point A and his subsequent self-talk.

Two months before his visit to the institute, Mr. Johnson had experienced a very frightening event. Filled with horror, he had watched helplessly as his junior partner developed chest pains and died while sitting at his desk. Weeks later Mr. Johnson himself experienced pressure in the lower part of his chest and immediately visited his physician.

After telling Mr. Johnson that "The electrocardiogram shows changes," the physician advised him to lose weight, stop eating eggs, quit smoking, and slow down. However, Mr. Johnson's *interpretation* of these instructions, coupled with his vague knowledge of medicine, resulted in an A-B-C pattern of stress. After hearing the doctor's instructions (Step A), Johnson's self-talks (Step B) included:

170

"I must have serious heart trouble" and "I must be going to have a heart attack." These self-talks ultimately resulted in Step C—what he *thought* having a heart attack would be like.

Within a month, these negative self-talks had crippled Mr. Johnson to such a point that he and his very distressed wife came to my office. Mrs. Johnson spoke for her husband as he sat and watched— his face ashen gray. She told me that since the doctor had mentioned that her husband's electrocardiogram had "shown changes," Johnson had drastically altered his level of activity. Whey they traveled, she had to carry all of his bags for him. He was afraid to climb stairs. Mowing the lawn was out of the question. He had become subdued, sad, sleepless, and fearful of any physical task. He was stressed to his limit. The more Mrs. Johnson described her husband's symptoms, the less I was inclined to diagnose heart disease. Instead, I suspected a problematic gallbladder. Mr. Johnson's exercise electrocardiogram was perfectly normal; however, minor EKG changes can be associated with gallbladder disease. I ordered specialized tests to differentiate between the two, and they demonstrated evidence of a few small gallstones.

Mistaking gallbladder disease for heart disease is a common diagnostic error. The first doctor simply might have been incorrect in his diagnosis. However, the recommended lifestyle changes would have also been appropriate for gallstones; and so the doctor may have simply failed to relay his true diagnosis adequately. A third scenario was that Mr. Johnson had misinterpreted all that the doctor had said. Regardless, by the time I saw them, both of the Johnsons desperately needed some stress-relieving information and improved perceptions. Before the end of the hour I had witnessed a transformation. Mr. Johnson looked pink and embarrassed, but relieved; Mrs. Johnson mirrored his reactions. Twenty years later, he is fit and fine. Even better, we can now laugh about the ABC's of his crippling self-talk.

The process of altering self-talks in a more positive, realistic direction is often slower than in the case of the Johnsons; but the results can be just as dramatic.

> **Much of the stress in our lives occurs because of a mismatch between expectation and reality.**

HOW CAN YOU TAKE CHARGE OF YOUR SELF-TALKS?

Stressful situations occur every day. As you experience them, monitor your own self-talks and listen for the kind of trap Mr. Johnson fell into. Amid the chorus of "I saids" and "They saids," remember your *reaction* to the event. Others may say what they like—you have no control over this. However, you *can* choose to react in a positive rather than a negative way and, in doing so, lighten your load and preserve your own health.

For example, after a hard day's work, it's irritating to become stalled in a line of slowed cars. The traffic jam is a reality you cannot change; and yet your reaction to it can be an irrational belief that the world had suddenly turned against you. This kind of ruminating, negative self-talk can change an ordinary traffic jam into a pressure-cooker experience. Negative self-talks such as "I hate this"; "This always happens to me;" "Why can't the mayor or the city council do something about this bottleneck?" can churn up all sorts of gastric juices.

More appropriate, healthful self-talk could be: "I'm not going to let a traffic jam take bites out of my heart muscle"; "I can make some notes and answer those letters I brought along"; "Now I can listen to that new tape"; "I'm just going to sit here and watch the stress reactions of everybody else."

CHAPTER 10

TIME MANAGEMENT
GETTING THE CLOCK ON YOUR SIDE

"There aren't enough hours in the day!" is a common lament in my clinical practice. Often this kind of stress comes from an inability or an unwillingness to manage time. One such client was Sheila.

When I first met her, Sheila was a bright, motivated achiever who taught laboratory science at a public high school. In her desire to show her competence, she spent hours grading daily lab reports and giving each student as much personal attention as she could. In college, she had been a competitive swimmer, and so now her nonclassroom duties included coaching the girls' swim team.

Everything was done to perfection. She did not, however, realize that a week has only 168 hours. She slept 46 hours a week, ate for 10 hours, taught for 22 hours, graded papers for 21 more, and coached swimming for 15 hours. In addition, she spent 40 hours each week preparing lessons and reading professional literature. With such a schedule, she had little time to cook or even move from classroom to gym. In her commitment to achievement, she had forfeited the time necessary for having a life of her own. However, she was soon to discover that time management was vital to her life.

During the third winter at this pace, Sheila experienced four successive strep throat infections. She began to slow down; she felt easily fatigued; and she began to notice inappropriate mood swings. This was unusual for a young woman in her prime. When she finally went for a medical checkup, her physician's findings were ominous:

- She was twenty pounds underweight.
- Her laboratory tests revealed abnormal cells in her blood.
- There were questions about cancer cells in her lymph nodes.

Her physician's immediate prescription was chemotherapy and total rest. Sensibly, Sheila resigned her teaching position and decided to put all of her energy into rebuilding her health. The first step was to sleep 8 hours each night. Next, she examined her eating habits. During Sheila's hectic days, high-fat and high-sugar fast foods seemed a time-saving necessity; but once she slowed down, she returned to a healthy diet of mostly complex carbohydrates.

Within six months, Sheila was told that her cancer had gone into remission, and her doctors said they could find no signs of abnormal cells. That was fifteen years ago; since then she has had no recurrence of her medical problems.

When she returned to teaching, Sheila decided that her new habits were necessary to her survival. Key to this strategy was a plan for time management. She began by taking on only those commitments that she knew she valued and could handle. After a normal work day, she took time for herself. She began to be more selective in her personal relationships, spending time with people she truly enjoyed and avoiding those she found to be emotionally draining. She was still a dedicated woman, but her zeal for perfection was balanced with a commitment to her own health. She learned that always saying yes—squeezing as much as you can into every day—is not the ultimate answer. All people need time to relax, time to play, time to work, time to rest, time to sleep, and time to enjoy themselves if they are to avoid the physical effects of stress.

> **Manage your time as if your life depended on it—because it does.**

If you feel that you are always "out of time" and this is creating feelings of anxiety, change the way you manage time now. However, time management is more than merely cramming *more* into the same twenty-four hours. As Mahatma Gandhi once said, "There is more to life than just increasing its speed."

THE SCIENCE OF TIME MANAGEMENT

What we think of now as time management practices were made possible with the advent of the mechanical clock; but it was the stop watch that enabled Frederick Taylor, the "father of time management," to develop the science of time and motion study.[1] This new focus spawned the era of "efficiency experts" and led to such dubious industrial contributions as a study entitled "The Science of Shoveling."

Charlie Chaplin lampooned time and motion studies in his classic silent movie, *City Lights*. In the film, Charlie depicted the frantic efforts of a factory worker as he continued work on an assembly line while trying to eat an ear of corn as it was automatically served on an electric rotor. The contraption had been the work of an efficiency expert who had decided that workers could maximize productivity if they didn't have to stop for lunch. Predictably, the errant robotlike device began to scatter both food and manufactured product in all directions. The ever-patient Charlie was finally enmeshed with the gears and carried off while the assembly line continued mindlessly. Although exaggerated, this kind of dehumanization was commonplace until everyone agreed that it seldom increased efficiency or quality.

However, when employees perceive that change is being instituted out of a concern for their well-being, both efficiency and quality will increase. This phenomenon was first identified in the Western Electric experiments conducted at Hawthorne, Illinois. In what was later termed the Hawthorne Effect, scientists concluded that as long as change is positive, even insignificant alterations, such as new lighting or repainted walls, will result in measurable improvements in productivity. The study also revealed that simply being told that they were being studied increased worker production.

PERSONAL TIME MANAGEMENT

Although the cliché "time is money" may not be completely accurate, there is a significant relationship between the two. For example, an adequate income can allow you to employ others to perform routine tasks, thus increasing your productivity and insuring time for leisure. Generally we see such delegation and efficiency in positive terms; and yet there are those individuals who feel compelled to work all of the time. To them, leisure time means *wasted* time.

If done properly, time management not only helps people to fill in the hours, but it also can allow them opportunities to reflect upon the pleasures and joys of life. As noted in the Quality of Life Index, setting aside time for conversation and interactions with relatives and friends is good for your health. After-dinner conversation, hobbies, three-day vacations, and professional development should be seen as critical and important investments in your mental, physical, and spiritual well-being.

"Whoever has my time, has my life."

—**Bruce K. Munro, Ph.D.**

TIME MANAGEMENT BEGINS WITH TIME ANALYSIS

The goal of time management should not be the elimination of relaxation time; rather it should be the elimination of life's real time wasters and redundancies. Start by identifying *how* you spend the hours of the day. Keep a time journal or hourly log for a few days, taking special note of repetitive tasks and the amounts of time in which you are merely waiting or searching for something. These are the activities that can cause anxiety and increased stress. For example, have you considered what seemingly endless, nonproductive staff meetings may be doing to your stress level? How many minutes in the day are you stuck on the telephone? Did you ever measure how many points your blood pressure rises when you are put on hold? You don't need a clumsy dictionary-size book to get started. Find a handy pocket notebook or purse-size exercise log at your local office-supply store. Carry it with you and begin to record the events in your life. When completing your daily log, be sure to record the following:

- the starting time of each task
- how much time the task took
- the type of activity (phone call, letter, conversation, etc.)
- the purpose of the activity
- whether or not the task was completed
- an indication of which tasks felt stressful and which did not

Make sure your list is detailed and specific rather than general. You might even find it useful to grade your activities on a 1 to 10 basis (1 = low stress; 10 = high stress).

Next, survey the day's events and ponder these questions:

- What are the tasks that occupy most of my time?
- Are these things that I need or want to be doing?
- Do these activities reflect my values?
- Is there a better way to order the tasks I am currently doing?
- Is there a more satisfactory way to organize what I do?

Your third step is to evaluate what you have recorded. Go back through your daily log and assign a value to each task. Record a plus (+) if the task was useful and a minus (−) if the task only wasted time.

Good time management is value-based.

Reviewing your list of pluses and minuses can be very enlightening. Notice how much time slipped past because you lacked organization, or how much time was consumed in partially completed tasks. Most important, note the levels of stress associated with each activity.

Do you see a pattern? For example, do you feel anxious (the FUD factor) when something is not completed, or are your activities stimulating and rewarding (NICE—new, interesting, challenging experiences)?

The following review can help you develop a plan for organizing, controlling, or eliminating those tasks that cause stress disproportionate to their value. For each task ask yourself:

1. How can I cut down its frequency, or perhaps do it during a nonstressful time of the day?
2. Can I simplify or restructure the task so that I can be more efficient?
3. Is there another way I can do the task so that it will be less stressful?
4. Is the task necessary at all?
5. Can I delegate the task to someone who might do it more effectively?
6. Have I allocated sufficient time or resources for the task to be completed to my satisfaction?
7. Am I too compulsive about doing the task perfectly? Or do I recheck myself again and again?

A good job doesn't have to be a perfect job! The question is, did it get the job done?

MANAGING TIME AND STRESS IN THE SHOPPING LINE

Have you ever watched a line of people when someone else tries to break in? No doubt you have seen the adrenaline flow. What you can't see is the progressive damage being done to the walls of their arteries or hearts. In reacting to a line-crasher, these individuals may be penalizing only themselves.

The time wasted either shopping without making decisions or waiting in line at stores provides two major opportunities for stressful reactions. These two situations can be controlled by: (1) knowing why you have gone to shop; (2) taking a list (complete with price limits); (3) shopping during nonpeak hours; and (4) leaving the kids safely at home.

MANAGING TIME AND STRESS IN TRAVEL

A friend of mine always keeps a stack of professional journals, novels, and interesting books, in the trunk of his car—just in case he experiences a delay or a breakdown. Travel is full of seemingly empty moments, and the best way to keep them from being wasted is to plan ahead. Even a pad and pencil in your car glove compartment can become a powerful, creative tool when a freeway accident stalls traffic.

What about the way your gastric juices begin to flow when you hear the words "Flight XXX has been delayed because of mechanical problems"? Modern air travel provides many opportunities for wasted time and added stress. Again, be prepared. If you travel frequently, consider paying the difference between a cramped tourist-class seat and a business- or first-class seat. Use it as an opportunity to enjoy a well-earned rest without interruption; or if you *must* turn each flight into a work session, first class can at least give you a more comfortable and a more productive environment. In fact, much of the book you are now reading was dictated, edited, and refined at 32,000 feet above sea level—in a first-class seat. Since my heart attack, I even use first-class travel to limit my business commitments. If the organization for which I am speaking or consulting won't pay first-class travel, I don't go. I can't afford to waste the time I would spend uncomfortably in a coach-class seat. My clients won't get their money's worth if I'm exhausted when I get there, and so ultimately this is giving clients more for their investment. If I'm making the journey for a benefit or for deserving, low-budget group, I'll pay for a first-class ticket myself. One heart attack is enough!

If I find myself with an extra hour as I wait for a plane, I make sure that I have a book to read, some letters to answer, a manuscript to write, or a walk to take. Occasionally I just sit and watch the chaos around me, turning what could be boring and stressful time into people-watching relaxation time.

Once aboard the plane, take a nap—and never leap to the aisle the moment you reach your destination—unless you're wearing a complete football uniform! Stay seated and cover your head. This will allow all of the Hot Reactors to blow *their* corks, drop their belongings from the overhead bins, jam the aisle, and poke other people's posteriors while waiting to burst out of the plane's door. You'll have an extra five minutes to relax and you'll escape the wrestling match between those travelers exchanging a comfortable seat for standing-room-only accommodations at the baggage claim area. The bottom line: rushing around usually gets you nowhere.

I also recommend using the express reservation and checkout services of hotels and car rentals. In time, the bill gets to me anyway, and it's an added pleasure *not* to stand in early-morning or late-night check-in lines with several flaming Type-A, "anger-outward" personalities.

MANAGING TIME AND STRESS IN HOUSEHOLD CHORES

Chauffeuring the children is often cited as a "pet hate" among overstressed homemakers. I recently saw a bumper sticker that read, "If a woman's place is in the home, why am I always in the car?"

If this sounds familiar to you, perhaps you should reevaluate the time spent catering to the "wants" and not necessarily the "needs" of your children.

Children don't need to be engaged in structured activities every minute of every day. Daydreaming, reading, and playing with friends can be just as important as regimented schedules, organized sports, or cultural events. Even well-intended activities such as Little League can be emotionally draining—and not much fun. It's possible that your child may get more exercise and acquire greater ego support by simply riding a bicycle around the neighborhood. You might also consider joining a car pool to reduce the number of times you will have to experience the "joy" of being your children's chauffeur.

An equally good plan for time management is to think of the time spent driving with a child as an opportunity for active parenting. You are a less threatening authority figure while keeping your eyes on the road and both hands on the steering wheel. Perhaps your child will feel more free to express his or her concerns or enthusiasm. Drive carefully and listen closely.

Today it's normal for both parents to work, and while mechanical devices can be great time-savers, the best "labor-saving device" may be your partner. Sit down with your spouse and look for ways to reduce or eliminate frustrating household chores. The following check list might help:

1. Is it necessary to do this at all?
2. Is it necessary to do this task so frequently?
3. What would happen if the task simply weren't done?
4. Is there an alternative?
5. Could someone else do it?

These simple questions can help you to sort out priorities so that you can find the time you need for the important parts of your life.

WASTED OPPORTUNITIES

Recently while speaking to a group in Hong Kong, a friend made the point that at first didn't strike me as a time-management hint. He said, "It takes a long time and considerable expense to get to Hong Kong; and coming here isn't something that happens all of the time. While you are here, keep this point in mind—if you see it, like it, can afford it, and *don't* buy it, you'll have to carry the emotional baggage for years."

He went on to tell of a trip his mother-in-law made to China when she was younger. During the trip she fell in love with a jade tea set, but she decided to pass it by. All through her life, even as she reached her eighties and nineties, she thought of that beautiful tea set and spoke often of how she had missed a wonderful opportunity.

"Spare yourself such anxiety," he said. "You don't want to completely overrun your bank account; but if you see something in a once-in-a-lifetime place, and you even suspect it would make a difference to you or to someone else—get it!"

His point was that the chronic burden of a lost opportunity is a needless form of self-deprecating, time-wasting stress.

OTHER TIME-SAVING STRATEGIES

1. "A place for everything, and everything in its place." I find that a great deal of time is wasted in the hunt for misplaced items; and many of my patients cite eyeglasses and keys as the primary culprits. Therefore, I'm amazed that so few of them have implemented the simple solution of having a spare pair of glasses or an extra set of keys. This precaution can be a great time and stress saver. Then get into the habit of placing these vital items in the same place in your home or office. You're less likely to face the exasperating problem of lost keys if they're *always* kept in your center desk drawer.

2. Handle each piece of paper as few times as possible. When you pick up a note, letter, or file, make an immediate decision and act upon it. This means that, as you go through the mail:

- Stand near a wastebasket, so that you can throw out the unnecessary junk.
- Delegate to others.
- Act on those items that require your immediate attention.

3. Learn how to control the telephone. The telephone can be a great time saver, as we've all seen in the ads telling us to "let our fingers do the walking"; but as I've already pointed out, the phone can also be a great time waster. People often ramble in long, meaningless conversations, apparently oblivious to the fact that you may have been busy when the phone interrupted. Breaking off such a conversation can be tricky; but if the phone call isn't going anywhere, you can terminate it. Do it politely, but do it!

Practice termination phrases such as: "Frank, I'd love to talk longer, but I must move on to my next appointment," or "Can I get back to you when I have an answer?"

Consider investing in a telephone answering machine. Such a device can be a disappointment when you are the one placing a call; but it can be a great stress saver by screening incoming calls. An answering machine allows you to eliminate hucksters, heavy breathers, and wrong numbers; more important, you can avoid calls that will waste your time. The new caller ID service will provide additional help in controlling annoying incoming calls.

Another telephone-control mechanism is the automatic-dial feature. A number of pocket-size automatic dialing systems are now available. This can be especially helpful when you are traveling and trying to make many calls during a break between planes.

When calling others, be considerate of their time schedules by always having an agenda in mind and by mentally checking off items as the conversation progresses. In addition to saving time, your message is more apt to be really heard.

4. Take charge of deadlines. Deadlines will help you define goals for specific tasks, but they also can cause a great deal of stress. I've found that as long as you allow time for Murphy's Law ("Anything that can go wrong will."), you can keep a seemingly formidable task in perspective by breaking it into a series of smaller, more manageable deadlines.

5. Learn to delegate both at work and at home. When you have more of a load than one person can carry, it's time to work on your skills of delegation. It's unrealistic to think that you can load *everything* on your own shoulders. I have found that this kind of perfectionism is often the manifestation of an inability to trust the competence of others—combined with an ever-present fear of failure.

Despite our best efforts, we all have days that begin with nothing working at all. The likelihood is it won't get better unless we take charge. So, if you can, stop everything, close the door, turn off the phone, take five minutes to rethink your plan for the day, and start again. It's like making a home video. If you don't like it the first time, stop, rewind, and do it again.

CASE PROFILE: PHILLIP DONATO

Phillip Donato had a time/stress overload that could have resulted in potentially fatal physical repercussions. He was a restaurant manager who felt compelled to involve himself in every phase of his restaurant's operations. Keeping all things under his immediate supervision, Phillip had moment-to-moment input on marketing, housekeeping, accounting, purchasing, and the management of personnel. When guests came into his restaurant, Phillip made it a point to greet them all. He inspected each table, and he regularly checked the cleanliness of the restrooms.

At home, his management style was the same. With the same compulsion he directed all activities of his wife and five children. As if that weren't enough, he extended this stewardship to several girlfriends. He defined his aim in all of these activities as the need to be "Mr. Nice Guy." His self-talks included phrases such as:

"We always have space for one more party."
"There's no time like the present."
"Maybe other people can't handle it; but I can—and I will."
"Sleep is for lazy people."
"I'm smarter and tougher than anyone else."
"I've got to be on top of every job to see that it's done right."

When things didn't go the way he wanted, Phil became cranky and irritable. He turned from Dr. Jekyll into Mr. Hyde. His outbursts were unpredictable, and so he sometimes reacted with anger to seemingly unimportant and inappropriate problems. No one could understand what had changed and why he was angry. His family, friends, and employees were alarmed when this unexpected behavior occurred.

As you might suspect, he soon developed a mechanism for keeping himself calm—a couple of martinis became his method for maintaining "equilibrium."

In his own mind, Phillip was the ideal manager; and no one could dispute that he certainly was an active one.

The restaurant owners required periodic health evaluations for all managers, and so Phillip reluctantly fulfilled his duty and came to the institute. He was overweight, exhausted, and tense. Tests revealed a blood cholesterol level well into the danger zone. His blood pressure was above normal; and physical and psychological stress tests revealed that while he had not yet developed coronary heart disease, he was a super Hot Reactor.

Our plan of therapy was to teach Phillip to cool his compulsions with a self-defined intervention program that would help manage his life. Together we identified the most critical problem: Because he gave everything the same priority, he was unable to delegate.

His life reminded me of a question in a grammar school English final. "What's wrong with the following sentence? 'Paul Revere got on his horse and rode off in all directions'?"

Phillip needed time management in the worst way. Essentially, he needed to reduce stress and correct his compulsive headlong rush into physical disaster.

In our first therapeutic session, I asked Phillip to list all of his responsibilities and place them in order of importance. Next I asked him to estimate how much time per week he spent on each item. Immediately we could see that both his management and his time were out of whack. Even he recognized that no human being could cram thirty-six hours into a twenty-four-hour day.

The next step was for him to define his own values and priorities. While he needed to take blood-pressure medication initially (to gain immediate physiological control), our main goal was for him to learn relaxation techniques and to develop an exercise program. He needed time-management skills, and he needed to practice new self-talks. These would include:

"I can't do it all. No one can."
"I don't need to do it all."
"I'll concentrate on the tasks that need my most immediate attention."
"A drink of alcohol may be a reward after a tough day, but I can control the stress myself."
"Drinking to stop my pain can be replaced by delegating authority."
"I've got a good staff; I need to let them do what I know they can do."
"Is it worth dying for?"

As his professional life came under close scrutiny, Phillip was also able to reevaluate his personal life. He recognized that he really loved his wife and children and didn't want to risk losing them because of his extramarital affairs. Soon he was able to confess that these physical relationships really arose from feelings of low self-esteem and the

185

seeking of conquest and achievement instead of love and respect. Equally insightful was Phillip's observation that these affairs usually came when he felt out of control, unsuccessful, or unfulfilled at his work—and that they only added to rather than eased his burdens. As a Swiss physician once told me, "The problem with an extramarital affair is that it takes too much time."

Six months later we tested Phillip and discovered a different man. He had reorganized his life strategies to include the following goals:

- Learn to give the right priority to the right tasks.
- Delegate jobs, and occasionally check to see if a quality job is being done.
- Learn to "go with the flow."
- Enjoy the feeling of being in charge of my life.
- Don't sweat the small stuff; it's *all* small stuff.

The end result was that Phillip also began to control his physiology. His metabolism began to respond to his less stressful lifestyle; and as a result, his weight and his cholesterol levels dropped. While still engaged in the same "stressful" career, he discovered that when he was relaxed, he could do a much better job. Everyone recognized his progress and renewed self-esteem, including the nurse who recorded his cholesterol levels. The change on the outside had mirrored change on the inside. Phillip had become a Cool Reactor.

IT CAN BEGIN WITH ONE SIMPLE WORD

Time management often pivots on your ability to say one simple word: "No." Important events and well-intended people can virtually overrun your life, demanding time that is not available, asking for decisions or commitments you cannot fulfill. This mismanagement of time, coupled with the need to be all things to all people, can produce relentless stress. Each of us can take ultimate responsibility for such a state. Each of us can learn to manage time—and, in doing so, to manage our relationships with others. This is not something that will

186

simply just happen. Learn to evaluate the choices in your life and to keep minor tasks from crowding out the ones that are really important to you, your values, and your goals.

When it is properly managed, time becomes a strength and an ally rather than a source of stress.

PART III

THE HABITS OF HEALTH

CHAPTER 11

NUTRITION

PUTTING PRUDENCE IN THE PANTRY

A critical principle for reducing stress in your life is knowing what you can do for yourself. Nutrition is one area where you really *can* have control—that is, if you can sort through the nutritional "breakthroughs" being announced daily to find the information that applies to you. In this chapter, we have distilled most of what you need to know to stay on a heart-healthy path.

One of the most important recent advances in our knowledge of how nutrition affects the body is the relationship between stress, too much blood cholesterol, and body fat or obesity. Stress affects weight and cholesterol by producing cortisol, which (in addition to other functions) causes your body to retain salt, while stimulating the appetite for more salt. Stress also changes your ability to metabolize carbohydrates through the actions of both cortisol and catecholamines. If that wasn't enough, catecholamines, like caffeine, can stimulate your appetite and sweet tooth.

We need a certain amount of body fat. Because it is layered under the skin and around the organs, it helps cushion the body against injury. Fat also insulates the body from cold and provides fuel for endurance activities. It aids in the utilization of fat-soluble vitamins, and it is essential for the synthesis of prostaglandins (hormonelike substances) and other important body chemicals.

Problems arise only when we carry too much fat. In medicine we deal with obesity from two perspectives. The first is the cosmetic effect of body fat and the stress brought on by social pressures to maintain a trim appearance. The second is the myriad of health risks inherent in being "obese."

The concept of cosmetic beauty is ever-changing. For example, at the turn of the century, Lillian Russell was the world's reigning sex goddess—the model to which most women aspired; and yet, during most of her adult life, Miss Russell held her hourglass figure to a robust 186 pounds. The body weights of Miss America contestants have declined steadily throughout the history of the pageant; and I suspect that if she were alive today, movie producers would insist on putting Marilyn Monroe on a diet. As a society we seem obsessed with the goal of looking thin. Obviously, extreme dieting regimens can have severe physical and psychological ramifications. A preoccupation with being thin can be just as unhealthy as being fat. However, as a cardiologist concerned with physiological stress, I look beyond cosmetic values to the health risks associated with obesity— of which there are many!

THE HEALTH RISKS OF OBESITY

Dr. C. Wayne Callaway, Associate Clinical Professor of Medicine at George Washington University, has made significant contributions toward understanding the complexities of obesity; and we have utilized many of his findings in formulating the weight management guidelines used at the Institute of Stress Medicine.[1]

Although clinical evidence long pointed to a correlation between heredity and obesity, it is just recently that science has confirmed this significant link. Heredity governs the body's basic fat distribution development; and in the broad sense, the body's fat formula is somewhat locked in at birth. Or as I once heard someone say, "God created chihuahuas, and He created St. Bernards."

In practical terms, this means that if there are a number of obese adults in your family, it may be very difficult for you to gain control over your genetic predisposition. Family patterns of poor food choices and overeating may also predispose you to being overweight.

We used to think that the number of fat cells increased only during infancy and adolescence; however, more recent research has suggested that the number of fat cells actually can increase at any age. Once fat cells are formed, they are with you for life. Or, as the saying puts it, "A minute on the lips; a lifetime on the hips."

Fat cells shrink in size as you lose weight, but their number does not decrease. This is the real tragedy of extreme deprivation diets. After a period of starvation, fat cells will shrink and the individual will appear thinner; but the moment normal eating is resumed, the cells will regain size or get bigger.

Liposuction, or the surgical removal of fat cells in an isolated area (usually the stomach or thighs), has recently gained in popularity. Unfortunately, this extreme measure can have less than satisfactory results. Particularly if you don't learn to manage your eating habits or if you don't increase your level of physical activity, you'll get fat again—but in a different place. Fat cells in other parts of your body will simply expand or multiply in number.

WHERE ARE YOU FAT?

Another recent discovery correlates the distribution of body fat with the risk of certain illnesses. When we're considering the risks for hypertension, diabetes, and coronary heart disease, the *location* of your fat deposits is more important than how fat you are. If your fat is located in the so-called saddlebags, or the sides of your hips, you are described as having a pear-shaped figure. This is generally associated with a *lower* risk of cardiovascular disease. On the other hand, if your fat is concentrated around the middle and you look more like an apple on a stick, your risk of coronary heart disease appears to be considerably *higher*. Physicians have come to nickname this correlation the "gut-to-butt" or "belly-to-bottom" ratio. You can determine your own ratio by measuring your hips and waist in the following manner:

1. Measure the circumference of the smallest part of your waist below the rib cage and above your navel.
2. Put your heels together and measure the circumference of your hips at the largest protrusion of your buttocks.
3. Divide your waist measurement by your hip measurement.

Women with a waist-to-hip ratio of .80 or more seem to be at a heightened risk for coronary heart disease. A ratio of .95 or more marks a significant risk for men.

Furthermore, results from a study conducted by Dr. G. A. Bray

193

indicate that the ratio associated with increased risk differs depending on your age.[2] As seen in the graph on page 195, lower levels of excess abdominal fat are associated with reduced risk for heart disease in men less than forty years old. Higher levels are associated with increased risk. A ratio greater then 1.0 puts men into the very high risk category. Perhaps the beer belly that begins to appear around the age of thirty is not as harmless as was once thought.

HOW TO DETERMINE IF YOU ARE OBESE

Generally accepted guidelines to determine if a person is medically obese include the following:

- Many experts define obesity as 20 percent above desirable body weight values. Furthermore, top researchers and the National Institutes of Health agree that weight above this percent is considered to be hazardous to health.
- While previous tables for ideal body weights were based on height and weight ratios established by the insurance industry, a more accurate measurement is obtained by calculating the percentage of total body weight that is composed of fat tissue.
- Exact clinical guidelines for "ideal" percentages of body fat have not been established and are still commonly disputed. Current recommendations for acceptable ranges for body fat are fairly broad: for men, 12 to 25 percent of total body weight; for women, 18 to 30 percent of total body weight.

The institute recommends that ideally men be 12 to 15 percent fat and women be 18 to 22 percent fat. Body composition goals, however, are tailored to each patient's needs as determined by their individual health evaluation, personal fitness, and ideal weight goals. For persons coming into the clinic with excessive percentages of body fat, we prescribe a regimen that encourages progressive weight loss resulting in fat percentages that may be slightly above the "ideal."

It is difficult for an individual to measure his or her body fat accurately. I suggest you see an expert to have your body fat assessed by one of the three most commonly used methods—skin-fold calipers, bioelectrical impedance analysis, or underwater weighing.

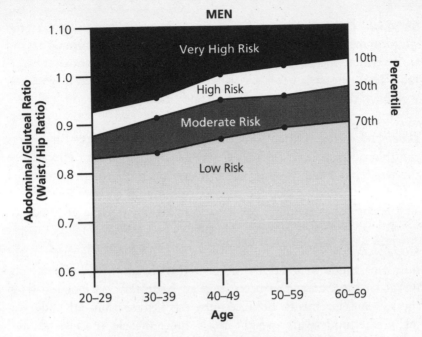

MEN

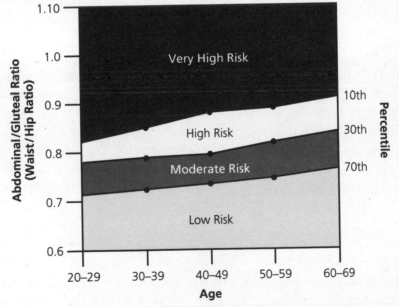

WOMEN

Skin-fold Calipers. In the hands of an expert clinician, this is the simplest method. Skin folds in several areas of the body are measured to determine the thickness of the layer of fat directly under the surface. These measurements are then equated with age, sex, height, and weight to determine the percent of body fat.

Bioelectrical Impedance Analysis (BIA). BIA introduces an imperceptible electric current across electrodes that have been attached to the wrist and ankle. Because fat and lean tissue conduct electricity at different resistance rates, the percent of body fat can be determined. The leaner the individual, the less electrical resistance registered.

Underwater Weighing. In this, the most accurate of the three methods, a person is weighed first in air and then again while being submerged underwater. The percentage of body fat is calculated from the two measurements. Because muscle is heavier than fat underwater, greater underwater weight means more muscle and less fat, and vice versa. Remember, fat floats. Underwater weighing is done clinically only in a specialized laboratory or athletic facility, and it is both time-consuming and potentially uncomfortable. The minor increase in accuracy is overshadowed by the added expense and inconvenience.

Body Mass Index. Physicians who do not have the measuring equipment just listed may rely on the body mass index (BMI) for *estimating* degree of body fat. This is a reasonably good system. Many experts agree that health risks increase when the BMI is above 27.

To find your BMI use the chart on page 197. Place a ruler or the edge of a piece of paper between your weight on the left (without clothes) and your height on the right (without shoes). The BMI and your risk is read from the middle scale.

THE DIETING YO-YO

If you don't like what the BMI has told you, restrain your impulse to start on a crash diet tomorrow. By now I hope the research on diets is well known: You can actually become *fatter* after lowering

NOMOGRAM FOR BODY MASS INDEX

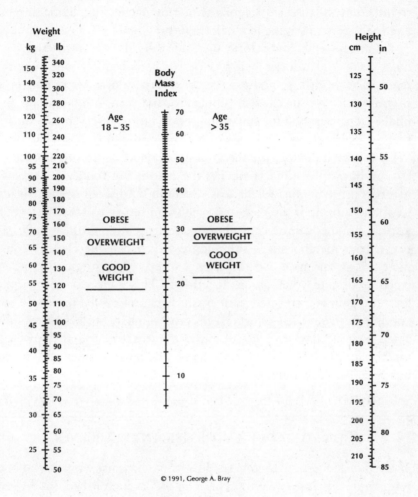

© 1991, George A. Bray

your metabolism through starvation or chronic, extreme low-calorie dieting.

Observations of this phenomenon were first made immediately after World War II, when studies of concentration camp survivors revealed that many of them had survived on food intakes of only 300 calories a day. Recent research shows that, under starvation conditions, the body compensates for reduction in the amount of calories eaten by shutting down the metabolism to a minimum survival level.

197

As can be expected, people living on 300 calories a day are neither physically nor mentally active; and they are much more vulnerable to infection and disease. A similar situation occurs in individuals who routinely go on extreme low-calorie diets.

By an extreme low-calorie diet, I mean dietary restrictions of more than 500 calories below a person's daily metabolic requirement. The body's response to such severe caloric restriction is a primitive survival mechanism similar to that seen in hibernating animals. In preparation for starvation, body fat is preserved as a future fuel source and weight loss slows. The end result is a Catch-22. With repeated dieting, the metabolism is depressed more and more so you have to continue reducing the amount of food you eat, just in order to maintain weight loss. Eventually, discouragement leads to abandonment of the diet; and when you return to what was your normal pre-diet caloric consumption, you rapidly put on weight because your metabolism is still suppressed. When the cycle is complete, your ultimate weight may exceed your original pre-diet weight—despite your agonizing efforts. This roller-coaster weight loss and gain is associated with crash diets and results in people becoming fat from their efforts to become thinner. Studies have indicated that it may take up to three months to raise the lowered metabolic rate back to a normal level; but by this time, self-esteem has been seriously damaged.

HOW TO BECOME A MORE EFFICIENT FAT BURNER

The critical question becomes: How can you raise your metabolic rate, and still lose weight? This can be accomplished in several ways.

1. **You need to eat.** The body's metabolic rate rises with an increase in caloric intake but appears to slow way down if food intake is dropped to more than 500 calories below total energy expenditures. (Remember the concentration camp survivors.) The key is to maintain metabolic rates at normal levels.

198

2. **Increase physical activity.** Exercise is the best way to increase metabolism and burn fat. Obviously, you can't starve and maintain a high metabolic rate and a high level of physical activity at the same time. A serious condition known as *anorexia nervosa* can occur when an individual combines starvation with a physical addiction to exercise (such as jogging); and it is most often seen in females due to the intense social pressure to become thin and fit.

3. **Eat a diet high in carbohydrates and low in fat.** Eating fat will add more pounds than will eating carbohydrates. Some studies suggest that the body converts fats of all types into body fat more efficiently than it converts either carbohydrates or protein. The energy used in converting fat is very low, while the energy used converting carbohydrates to body fat is much higher. This means that it costs the body more calories to metabolize complex carbohydrates than fat. Given *the same calorie content* for a portion of fat or of carbohydrate, you will gain more from the fat than from the carbohydrate!

    Thus carbohydrates not only *supply fewer* calories per gram (4 rather than 9), they also are a *more expensive* fuel.

4. **Avoid less healthy methods of stimulating metabolic rate.** Thyroid excess (such as taking too much thyroid medication), nicotine, diet pills, and fever are among the less desirable ways to increase total metabolic rate. As mentioned earlier, increased caloric intake will also increase metabolism; however, unless you counter the increased food intake with exercise, you'll create yet *another* Catch-22 situation.

Your normal dietary requirements are influenced by factors such as age, sex, body size, and general state of health; and they should be established in consultation with your physician. A weight reduction plan would then include a balanced diet, a caloric intake of no more than 500 calories below your individual requirements, and a sensible aerobic exercise program that is done three or more times per week.

If you have had the diet roller-coaster experience and suspect that you have lowered your metabolic rate to an inappropriate level, I recommend that you ask your physician to measure your basal metabolic rate. By determining if your basal metabolism is high or low, your physician can more accurately prescribe your daily caloric requirements and monitor metabolic changes over time.

Even minor changes in caloric intake (5 to 15 percent) combined with exercise can mean pounds per year. Early in such a program you may not notice any overt weight loss, but progress can still be occurring at the cellular level. Then, after your metabolic rate returns to normal, your diet/exercise program will be more likely to produce a permanent weight loss.

Remember that the metabolism is a slow learner (even slower with age) and very dutiful. Over the years it has done what your brain prescriptions told it to do, whether right or wrong. So it will take some time and sustained new brain prescriptions before your metabolism finally responds. Expect to wait a few weeks or even several months to see your weight change. Pick a weight-control system that is slow, steady, scientifically sound, and sustainable—and be patient.

To lose weight

Modest reductions in calories. Moderate increases in activity. That's the only sure way to lose weight. Sadly, it's not a message that plays well on cable TV.

ARE MY CHOLESTEROL LEVELS KILLING ME?

The war on cholesterol has been well funded by the federal government. Virtually every American is now convinced that cholesterol is Public Enemy Number One. My first job is sometimes to persuade patients that there are other things that need their attention.

Keep in mind that cholesterol is required by every cell in the body for its metabolism. It's a basic building block for the survival chemicals (including cortisol) that allow us to go for extended periods

200

without food and water. It is also a basic building block for the sex hormones. So cholesterol is not all bad.

Many of my new patients are unaware of the relatively large number of people who live into their 80s and 90s with cholesterol levels that are considered by some experts to be in the high risk category. Many do not realize that as you age, cholesterol levels diminish in predicting risk.

The bottom line is that cholesterol is an important factor. *How* it becomes elevated is critically important; how old you are is important; your family risk is important; and how your cholesterol levels relate to your other risk factors is important. But blood cholesterol is only one thing to consider, and it is influenced as much by your mental prescriptions as by your meal preparation.

Indeed, the last word on cholesterol has yet to be written by the researchers. For now, I consider blood cholesterol elevation a statistical risk based on large population studies that may hit or miss you. It's like not wearing your seat belt. Certainly you are better off avoiding the risk, but high cholesterol is not an absolute death sentence.

So use the material that follows in balance with the rest of your health portfolio—and avoid cholesterol guilt trips.

I recommend blood cholesterol levels based on the presence or absence of risk factors for coronary heart disease. These include family history, being male, cigarette smoking, elevated blood pressure, diabetes, and HDL cholesterol below 35—as well as the contributing factors of sedentary living and excessive body fat.

RECOMMENDED BLOOD CHOLESTEROL LEVELS

150 to 180 milligrams per deciliter (mg/dl) for individuals with one or more risk factors.
Less than 200 mg/dl for individuals with *no* risk factors.

If you have the risk factors mentioned earlier, research has shown that for every 1 percent an individual lowers his or her blood cholesterol level, the risk of coronary heart disease decreases approximately 2 percent. If you do not have those risk factors, there may be no reason for you to change your dietary intake of cholesterol and saturated fat if your blood cholesterol levels are within the guidelines just outlined. In addition, as I tell my patients, characteristics of people, like those of cars, vary greatly. Cars have different types of engines and burn different types of fuels with differing degrees of efficiency. What is good for one person may not be good for the next.

A SHORT COURSE IN BLOOD FATS

The complex chemistry of blood fats has become a part of everyday jargon. However, the terms are still confusing to most of us; and so I'd like to offer a brief glossary.

• **Lipid:** A general term for fats that include triglycerides, phospholipids, and sterols.

• **Cholesterol:** A sterol that is carried throughout the bloodstream by lipoproteins. Most cholesterol is produced by the body; it is a key component of cells and several hormones.

• **Lipoproteins:** Combinations of lipids and protein. Lipoproteins transport lipids from the liver through the blood into the cells.

• **Total Cholesterol:** The figure given in blood lipid analysis of all the cholesterol, including HDL, LDL, and VLDL cholesterol.

• **HDL:** High-density lipoprotein, a subcategory of cholesterol, often called "good" cholesterol.

• **LDL:** Low-density lipoprotein, a subcategory of cholesterol, often called "bad" cholesterol. Lp(a) is a particularly dangerous LDL particle, newly recognized as a separate risk factor.

• **VLDL:** Very-low-density lipoprotein, a major transporter for triglycerides that also carries some cholesterol.

• **Triglycerides:** The actual fats in the body and the blood. Ninety-five percent of the lipids in food and in our bodies are triglycerides. Some people show high blood triglyceride levels when they consume excessive amounts of simple carbohydrates (sugars) or alcohol.

Nevertheless, a reduction in total calories, total fat, saturated fat, and cholesterol is believed to be sensible for the U.S. population as a whole. It is *imperative* for people who are overweight, have high blood pressure, have diabetes, smoke, or have a family history of breast, prostate, or colorectal cancer.

The total amount and type of fat consumed is far more important than the amount of cholesterol consumed.

GOOD CHOLESTEROL AND BAD CHOLESTEROL

Ongoing research continues to expand our understanding of the role played by high-density lipoprotein (HDL) cholesterol and low-density lipoprotein (LDL) cholesterol. An easy way to distinguish the two is to think of HDL as "healthy" or "good" cholesterol and LDL as "lousy" or "bad" cholesterol. This good/bad differentiation is necessary because we are now certain that blood cholesterol levels associated with high levels of LDL are notorious for promoting atherosclerotic plaque formations, or hardening of the arteries.

The National Institutes of Health (NIH) has developed the following scale regarding LDL cholesterol levels:

Desirable	Below 130 mg/dl
Borderline	130–160 mg/dl
High Risk	Over 160 mg/dl

The NIH has further determined that people at high risk for coronary heart disease (having one or more of the previously discussed risk factors) should have an LDL level *below* 130 mg/dl. For people at low risk, an LDL less than 160 mg/dl is regarded as acceptable. I encourage *all* of my patients, regardless of risk factors, to keep LDL levels below 130 mg/dl.

It isn't enough simply to lower your level of LDL cholesterol. Because of increased evidence that coronary artery disease is also the

203

outcome of a contest between LDL cholesterol and HDL cholesterol, you should also strive to increase HDL, or "good," cholesterol levels. The ratio of HDL and total cholesterol level reflects this balance, and it can be calculated with the following formula:

$$\frac{\text{Total Blood Cholesterol}}{\text{HDL Cholesterol}}$$

An example of a good risk ratio would be:

$$\frac{\text{Total cholesterol 203}}{\text{HDL cholesterol 56}} = 3.6$$

An example of a bad risk ratio would be:

$$\frac{\text{Total cholesterol 380}}{\text{HDL cholesterol 26.6}} = 14.6$$

The consensus of researchers today is that a total cholesterol to HDL cholesterol ratio of no more than 4 to 1 (or 4.0) is the highest acceptable value.

Because so many studies have shown that ratios below 4.0 are associated with the least amount of risk, I strongly recommend maintaining your cholesterol to these standards.

(Note that some laboratories report the values inversely—that is, the percentage of HDL cholesterol to total cholesterol. In those cases, a percentage of 25 percent or higher is desirable. It is also important to find out if the laboratory conducting the analysis is one of the six national reference laboratories, or uses certified reference methods, such as the College of American Pathologists [CAP] quality assurance. Results from uncertified labs often vary widely.)

Make sure your doctor reports and explains all the elements of your blood fat studies discussed above.

> ### HOW TO IMPROVE THE RATIO OF HDL CHOLESTEROL TO
> ### TOTAL CHOLESTEROL
>
> - **Stop smoking.**
>   Smoking *lowers* the good or HDL cholesterol.
> - **Reduce the amount of saturated fats in your diet.**
>   Saturated fat raises total cholesterol.
> - **Take up some form of aerobic exercise.**
>   You should walk, jog, or swim, or the like for at least thirty minutes three times a week. Aerobic exercise raises HDL cholesterol.
> - **Maintain a healthy weight.**
>   Losing weight decreases total as well as LDL cholesterol.

MENTAL STRESS AND BLOOD CHOLESTEROL

The liver produces blood cholesterol during chronic mental stress, or when a person needs to be vigilant for a long period of time. Elevations of blood cholesterol have been demonstrated in medical students before examinations. Blood cholesterol levels of naval air pilots on active duty have been shown to correlate with their degree of moment-to-moment control over the aircraft they fly. The lowest levels occur in older pilots who fly transport aircraft. The highest levels occur in young pilots who fly carrier-based fighters.

Drs. Meyer Friedman and Ray Rosenman made similar observations in tax accountants, whose cholesterol levels rose dramatically from the first of January to the fifteenth of April.[3] Our studies have shown that Hot Reactors produce their own cholesterol. In most cases, as they cool off, their blood cholesterol levels glide downward.

Dr. Dean Ornish, an expert in the field of stress medicine, emphasizes that controlling stress is critical to lowering blood cholesterol levels as well as to reversing atherosclerotic obstructions in the blood vessels.[4]

As a result of the campaign against cholesterol, we are now seeing patients who are carrying extra stress about their cholesterol levels! This is dangerous not only in itself, but because it may be distracting them from other serious issues.

My patient Albert was a classic example. Albert was an accountant and a darn good one. He prided himself on his tireless dedication to accuracy and integrity. But, at age 45, in a cholesterol screening at his firm, he was found to have a blood cholesterol level of 260 mg/dl. His HDL (good cholesterol) was low and his LDL (bad cholesterol) was high.

Albert attacked the problem with the same zeal and intensity he generated in balancing his clients' accounts. He immediately reduced his dietary fat to 10 percent, started jogging two miles per day, and bought a scale to weigh his food. He lost 12 pounds to achieve an ideal BMI, and had his blood cholesterol checked weekly. Two months later he was horrified to realize that with all this effort and sacrifice his cholesterol level had only slid to 237—23 points—a lousy 9 percent reduction and a life of misery. By the time he started our program, Albert was loudly proclaiming, "I'm doomed."

But in reviewing Albert's Quality of Life Index, we discovered he had other problems: specifically a bulimic daughter, the apple of his eye, and an 86-year-old mother who was becoming forgetful and accident prone. His wife of twenty years was in a panic over Albert's new-found paranoia and had considerable guilt over his high cholesterol, assuming her cuisine was the culprit. Albert wondered about that too.

During our evaluation sessions, I suggested counseling for his daughter, a retirement home for his mother, and the stress control techniques outlined in this book. I explained to Albert that his overburdened knapsack was contributing to his brain's prescriptions for cholesterol production. He was amazed, relieved, and a delight to work with.

Albert recruited his wife's assistance with the family problems. Both of them received absolution from our registered dietitian. We actually raised his dietary fat intake to 20 percent. His meals became palatable again. We also suggested he walk instead of jog because he was beginning to get traumatic arthritis in his feet.

Twelve months later Albert's daughter's problem was controlled and his mother was secure, accustomed to—if not thrilled with—her new environment. Albert's cholesterol now hovers around 200 and occasionally dips to about 187—acceptable because his family incidence of heart disease is not high and the remainder of his health portfolio is well balanced. His wife has also let go of undeserved guilt over Albert's cholesterol. We had cured Albert's presenting condition: cholesterolmania.

> "*Cholesterolmania,* an exaggerated and unreasonable enthusiasm for knowledge about and fear of dietary and plasma cholesterol."
>
> Robert E. Olson, M.D., Ph.D.[5]

OTHER FACTORS THAT AFFECT LIPID LEVELS

When you undergo blood tests for cholesterol, remember that there are other extraneous factors that can affect the levels of cholesterol and lipids. For example:

• During her menstrual period, a woman's LDL level is lower and her HDL level is higher.

• Birth control pills raise the LDL levels and lower the HDL levels.

• Many diuretic drugs will raise both triglycerides and total cholesterol.

• Antihypertensive medications (specifically, beta blockers) lower HDL levels and raise triglyceride levels.

• Anabolic steroids raise total cholesterol.

• In order to obtain accurate triglyceride values, you should fast for 12 to 24 hours.

• Blood drawn from a prone position is more dilute and thus yields lower cholesterol values. Standing raises total cholesterol, so any blood sample should be taken in a sitting position.

• Cholesterol levels respond to the seasons. The highest levels are recorded in December and January, while the lowest are recorded in June.

• Blood cholesterol levels increase during pregnancy and may remain elevated for up to 20 weeks after delivery.

• Estrogen may raise HDL levels, although this effect is reduced when progestins are added. Estrogen replacement therapy, both with and without progestins, will lower total cholesterol.

• "Milking" or squeezing the finger to get blood for a fingerprick dilutes the sample and can artificially lower total cholesterol readings.

THE AMERICAN DIET MAY BE HAZARDOUS
TO YOUR HEALTH

In order to lower your risk of heart disease, you must pay attention
to dietary fats as well as to blood fats. Our bodies need some fat in
the diet in order to function normally. However, susceptibility to
diabetes, hypertension, atherosclerosis, obesity, and heart disease are
clearly increased by diets that are *too high* in total fat, saturated fats,
and cholesterol.

The typical American derives approximately *37 percent* of his or
her calories from fat! Most nutrition experts agree this is too much,
and there is general consensus that a more healthful percentage
would be 30 percent or less. This is the recommendation of the American Heart Association and of the Dietary Guidelines for Americans.
The Institute of Stress Medicine's policy is to take a more aggressive
approach. We recommend to our clients that they aim for *20 percent
of total calories in fat.*

Research by Dr. Ornish has shown that lowering of fat in the diet
to less than 10 percent of calories and the diligent practice of stress
management techniques for one hour each day can arrest the progression of documented coronary heart disease.[6] Furthermore, the
disease process *regressed* in 82 percent of the individuals who followed the Ornish regimen. Of those adhering to the American Heart
Association recommendation of less than 30 percent of calories as
fat, 53 percent of the group had *further progression* of the disease
process, 42 percent had regression, and one patient (5 percent) had
no change.

As a result of these findings, Dr. Ornish suggests that "conventional recommendations for patients with coronary heart disease
(such as 30 percent fat diet) are not sufficient to bring about regression in many patients. Stress management practices are necessary to
achieve reversal of coronary disease."[7]

In my opinion, fat reduction *below* 20 percent of calories may be
overdoing a good thing for most people. Anyone considering such a
regimen should first consult his or her physician. Our experiences at
the institute have shown that when beginning a low-fat diet, just
about everyone needs strong motivation as well as the supervision of
a physician-nutritionist team if long-term compliance is to occur. In-

dividuals who already have documented disease (such as stroke or heart attacks) have reason to be motivated; and they are more likely to greatly reduce fats in their diets.

WAYS TO REDUCE THE CONSUMPTION OF FAT

There are only a limited number of ways to reduce the amount of fat in the diet, since carbohydrates and proteins are the only other viable sources of energy for the body.

(Alcoholic beverages also provide dietary calories, but we do not recommend considering them as a viable source of energy.)

Most nutritionists agree that 55 to 65 percent of total calories should be derived from carbohydrates, of which 45 to 55 percent should be in the form of complex carbohydrates. This means that simple carbohydrates—the sugary sweets—should not exceed 10 percent of total calories. Another 15 percent of calories should be made up of protein.

However, at the Institute of Stress Medicine, we recommend a higher proportion of complex carbohydrates:

• 67 percent of total calories should come from carbohydrates, with 57 percent or more being complex and 10 percent or less being simple carbohydrates.

• 13 percent of total calories should come from protein.

• 20 percent of total calories should come from fats.

Reducing fat in the diet to extreme limits (10 percent or below) can make the food very unpalatable. You also may have problems in absorption of fat soluble vitamins. In addition, when fat is reduced that much, you have to eat a lot of carbohydates to compensate. This can trigger triglyceride elevation, insulin resistance, and blood-sugar elevation. It can even lead to more serious complications like the inflammation of the pancreas (pancreatitis).

WHAT TYPE OF FAT SHOULD YOU EAT?

Not all dietary fats are created equal. In addition to limiting overall fat intake, you need to focus on the specific kind of fat to avoid. Although your body controls how much cholesterol is synthesized or

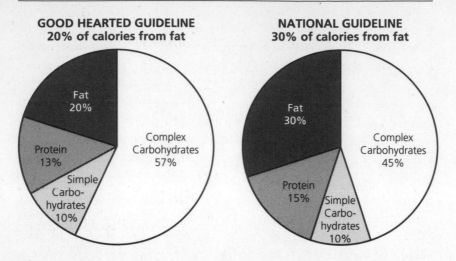

GOOD HEARTED GUIDELINE
20% of calories from fat

Fat 20%
Protein 13%
Simple Carbo-hydrates 10%
Complex Carbohydrates 57%

NATIONAL GUIDELINE
30% of calories from fat

Fat 30%
Protein 15%
Simple Carbo-hydrates 10%
Complex Carbohydrates 45%

produced, research has shown that saturated fat intake is directly related to significant increases in blood cholesterol levels. When you eat foods high in saturated fats (found primarily in animal products, hydrogenated vegetable oils, or tropical oils), your liver is stimulated to produce more blood cholesterol.

In this area, again, the Institute of Stress Medicine takes a somewhat more conservative approach than national guidelines, such as those of the National Research Council. The following table shows how we compare.

Institute of Stress Medicine Guideline 20% of total calories from fat		National Guideline 30% of total calories from fat
less than 7%	saturated	less than 10%
less than 7%	polyunsaturated	7 to 10%
less than 7%	monounsaturated	10 to 15%

National Research Council guidelines also specify that total cholesterol intake should be no more than 300 mg daily.[8] We tell our patients to limit cholesterol to 100 mg for every 1,000 calories consumed per day, with 300 mg as the upper limit.

A SHORT COURSE IN DIETARY FATS

- **Saturated Fats:** Primarily those that remain solid at room temperature; best illustrated by animal fats in meats and dairy products.
- **Hydrogenated Fats:** Unsaturated vegetable oils that have been artificially hardened, making them into saturated fats.
- **Exceptional Saturated Fats:** "Sneaky" saturated fats that remain liquid at room temperature. These tropical oils include palm oil, palm kernel oil, and coconut oil. Beware! These saturated forms of vegetable oil are as artery-clogging as are any of their animal fat cousins.
- **Unsaturated Fats:** Primarily those that remain liquid at room temperature, including most vegetable fats. They are divided into two categories; both play an important role in good nutrition.
- **Polyunsaturated Fats:** The most unsaturated fats, these include safflower, sunflower, corn, cottonseed, and soybean oils.
- **Monounsaturated Fats:** The least unsaturated fats, these include olive oil, canola oil, and peanut oil.

Among the unsaturated fats, canola and olive oils are highly recommended because they are high in monounsaturated fat and relatively low in saturated fat. These oils may be as or more effective in lowering blood cholesterol than are polyunsaturated fats. Monounsaturated fats appear to have an advantage over polyunsaturated fats because they actually appear to lower the "lousy" LDL cholesterol levels in the blood without reducing the amount of the "healthy" HDL cholesterol levels. Polyunsaturated fats such as safflower, sunflower, corn, soybean, and sesame oils have been shown to reduce both the *good* and bad forms of cholesterol.

Tip: *Check the label* of your margarine to make sure the brand you are using is not high in saturated fat. There should be no more than 1 gram of saturated fat per tablespoon serving (14 grams).

211

Guide to Oil Types

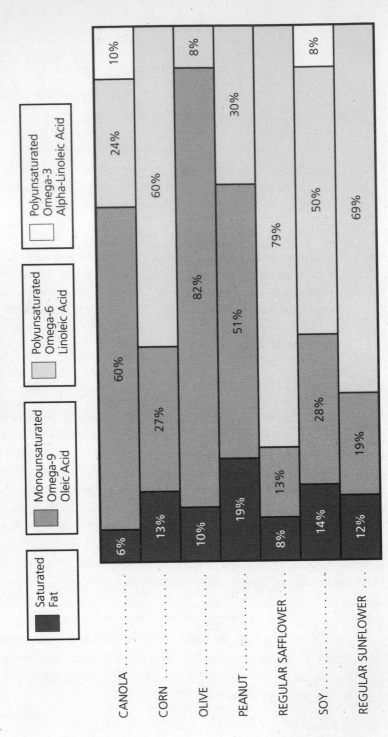

CAN CONSUMING CERTAIN KINDS OF FATS LOWER CHOLESTEROL?

Eskimos who subsist on blubber and other marine fats have virtually no coronary heart disease. Studies of their diet have led to the conclusion that not all polyunsaturated fatty acids are created equal. The fat found in the fish that the Eskimos most commonly eat is composed of long chains of omega-3 fatty acids.

Omega-3 (*alpha-linolenic acid*) and omega-6 (*linoleic acid*) are two fatty acids considered essential for good health. Of the two types, we know more about omega-3 fatty acids. Two of these, EPA (*eicosapentaenoic acid*) and DHA (*docosahexaenoic acid*) are purported actively to increase HDL cholesterol and reduce triglycerides in the blood in some people. In addition, they appear to keep the blood thin, which may in turn prevent the formation of clots that could cause blockages in the arteries. This may be their major effect.

However, this does not mean that you should carry a hip flask full of EPA, to be quaffed during stressful moments in an effort to prevent a heart attack. When these oils are taken in excessive quantities, complications can result, including Vitamin E deficiency and thrombocytopenia (a platelet deficiency that can lead to bleeding throughout the body, including the brain). Another disadvantage of overoiling is that the unmistakable odor of fish oil will emanate from your body, thus making you smell like an ambulatory fish cannery.

> **Both the American Heart Association and the National Heart, Lung, and Blood Institute believe there is inadequate data to support a recommendation to use fish oil supplements for the prevention or treatment of coronary heart disease. These organizations have gone on record against their use. Fish oil supplements should be taken only under a physician's guidance.**

A practical alternative to using supplements is simply to eat cold-water varieties of fish two to three times a week. (Crushed flax seeds can provide vegetarians with a rich dietary source of omega-3 fatty acids.)

All fish and shellfish contain omega-3 fatty acids, but oilier, fattier fish are the richest sources.

A rule of thumb: the darker the fish's flesh, the higher the fat and omega-3 fatty acid content.

Fish Rich in Omega-3 Fatty Acids

Anchovies	Lake Trout	Sablefish
Bluefish	Mackerel	Salmon
Catfish	Mullet	Sea Herring
	Rainbow Trout	Sturgeon

Fish Moderate in Omega-3 Fatty Acids

Albacore Tuna	Ocean Perch	Rockfish
Cod	Orange Roughy	Sea Trout
Halibut	Red Snapper	Shellfish
		Shrimp

Fish Low in Omega-3 Fatty Acids

Flounder	Lake Perch	Sea Perch
Haddock	Pike	Swordfish
		Whiting

When selecting canned fish, choose only those packed in water. The vegetable oil used in canned fish is not an omega-3 rich oil and it also contributes to added fat.

We recommend not to overdose on fish oil or *any type* of polyunsaturated fatty acids. There is evidence that consuming more than the recommended 7 percent of calories from polyunsaturated fats could increase the risk of developing gallstones, certain cancers, and possible suppression of the immune system. Always keep in mind, fat is fat. The excessive intake of *any type* can lead to obesity and an increased risk of many of the lifestyle-related diseases just discussed.

PHARMACOLOGICAL TREATMENT OF HIGH BLOOD CHOLESTEROL

Patients frequently ask me questions about lipid-reducing drugs, which are being introduced in increasing numbers. As a cardiologist, my response is simple: Drugs should be reserved for special patients who require them. Almost all lipid-lowering drugs on the market have been associated with side effects that were not apparent when the drugs were first put into use. Therefore, it is my policy to reserve drug treatment for individuals who have the highest risk for medical complications and who cannot successfully reduce their blood cholesterol, LDL, and triglyceride levels or raise their HDL levels with just dietary and lifestyle (exercise) modifications. Recent results suggest that medication can provide a significant reversal of coronary blockage when dietary restrictions fail to do so.

Many of my patients have also heard of treating high cholesterol with niacin and ask if they can try it. When given under a physician's direction, niacin is a tried-and-true method for lowering triglycerides, total cholesterol, and LDL, while raising HDL. It is quite effective, relatively safe, and inexpensive. While it has unpleasant side effects (hot flashes and generalized itching), these usually disappear in two to three weeks when the doses do not exceed 500 milligrams three times per day. One baby aspirin taken 15 minutes before the niacin can help to diminish flushing and is often recommended during the first few weeks after a person begins taking niacin.

But you should never attempt to self-dose with niacin. It occasionally produces liver damage, reactivation of peptic ulcers, heart rhythm disturbances, problems with glucose tolerance, and jaundice. (The long-acting niacin preparations have been found to be more toxic to the liver than the short-term ones.)[9] When taken with hypertension medication, niacin may cause a drop in blood pressure, fainting, or problems with the central nervous system. Fortunately,

215

such side effects are almost always reversible when the dosage is lowered or discontinued.

PROTEINS

Proteins (from the Greek word meaning "of prime importance") are the second part of the nutritional trinity of fats, proteins, and carbohydrates. A single protein may contain up to twenty (some researchers say twenty-two) structural units called *amino acids.*

Nine of these amino acids are essential—meaning that they are indispensable to body function, and the body cannot manufacture them. Antibodies, enzymes, hormones, hemoglobin, and muscle tissue are just a few examples of body components made up of proteins containing these essential amino acids.

Furthermore, amino acids are necessary for the proper functioning of the body. For example, *tyrosine* is a building block of the hormone noradrenaline; it also functions as an antidepressant. *Tryptophan,* a component of *serotonin,* is another important brain chemical, a primary function of which is to induce sleep. Most experts agree that in order to keep all of these chemical reactions in balance, 15 percent of a person's diet should be made up of protein. We recommend a more conservative figure of no more than 13 percent protein in a total diet because most protein sources are animal and, as such, are high in both saturated and total fat.

SOURCES OF PROTEIN

Meat from animals (pork, beef, lamb, poultry, fish, and shellfish) as well as dairy products constitute the primary sources of protein in the average American diet. Unfortunately, both contain a large amount of saturated fat. Poultry (especially white meat without skin), fish, shellfish, and skimmed milk products are preferable to other choices such as marbled beef, lamb, and whole milk products; the white meat of turkey has one of the lowest fat contents of all animal proteins.

Foods containing protein such as legumes (lentils, dried beans, and peas) and grains (rice, oats, wheat, barley, millet, and so on) are healthful choices because they are high in fiber and low in fat. Unlike meat and milk products, most sources of plant protein have no (or very little) saturated fat. Grains and legumes also have a secondary benefit of being less expensive than most animal protein.

Meat, milk, and eggs are considered to be *complete* proteins because they provide all nine of the essential amino acids; foods derived from plants are called *incomplete* proteins because they are lacking in one or more of these elements. This "shortcoming" is easily overcome by eating complementary sources of vegetable protein. The classic example is the dish of rice and beans, which contains all nine essential amino acids. You also can insure a complete complement of amino acids by eating small amounts of meat, eggs, or milk products along with incomplete protein sources. Egg whites are particularly good for this purpose since they contain no cholesterol.

The following chart can help you combine incomplete proteins in nutritious alternatives to meat, milk, and eggs.

DAIRY PRODUCTS HIGH IN PROTEIN AND LOW IN ANIMAL FAT

Skimmed milk or 1 percent fat milk are also healthful selections for people who wish to reduce their intake of animal fats. They provide the same amount of calcium and protein as whole milk products but are low in or lack the fat. Fermented milk products, such as skim or lowfat buttermilk and yogurt, are also good protein sources and are often highly digestible by individuals who lack the enzyme lactase to digest the milk sugar lactose. In addition, the fermented milk introduces desirable lactobacilli into the intestine. These "good bugs" displace undesirable microorganisms in the intestines that can contribute to digestive problems.

CARBOHYDRATES

Carbohydrates, which complete the nutrient trinity, consist of sugars, starch, and fiber. Because they were considered fattening, carbohydrates used to be a dirty word to individuals who were dieting; but now nutritionists are touting their value and encouraging their increased use in weight control. Carbohydrates are classified as either

GUIDE TO COMPLEMENTARY PROTEINS

To get maximum nutritional benefits, combine proteins,
linking foods from groups connected with arrows. (The thinner arrows
connect food groups in which not all items are complementary.)

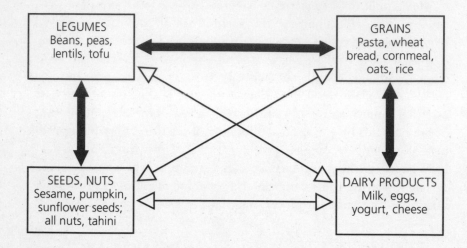

simple (containing glucose, fructose, and galactose) or *complex* (those rich in starch and fiber).

Simple carbohydrates, or *mono-* and *disaccharides,* can be found in fruits, honey, milk, malt, and table sugar. Complex carbohydrates, or *polysaccharides,* are found in foods such as grains, potatoes, breads, rice, pasta, cereals, and legumes (dried peas and beans). As mentioned earlier, I recommend eating 67 percent of your calories in the form of carbohydrates (most of which should be complex) and limiting the intake of simple sugars to no more than 10 percent of calories.

THE HEALTH BENEFITS ASSOCIATED WITH FIBER

Complex carbohydrates have added health benefits because they are considered to be nutritionally dense. That is, they contain large amounts of vitamins and minerals and are rich in fiber. Fiber, the indigestible portion of complex carbohydrates, is found in fruits, vegetables, grains, potatoes, and legumes. Because the body cannot break down fiber, it contributes no calories to the diet.

There are two basic types of fiber.

Insoluble fiber (usually called roughage) is composed of the woody, structural parts of plants—such as fruit and vegetable skins, seeds, and the outer coating, or bran, of grains such as wheat kernels. In addition to their high fiber content, much of grains' nutrition is concentrated in the hulls; refined complex carbohydrates that have had those hulls removed (such as white flour and white rice) are less desirable. That's why the term "whole grain" has become such a buzz word for today's health advocates.

Soluble fiber is a substance that dissolves and thickens in water to form a gel. These fibers are found in a variety of whole grains (such as oats and barley), legumes, fruits and vegetables (such as apples and the pulpy part of citrus fruits), psyllium seeds (the source of Metamucil), and seaweed (the source of agar).

Insoluble fiber causes food to pass more rapidly through the intestinal tract. Inclusion of this roughage in the diet may prevent the buildup of carcinogenic compounds that would otherwise ferment in the large intestine, reduce the risk of colon cancer, and reduce symptoms of diverticular disease and some types of irritable bowel syndrome.

Soluble fiber, on the other hand, is a binding agent that has been shown to lower blood cholesterol levels. We know that pectin can block the absorption of cholesterol from the small intestine back into the bloodstream; everyone is probably familiar with oat bran, the nationally acclaimed conqueror of elevated blood cholesterol levels. Soluble fiber also keeps the blood sugar level more constant. By forming a gel in the gastrointestinal tract, this type of fiber slows the absorption of nutrients into the bloodstream, thereby avoiding peaks and valleys in the blood sugar level. This is important because sudden elevations and depressions in the blood sugar level are associated with mood swings; as you can imagine, people tend to respond more to stress when they are moody. Conversely, stress itself can also be a factor in erratic shifts in blood sugar levels, completing a destructive cycle of stress and nutritional intake. (Because fiber slows digestion and delays the absorption of sugar, it is also helpful to diabetics in the control of blood sugar, by lowering the peak demand for insulin after a meal.)

Finally, both kinds of fiber have some value in weight control by adding bulk to the meal and enhancing feelings of being full or satisfied.

DIETARY FIBER RECOMMENDATIONS

I recommend that a healthy adult eat 15 grams of dietary fiber per 1,000 calories consumed. For the average adult this amounts to 20 to 35 grams per day.

A word of caution: Increasing your daily consumption of too many foods high in fiber, too fast, can cause gas, severe stomach cramps, and diarrhea.

It's vital to drink adequate amounts of fluid to allow the fiber to expand and move through the digestive system; complications can most certainly occur if large amounts of fiber supplements are taken without increasing fluid intake. Overall, I feel that unless supplements are prescribed by your physician, you should avoid fiber bars, tablets, and pure bran. Instead fulfill your fiber requirements by eating a variety of grains, legumes, potatoes, fresh fruit, and vegetables.

FOODS HIGH IN
SOLUBLE AND INSOLUBLE DIETARY FIBER

Water Soluble (pectins and gums)

FUNCTION: *Binding* agents that have been shown to reduce blood cholesterol levels.

SOURCE: Legumes (dried beans, peas, lentils)
Fruits (primarily apples, oranges)
Vegetables, oats, oat bran, barley

Water Insoluble (celluloses, hemicelluloses, and lignins)

FUNCTION: *Bulking* agents that aid in regularity.
SOURCE: Wheat bran
Whole grains
Vegetables

Recommended Daily Intake = 15/gm per 1,000 calories consumed

	Serving Size	Total Fiber (grams)	Soluble Fiber (grams)	Insoluble Fiber (grams)
VEGETABLES				
Peas	*	5.2	2.0	3.2
Parsnips	*	4.4	0.4	4.0
Potatoes	1 small	3.8	2.2	1.6
Broccoli	*	2.6	1.6	1.0
Zucchini	*	2.5	1.1	1.4
Squash, summer	*	2.3	1.1	1.2
Carrots	*	2.2	1.5	0.7
Tomatoes	*	2.0	0.6	1.4
Brussels sprouts	*	1.8	0.7	1.1
Beans, string	*	1.7	0.6	1.1
Onions	*	1.6	0.8	0.8
Rutabagas	*	1.8	0.7	1.1
Beets	*	1.5	0.6	0.9
Kale greens	*	1.4	0.6	0.8
Turnips	*	1.3	0.6	0.7
Asparagus	*	1.2	0.3	0.9
Eggplant	*	1.2	0.7	0.5
Radishes	1/2 cup raw	1.2	0.3	0.9
Cauliflower	*	0.9	0.3	0.6
Beans, sprouted	*	0.9	0.3	0.6
Cucumber	1/2 cup raw	0.8	0.5	0.3
Lettuce	1/2 cup raw	0.5	0.2	0.3
FRUITS				
Apple	1 small	3.9	2.3	1.6
Blackberries	1/2 cup	3.7	0.7	3.0
Pear	1 small	2.5	0.6	1.9
Strawberries	3/4 cup	2.4	0.9	1.5
Plums	2 medium	2.3	1.3	1.0
Tangerine	1 medium	1.8	1.4	0.4
Apricots	2 medium	1.3	0.9	0.4
Banana	1 small	1.3	0.6	0.7
Peaches	1 medium	0.7	0.5	0.2
Cherries	10	0.9	0.3	0.6
Pineapple	1/2 cup	0.8	0.2	0.6
Grapes	10	0.4	0.1	0.3
BREADS, CEREALS				
Bran (100%) cereal†	*	10.0	0.3	9.7
Popcorn	3 cups	2.8	0.8	2.0
Rye bread†	1 slice	2.7	0.8	1.9

	Serving Size	Total Fiber (grams)	Soluble Fiber (grams)	Insoluble Fiber (grams)
Whole grain bread†	1 slice	2.7	0.08	2.6
Rye wafers†	3	2.3	0.06	2.2
Corn grits	*	1.9	0.6	1.3
Oats, whole	*	1.6	0.5	1.1
Graham crackers†	2	1.4	0.04	1.4
Brown rice	*	1.3	0.0	1.3
French bread†	1 slice	1.0	0.4	0.6
Dinner roll†	1	0.8	0.03	0.8
Egg noodles	*	0.8	0.03	0.8
Spaghetti	*	0.8	0.02	0.8
White bread†	1 slice	0.8	0.03	0.8
White rice	*	0.5	0.0	0.5
LEGUMES				
Kidney beans†	*	4.5	0.5	4.0
White beans†	*	4.2	0.4	3.8
Pinto beans	*	3.0	0.3	2.7
Lima beans	*	1.4	0.2	1.2
NUTS				
Almonds	10	1.0		
Peanuts	10	1.0		
Walnuts, black	1 tsp. chopped	0.6		
Pecans	2	0.5		

Currently, researchers use different methods to analyze dietary fiber content of foods. Until a single testing protocol is adopted, precise fiber totals will vary from laboratory to laboratory. Meats, milk products, eggs, and fats and oils are not listed because they have virtually no fiber content.

*Indicates 1/2 cup serving size, cooked
†Indicates that the fiber analysis was carried out on cooked food rather than raw food.

VITAMINS

A few years ago, if someone had said to me, "Next you'll be telling people how to take vitamins," I would have laughed. We physicians considered vitamins a fringe approach to treating anything but vitamin deficiency itself.

But today, new research into antioxidants has made vitamins an important tool for cardiologists. In this section, I focus primarily on the vitamins and minerals that can counteract some of the effects of stress and aging, and on those that affect the heart and cardiovascular system.

The analysis of vitamins, their uses and misuses, begins with the standards established by our federal government. The Food and Nutrition Board has published RDAs (Recommended Dietary Allowances), or the recommended amounts of essential nutrients considered to be adequate to meet the physiological needs of healthy people. The RDAs for vitamins are estimated to *exceed* the requirements of most people.

However, the standards are not reliable guides for the nutrient requirements of individuals who engage in high levels of activity or for persons who are less than healthy (chronically ill, injured, recuperating, or taking medication). Smokers and those under stress (physical or mental) also do not fall within the average category. In other words, each individual is just that—an individual. Some people need more than the RDA for all vitamins, while others may get along on an RDA for one but still need supplementation for another. And while some people who eat huge quantities of food (such as professional football players) may get all of their RDAs simply by eating a well-balanced diet, others on weight-maintenance diets of 1,200 to 1,500 calories or less per day may not be getting enough needed nutrients.

BUT FIRST, A WORD OF CAUTION

Because of people's concern with the deterioration in the quality of our food supply, promotion by commercial enterprises, and the highly advertised claims of the health benefits of mega-vitamin therapies, 40 percent of Americans now take vitamin and mineral supplements. The results have not always been successful. News of toxicity from overdose appears more and more often in the scientific literature and lay press.

Most dangerous are the fat-soluble vitamins, excesses of which are stored in the body. The fat-soluble vitamins include A, D, E, and K. Symptoms of toxicity are seen most often with the overconsumption of Vitamins A and D; serious side effects have developed

223

in people consuming as little as five times the RDA of these vitamins.

In addition, Vitamin B6, which is a water-soluble vitamin, has been shown to be toxic if taken in doses in excess of 100 milligrams per day.

Therefore, I do not advocate mega-vitamin therapy in which patients ingest many times the RDA.

So what are you to do? Obviously, the first and safest thing to do is to increase your intake of foods rich in vitamins and minerals. This means eating generous amounts of fruits, vegetables, and whole grain cereals. If you still feel your intake is inadequate, or you have unusual needs, a vitamin supplement may be warranted, but only at safe levels: a supplement that supplies approximately 100 percent of the RDAs and never more than two to three times the RDA. Taking vitamins in excess of this should be done only under a doctor's supervision. And, remember, all the vitamin pills in the world won't make up for a fatty, salty diet that's lacking in fruits, vegetables, and whole grain cereals.

THE ANTIOXIDANT VITAMINS

Vitamins C, E, and beta-carotene (a precursor of Vitamin A sometimes referred to as pro-Vitamin A) are antioxidants. These antioxidant vitamins neutralize, deactivate, destroy, or prevent the formation of highly reactive, oxygen-containing free radical compounds. Free radicals can damage DNA, proteins, lipids, and carbohydrates, causing cell and tissue degeneration. Some of the diseases to which free radicals are thought to contribute are cancer, atherosclerosis, stroke, myocardial infarction, senile cataracts, Parkinson's disease, and rheumatoid arthritis. It has also been suggested that free radicals contribute to the aging process.

It is believed that these antioxidant vitamins work in a synergistic way—complementing each other in their antioxidant activities. However, prevention of specific diseases is associated with each.

Higher intake of Vitamin C is thought to protect against gastrointestinal cancer, age-related cataracts and is associated with lower blood pressure and increased levels of high-density lipoprotein (HDL). Citrus fruits are the most prevalent source of Vitamin C, and yet this vital substance can also be found in melons, berries, pineapple, broccoli, green peppers, and tomatoes. One source of Vitamin C, the cruciferous vegetables (members of the cabbage family), has recently received a lot of good press. Cabbage, cauliflower, broccoli, and Brussels sprouts in particular have been touted as appearing to strengthen the immune system against carcinogenic agents. Supplements of 100 to 500 mg/day of Vitamin C might be considered if dietary habits do not provide sufficient intake.

Higher intake of beta-carotene is thought to protect against lung and throat cancers and to decrease the risk for stroke, myocardial infarction, and heart disease from smoking. Good food sources of beta-carotene include carrots, yellow-fleshed squash, sweet potatoes, pumpkin, apricots, cantaloupe, peaches, and other deep-orange vegetables and fruit. If the diet is not adequate, consider a supplement of 6 to 12 mg/day.

A cautionary note: Some supplement labels list the total International Units (IU) supplied by beta-carotene and Vitamin A together and it is difficult to determine how much of the supplement comes from each. Remember, only beta-carotene is an antioxidant, and it is nontoxic; you don't need *any non-beta-carotene Vitamin A*, and high doses of it can be toxic.

Exciting news is appearing almost every day in medical journals about the role of Vitamin E in the prevention of cardiovascular disease. Higher intake is thought to prevent oxidation of LDL cholesterol and its absorption by blood vessels (a critical step in the development of atherosclerosis). A number of studies using supplements of 100 to 800 units of Vitamin E daily over a period of two or more years are underway at this time to confirm or deny this theory. Preliminary results suggest a 37 to 40 percent reduction in the risk of heart disease. Vegetable oils and whole grains are our best sources for Vitamin E. However, it is difficult to increase Vitamin E substantially by diet alone. For many people, it may be desirable to take a modest daily supplement of 50 to 400 IU. Fortunately, Vitamin E appears to be safe and has shown no side effects with consumption of large doses.

Vitamin E supplementation should not be taken by those with Vitamin K deficiency or with known coagulation defects, or by those receiving anticoagulation therapy.

Check with your doctor to see if supplementation with the antioxidant vitamins fits into your health portfolio.

In addition to their antioxidant properties, Vitamin A possesses certain anti-infective properties, Vitamin E is thought to enhance cellular immunity in the elderly, and Vitamins C and E are important in the healing of wounds. Vitamin C enhances the absorption of iron and aids in the fight against viruses. Both stress and smoking increase the need for Vitamin C; although there is little evidence that Vitamin C can protect us from catching cold, it does appear to make cold symptoms milder.

VITAMIN D

Vitamin D aids in the absorption and utilization of calcium. With the aid of sunlight, the body can make its own Vitamin D from a derivative of cholesterol. Foods high in Vitamin D include cod liver oil, butter, cream, egg yolk, liver, and fortified food products. Because of the dangers of saturated fat and cholesterol, I recommend that you select skim milk products or cereals fortified with Vitamin D and avoid the other fatty, cholesterol-rich choices.

The 1989 Recommended Dietary Allowance for Vitamin D for both adult men and women is expressed as 5 micrograms. Food labels often still use the old-style measurement of International Units or IU. Five micrograms equals 200 IU.

Too much Vitamin D can lead to excessive calcium deposits, contributing to hardening of the arteries. Other recent research indicates that a Vitamin D intake of four to five times the recommended allowance may set an individual up for cardiac complications by raising blood cholesterol levels and thereby increasing the risk of heart attacks.

VITAMIN B

The B vitamins, which I call the "morale vitamins," can lift your spirits or calm your anxieties. Several of the B vitamins are important co-enzymes in fat and carbohydrate metabolism. B6 is vital in maintaining a strong immune system; people with diabetes, women taking estrogen, or postmenopausal women tend to need more of this substance. While B6 is commonly prescribed in the treatment of premenstrual syndrome (PMS), as little as 600 milligrams a day can cause nerve damage.

Vitamin B12, which is essential for the formation of healthy red blood cells, is not found in food derived from plants. Therefore, vegans (vegetarians who also avoid eggs or milk products) should eat cereal or vegetable protein products that have been fortified with this substance.

MINERALS

Most minerals, including sodium, potassium, calcium, magnesium, iron, and the trace elements of copper, zinc, selenium, manganese, and iodine, are widely distributed in foods. Therefore, they are unlikely to be deficient in any diet.

As with vitamins, overdose is possible. Large doses of calcium can cause drowsiness and lethargy. Large doses of phosphorus hinder the absorption of calcium, and excess magnesium has a laxative effect. Excess iron can cause damage to the liver, pancreas, and heart, and recent research has raised concerns about high iron stores and the risk of myocardial infarction. Excess zinc may have an unfavorable impact on copper and iron metabolism, lipid profile (increased LDL and decreased HDL cholesterol), and immune function.

SODIUM

As many of you already know, common table salt is composed of sodium and chloride. It's the sodium component (40 percent by weight) that is negatively linked to certain diseases, including high blood pressure.

In fact, about one-third of all individuals with high blood pressure are sensitive to sodium chloride and can lower their blood pressure levels by simply cutting back or eliminating extra salt from their diets.[10] If you have high blood pressure or if you experience fluid retention, you should definitely make a trial of sodium restriction. Obtain individualized instructions from a doctor and/or dietitian for safe and sensible reduction of salt. Then determine whether—holding other factors constant—your blood pressure responds favorably.

I cannot overstate the fact that the American diet contains much more sodium than the body needs. On average, each of us uses from 4 to 20 grams of salt daily, including that which is already present in food (which is equivalent to 1 to 4 teaspoonsful). Our physiological need for sodium is only $2/10$ of a gram, or $1/10$ of 1 teaspoonful of salt!

The RDA for sodium has been placed at a safe level of 1,100 to 3,300 milligrams—that's 3 to 8 grams of table salt, or approximately $1/2$ to $1\frac{1}{2}$ teaspoonsful. However, this is many times more than our basic physiologic requirements. The National Academy of Sciences' latest report, *Diet and Health,* recommends that the average American adult limit total intake of salt to 6 grams or less per day.[11]

The easiest way to meet this goal is to remember that most of the sodium we need is naturally found in our foods. Cook with no salt or with only small amounts of salt. Add little or no salt at the table, and only after food has been tasted. You can learn to enjoy foods for their own taste, and your acquired taste for saltiness will fade over time. In fact, foods that you once enjoyed may start to taste unbearably salty! If you still miss that tang, I recommend the salt substitutes that you can now find in most supermarkets. Here are some further guidelines for reducing sodium in your diet:

• Limit your intake of salty foods, such as cured meats, prepared soups, and prepared frozen dinners with high sodium content, potato chips, pretzels, salted nuts and popcorn, cheese, pickled foods, and condiments such as soy sauce, steak sauce, and garlic salt.

• Read food labels carefully to determine the amounts of sodium in processed food and snack items. Watch for baking powder, baking soda, monosodium glutamate (MSG), sodium nitrate, sodium phosphate, sodium ascorbate, and sodium saccharin.

• When you eat out, order something individually prepared and ask that no salt be used in the preparation. For salads, ask for oil and vinegar on the side and mix your own. Bring along your salt substitute.

• When you fly, request the low-salt diet. Most airlines require at least twenty-four hours' notice, but if you notify them regularly your preference will be computerized and you can regularly fly with a low-salt diet.

THE SODIUM/POTASSIUM BALANCE

The dynamic functioning of the body's processes depends on the finely orchestrated movement of sodium and potassium ions in and out of the body's cells. Good health depends on these two minerals remaining in the appropriate balance. While reducing sodium chloride has been shown to help lower blood pressure, *adding* 2 or 3 grams of potassium has been shown to have an equally helpful effect. Specifically, we know that this amount of potassium can lower blood pressure by 3 to 5 mmHg. Sufficient potassium can be obtained through diet unless you do not eat complex carbohydrates or are taking certain diuretics. Some good sources of potassium are orange juice, bananas, dried fruits, and potatoes.

Individuals taking diuretics must be especially careful to maintain an appropriate sodium/potassium balance, because certain types of diuretics can extract sodium, potassium, and magnesium as well as fluid from the body's tissues.

CALCIUM

Both growing children and adults require adequate amounts of calcium for good health. The RDA for individuals of both sexes, ages eleven to twenty-four, is 1,200 milligrams. After the age of twenty-five, the RDA is 800 milligrams. I recommend slightly higher intakes for women after menopause. Increasing intake of dairy products such as low-fat or skim milk, low-fat or nonfat yogurt and mozzarella and

229

other part-skim milk cheeses would be the first choice. If supplements are taken, 500 milligrams is the amount I advise.

Infants, children, and elderly adults often have special nutritional needs, especially for calcium. Therefore, it's best to check with your physician when determining an adequate diet.

As is commonly known, dairy products are the most prevalent sources of calcium. Other sources include canned fish with edible bones (sardines and salmon) and dark, leafy green vegetables.

Adequate calcium intake seems to protect against the hypertensive effects of a high-sodium, low-potassium diet. By increasing calcium in the diet, some hypertensive patients have experienced significant decreases in their blood pressure levels.

However, excessive doses of calcium—that is, 4,000 to 5,000 milligrams per day—can cause a condition called *milk-alkali syndrome,* which damages the kidneys.

MAGNESIUM

Magnesium is required for bone formation as well as for proper brain and nerve function. Nervous tics, irritability, sleep problems, and muscle cramps may be related to insufficient amounts of magnesium in the diet. Good food sources of magnesium include nuts, legumes, cereal grains, dark green vegetables, seafood, chocolate, and cocoa. Some water supplies also have a high magnesium content.

Magnesium depletion may affect cardiac function by altering concentrations of calcium, potassium, and sodium in intercellular and extracellular fluids.

> **Acute and chronic stress lead to losses of both magnesium and potassium. However, supplementation of these minerals should only be done with a physician's close supervision.**

OTHER IMPORTANT MINERALS

Copper, which plays a role as a catalyst in the formation of hemoglobin, is widely available in so many foods, including shellfish, that copper deficiencies are rarely seen.

Absorption of copper can be inhibited by large doses of dietary *zinc* (50 milligrams, or three to four times the RDA). In addition, high intakes of this necessary mineral can also lower "good" HDL cholesterol in the blood and suppress immunity. *Selenium* works in conjunction with zinc to help remove heavy metals from the body and to enhance immunity. Both minerals have also been shown to have antitumor properties. Zinc occurs in animal foods, such as oysters, herring, milk, and egg yolks, as well as in whole grains. Deficiencies in selenium are virtually unknown as food sources are abundant.

Manganese is necessary for strong muscles and is found mainly in the plant embryo or germ of grains; while *iodine,* consumed primarily in seafood and iodized table salt, is necessary for a healthy thyroid gland and subsequent control of metabolism.

Perhaps the most well-known mineral is *iron,* a substance necessary for the production of red blood cells. While it is true that menstruating women have a greater need for iron, routine supplementation of this mineral is *not recommended* for postmenopausal women, men, and children. This is because the body has no way of ridding itself of an excess (except through menstruation); and an iron overdose can cause damage to the liver, pancreas, and heart. Good sources of iron are meats, legumes, and fortified grain products.

WHEN DO YOU EAT?

Our bodies require a fairly constant flow of blood sugar to fulfill the cells' relentless need for nutrients. Frequent meals and strenuous physical activity step up the metabolism. Conversely, the metabolism slows down between meals, when there is little physical activity, or when caloric intake is very low. Eating infrequent, large meals favors weight gain, and may also increase blood cholesterol levels. In addition, the body utilizes protein better with five or more meals a day.

When you eat can be almost as important as what you eat.

If most of your caloric intake occurs at meals eaten in the evening, you have a greater chance of gaining more weight than if the same number of calories were divided into three or four small meals throughout the day.

The brain needs a continuous supply of glucose in order to function; and so if you have not eaten an adequate breakfast or lunch, you may experience low blood sugar by midmorning or late afternoon. Signs of irritability, lack of ability to concentrate, shakiness, or a dragging feeling may be an indication that your blood sugar level is low. In this case, eating a healthful, late-afternoon snack (such as a piece of fruit) may make your drive home less stressful and perhaps safer.

Although I can't recommend gulping down even healthful food during the morning rush, there's no reason to skip breakfast entirely. Instead of having a coffee and danish at work, pack a health break of whole-wheat bagels, nonfat yogurt, fruit, or cereal. You'll be amazed at how this simple change of habit can help you maintain a steady energy level throughout the day. The bottom line is to incorporate daily a properly *balanced* and varied diet rather than to rely primarily on a single food or dietary supplement.

How are you to translate all this information into your daily routine? The simplest guidelines to follow are those published by the U.S. Departments of Agriculture and Health and Human Services.[12] In a nutshell:

- Eat a variety of foods.
- Maintain healthy weight.
- Choose a diet low in fat, saturated fat, and cholesterol.
- Choose a diet with plenty of vegetables, fruits, and grain products.

- Use sugars only in moderation.
- Use salt and sodium only in moderation.
- If you drink alcoholic beverages, do so in moderation.

These guidelines and the recommendations made in this chapter will allow you to take personal action regarding your diet. The results can be an overall improvement in your health as well as greater control of your life and your stress.

CHAPTER 12

EXERCISE

YOU DON'T HAVE TO
BE AN ATHLETE

The most startling thing we've learned about exercise in the last ten years is that it can be overdone. One of the hottest Hot Reactors I ever met was the fitness director of a health spa. He thought that he was Captain Wonderful, out there jogging for everybody all of the time. Actually, the man reminded me of a trained horse running around a track.

A few years ago, a 45-year-old runner given to overextending himself entered a long-distance race wearing a T-shirt imprinted with the message, "You have not run a good marathon unless you have dropped dead.—Pheidippides."

Legend has it that in 490 B.C., Pheidippides, the original marathon man, died minutes after running 26 miles, 385 yards to Athens to announce a victory over Persia in the Battle of Marathon.

Ironically, a week after entering the race, the middle-aged runner with the T-shirt collapsed during a long run, dead from coronary heart disease. It turned out that he had long ignored such distressing symptoms as severe chest pains.[1]

—Robert Brody, *Chicago Sun-Times*

When you begin your "commitment to fitness," as I've heard it called, ask yourself if you are entering such a program for your health or to satisfy some sort of competitive urge. There's nothing wrong with competition, until it literally drives you into the ground. Rather than making exercise a drudgery, work it into your lifestyle—make it something you can enjoy. This kind of lifelong activity is best when done for fun or diversion as well as for health. For example, aerobic exercise can entertain, keep you fit, and increase your immunity by literally helping flush out your system through the cleansing action of the lymphatic system. Most important to improving your quality of life, even the most moderate levels of aerobic exercise can provide the extra mental energy necessary for creatively solving stressful problems.

> **One critical value of both fitness and nutrition is that they give us the energy to cope with unavoidable life stresses.**

While intensive physical activity remains a controversial issue, there is general agreement among experts that regular, moderate aerobic exercise is essential to health and well-being. Regular exercise results in enhanced physical fitness, which includes cardiovascular endurance, flexibility, and muscular strength and endurance. It also improves mental fitness. In addition, researchers have discovered that a consistent aerobic exercise regimen can reduce insulin requirements in people with diabetes and reduce the complications often associated with the disease.

Contrary to common belief, increased activity does *not* necessarily increase the appetite. In studies of the caloric intakes of workers with different activity levels, the data indicated that sedentary workers consumed significantly more calories than did those who were moderately active.[2]

WHICH EXERCISE SHOULD YOU CHOOSE?

Physical activity involves two types of muscle contractions, *isotonic* (a *dynamic* action involving joint movement) and *isometric* (a sustained muscle contraction also called *static* because it occurs without visible joint movement).

One form of isotonic exercise has proven most beneficial for cardiovascular health, and it will be the primary focus of the chapter. This repetitive or rhythmic movement of large muscle groups is called *aerobic* because it requires a continuous supply of oxygen. Examples of aerobic exercise include walking, running, swimming, bicycling, rowing, stair stepping, aerobic dancing, and cross-country skiing— in short, anything that moves the body through space.

Aerobic exercise:

- increases the level of beneficial HDL cholesterol in the blood
- is associated with moderate declines in blood pressure
- helps dissipate accumulated stress chemicals in the bloodstream
- helps control weight

Without question, the last benefit is the most popular. The combination of aerobic exercise and a prudent diet preserves and promotes muscle and diminishes the loss of protein or muscle tissue. Even if your body weight does not change with exercise, your body composition will convert to more muscle and less fat. Furthermore, the increased metabolic rate achieved during aerobic exercise lasts for several hours. This bonus burn of extra calories is in addition to those used during the exercise itself.

In contrast, many isometric exercises are *anaerobic,* requiring less oxygen. As such, they do not result in the same overall health benefits as do aerobic exercises. In fact, my clinical experience demonstrates that some isometric exercises (such as straining during weight lifting) can actually overload the heart. (In technical terms, these exercises raise the mean blood pressure by increasing the peripheral resistance without increasing cardiac output.) For this reason, individuals with cardiac or blood pressure problems should limit the type and number of isometric exercises they perform. In fact, we have recorded tremendous blood pressure surges during the isometric testing of Hot Reactors who have visited our institute. In one case, an extreme Hot Reactor was able to become a Cool Reactor simply by reducing the weight-lifting component of his regular exercise workout and increasing the period of aerobic exercise.

But don't reject isometric exercise entirely, because, when properly done, it is a critical part of your health portfolio. As you age you need to maintain muscle strength in order to stay mobile and keep from falling. You don't need anything more elaborate than a series of simple exercises at home using common objects like gallon milk jugs and heavy rubber bands, as outlined by William Evans, Ph.D., and Irwin Rosenberg, M.D., in their book, *Biomarkers: The 10 Keys to Prolonging Vitality.*[3] Just be aware that if you are bearing down or straining during exercise, you are probably straining your heart as well.

AEROBIC EXERCISE

Aerobic exercise can be of two types: *continuous,* such as brisk walking, or *intermittent,* such as tennis or jog-walk programs. The continuous form of exercise achieves a more consistent heart rate for longer periods of time than that achieved during intermittent exercise. If you are less fit (especially after a long period of inactivity), intermittent aerobic exercise is your best first step; however, a greater training (and thus health) effect is attained by doing low-intensity, long-duration, continuous aerobic activity.

The stationary bicycle has gained in popularity as an aerobic exercise because sitting while exercising allows you to control the intensity of your work as well as your heart rate. Another excellent piece of equipment (although it's a bit more expensive and takes up more space) is the treadmill.

If the grim faces of people who walk or jog on a treadmill or who ride stationary cycles make you question the worth of these devices, take heart. There *are* other excellent forms of continuous aerobic exercise. Brisk walking or hiking can help you increase your cardiovascular endurance level and maintain it for a lifetime. I find dancing to some of my favorite tunes is a great way to exercise, loosen up, and reduce stress at the same time.

The *most effective* form of aerobic exercise is that which you do continuously for thirty minutes, three times per week. However, health gains are also seen with moderate levels of aerobic exercise, such as using the stairs instead of riding the elevator, parking farther away and walking to your destination, or riding your bike instead of using your car. If you have an exercise facility at your place of employment, use it! The good news is that the greatest immediate benefit is in moving from couch-potato status to a mild exercise program.

THE EXERCISE WORKLOAD

An important concept for you to consider before beginning an exercise program is the *workload* of each activity. When we write exercise prescriptions for our patients, we measure the workload in METs, or metabolic equivalents, the metabolic "cost" in oxygen of each activity. One MET represents the predicted amount of oxygen (3.5 ml/Kg) used while sitting quietly for one minute.

This is more reliable than measuring exercise by calorie expenditure, because the calories expended vary with body mass. The formula used to calculate METs takes into account an individual's body mass; thus the same number can be used to describe the amount of work performed by a large person and a small person.

The volume of oxygen used during aerobic exercise is predicted by dividing the METs produced during exercise by the METs produced while at rest. During exercise, the heart rate increases linearly with an increase in METs (or workload) until a maximum rate is achieved; then the heart rate plateaus.

For men, the heart rate increases approximately 8 to 10 beats per minute for each MET increase.[4] For women, it increases approximately 11 to 13 beats per minute for each MET increase.[5]

The heart rate increase per MET is *higher* in individuals who are not in good cardiovascular shape and *lower* in those who display the training effect from having participated in an aerobic exercise or sports program. And, as people age, the maximum heart rate attainable declines.

There are various ways to estimate your maximum predicted heart rate. If you are healthy and not using medication, the best method is to subtract your age from the number 220.

220 − age = maximum predicted heart rate

Thus for a forty-six-year-old man, the maximum predicted heart rate response would be about 174 beats per minute. This is the *maximum*, not the rate at which your heart should be working when you are training. Your training, or *target*, heart rate will be discussed below. Just as with your car, the maximum speed quoted by the manufacturer is far higher than it is safe to drive down the highway! If you have questions about your ability, always check with your physician.

Why are all of these calculations important? Let me answer by asking you to recall the people we've all observed taking daily walks through parks and neighborhoods. Depending on the fitness level of each person, the pace and length of that walk must reach specific levels if he or she is to reach target heart rate range and thus obtain the full training effect. Otherwise it's merely a casual stroll. Don't get me wrong—there's nothing wrong with a casual stroll; it's an excellent way to relax and reduce stress. But it's a very low-grade aerobic training exercise.

YOUR EXERCISE DOSAGE

I'm often asked, "How *much* exercise should a person do?"

The ideal "dosage" of exercise is the amount of activity necessary to promote your optimal health benefit (also called the *training effect*). This is the amount of exercise necessary to condition your heart by making it work more efficiently. It is also the amount that will maximize the benefit of your exercise for weight control.

The key components of an exercise program are easy to remember with the simple acronym FIT:

Frequency: how often, or the number of exercise sessions each week

Intensity: how hard, or the amount of energy expended during exercise

Time: how long, or the duration of each exercise session

It's important to note here that a regular exercise program can have some side effects for some people. This is especially true if you are over the age of forty, have a chronic health problem, or have one or more risk factors for coronary heart disease. For this reason, you must consult your physician before beginning any serious exercise program. I suggest asking for a treadmill test. This test will enable your physician to suggest a safe program that will also provide your optimal training effect.

> **I recommend that treadmill and other fitness tests be taken *before* initiating any exercise program or before taking part in any vigorous sport.**

FREQUENCY

The ideal frequency for exercise is three to five times each week. If exercise sessions are too widely spaced, there may be a loss of the training effect or other conditioning benefits. Furthermore, exercising less than three times per week will not produce significant improvement in heart and lung capacity or in weight control.

More frequent sessions of exercise can increase the risk of injury. Exercising on alternate days and allowing at least one day to recover provides time for muscles to rest or for the soreness from the previous session to dissipate.

Varying your activity can promote enjoyment and adherence. For those who prefer daily exercise, less intense activities can supplement the more vigorous target heart rate workouts. To round out such a fitness program, cardiovascular endurance training should be combined with exercises that promote an increase in flexibility and muscular strength.

INTENSITY

The intensity of your program is how hard you exercise. This is where you use your target heart rate. You can't measure the effectiveness of your program by the activity itself; it's how hard your heart is working that counts. Intensity is especially important to monitor if you are beginning after a long period of inactivity. Individuals with different levels of cardiovascular endurance will have different heart rate responses to a given workload. Someone with a high level of physical fitness (one who has been involved in a regular aerobic exercise program) can achieve a workload of 10 METs at 160 beats per minute, while a person with a low level of physical fitness may require 200 beats per minute to reach the same workload. The heart rate can thus be used to determine the pace that will allow an individual to maximize the benefits of exercise. Studies have shown that healthy individuals can develop and maintain cardiovascular endurance by raising the heart rate to a target range, between 60 to 80 percent of the individual's maximum predicted heart rate. This is the safe training range.[6]

I tell our patients to aim at a heart rate that is 75 percent of their maximum predicted heart rate. Going back to our forty-six-year-old man, his target heart rate is 75 percent of 174, or 130 beats per minute. Any exercise done at intensities of *lower* than 60 percent of the maximum predicted heart rate will not produce a training effect.

Keep in mind that injuries occur more often at higher intensities of training. This is especially true for people who exercise *too intensely* when they first start an exercise program. Moreover, an exercise that requires a heart rate higher than an individual's target heart rate range can force the body to resort to internal sources of quick energy. The exercise changes from aerobic to anaerobic. In such an event, carbohydrate or sugar stored in the muscles will replace oxygen as the preferred form of fuel. The result is that long-term weight loss will not occur as readily because sugar instead of fat calories will be burned. It's easy to see how many individuals wishing to control weight fall into this counterproductive exercise pattern. They try too hard, too fast, and come up short.

Whatever your target heart rate or safe training zone, a fair rule of thumb is to check your facial expression and ask yourself, "Am I having fun, or am I simply substituting one form of stress for another?" If an exercise is unpleasant, you are unlikely to make it a lifetime pursuit.

TIME

For effective cardiac conditioning, the aerobic portion of your workout should last thirty minutes. Caloric expenditure in such a session depends on your body weight and your maximum MET rate. If you are beginning an exercise program after being sedentary, I advise that you start with perhaps only a ten-minute aerobic period (equating for most people to between 60 and 80 calories) and adding five minutes to your workout approximately every two weeks.

As your cardiovascular endurance (aerobic capacity) improves, you can keep the level of exercise intensity constant and gain more benefits by exercising for a longer time. Conversely, if you are short on time, you can get the same effect by increasing slightly the intensity of the exercise. More intensity for lesser duration. Longer duration with lesser intensity.

> **You burn almost the same amount of calories whether you walk or jog a mile.**

High-intensity, short-duration exercise programs are more suitable for young, healthy people with high levels of aerobic fitness. For cardiac patients or persons with lower levels of aerobic fitness, exercise training sessions of low intensity with longer durations are preferable. Importantly, the adherence rate to low-intensity programs is much better because the rates of injury and burnout are much lower. Moderation is the key. The old saying, "No pain, no gain" is dangerous and utter nonsense!

THE SEQUENCE OF YOUR EXERCISE PROGRAM

If you are to avoid injury and maximize the training effect, every exercise workout must follow a specific sequence of events. This includes three stages.

1. Warm-up

   • light stretches
   • aerobic warm-up

2. Steady exercise at your target heart rate
3. Cool-down

   • aerobic cool-down
   • stretches to improve flexibility

For example, a fifty-minute exercise routine might include eight minutes of warm-up, thirty minutes at target heart rate, and twelve minutes of cool-down. (The warm-up and cool-down periods should be longer for beginners.)

The importance of the warm-up is twofold. First, light stretches done before exercise will limber, loosen, and warm the muscles and joints as a preventive measure against musculoskeletal injury. It's similar to warming up your old car on a cold day. Idling engines allows all the parts to be lubricated and running smoothly before moving the weight of the car. Light stretches should include exercises for the lower back as well as for the hamstring and calf muscles of the legs.

Second, an aerobic warm-up is done to slowly raise the metabolic rate to that required at your target heart rate. A slow rehearsal of the aerobic exercise is done to adjust the body's temperature, respiration, and circulation gradually to the upcoming metabolic demand of the target heart rate pace or intensity. The aerobic warm-up consists of gradually increasing the intensity of the exercise by slowly increasing the workload. For example, when cycling, the heart rate could be elevated slowly to target levels by progressively increasing the speed and/or tension.

The need for a cool-down period may not be as obvious, but it is just as important. Cars can be stopped and turned off abruptly. However, the human engine should not be slowed abruptly after aerobic exercise. It must be given time to readjust the physiology to a lower metabolic demand. During vigorous activity such as running, blood vessels in the legs open to maximize the flow of oxygenated blood that is required for the working muscles. In addition, the milking action or contraction of the leg muscles helps push the blood through the veins and back up to the heart. When muscle activity is stopped abruptly, blood tends to pool in the legs instead of being pumped back to a heart still beating at exercise levels. As a consequence, the volume of blood reaching the heart drops suddenly. This can threaten the supply of blood to the brain. The result may be light-headedness or syncope (fainting). Worse, the coronary arteries may not receive adequate amounts of blood, which can lead to heartbeat irregularities—even to heart attack or death.

> **Within the past five years I personally have lost three apparently aerobically fit medical colleagues to sudden cardiac death because they did not progressively cool down!**

The cool-down period gives the arteries in your legs ample time to constrict steadily, shunting the blood from the lower extremities back to the heart. Meanwhile, as the heart rate slows, oxygen requirements diminish, and the entire system stabilizes. In essence, the cool-down should be the reverse of the warm-up, and this normally takes about five minutes. When you are less aerobically fit (again, at the beginning of an exercise program), it takes more time for the heart rate to return to preexercise levels and so cool-down should be lengthened appropriately (usually up to twelve minutes).

The sustained stretches of the cool-down period are designed to improve flexibility. Muscles tighten following sustained vigorous exercise, and stretching helps prevent muscle soreness and leads to increased flexibility over time. I also recommend finishing with exercises to strengthen the abdominal muscles. You will find some guidelines for stretching and muscle strength at the end of the chapter.

WHEN TO INCREASE THE LEVEL OF EXERCISE

There will come a time when you may need to increase either the intensity or the duration of your exercise sessions. The degree of increase will be determined by your initial cardiovascular condition *and* your level of motivation. The greatest gains in aerobic conditioning can be seen in those who begin to exercise when they are aerobically out of shape—which is often a source of great motivation. Even walking ten to fifteen minutes a day can make noticeable differences in a beginner's aerobic capacity. In order to produce the same training effect, a person with a higher level of fitness will have to work at a more rigorous target heart rate.

Once you get into a set exercise regimen and exercise routinely at your target rate, maintaining your aerobic fitness takes less effort. Unfortunately, you can soon return to square one if you do *not* maintain that level of activity. In one experiment, trained and untrained persons were given twenty days of bed rest followed by sixty days of exercise training. Besides demonstrating the deconditioning effects of prolonged bed rest, the results showed that the trained persons needed forty days of exercise to achieve their preconvalescent maximal aerobic level; the untrained individuals achieved their preconvalescent maximum levels in only fourteen days.[7] The conclusions are clear:

1. It takes longer to reach higher cardiovascular endurance levels than it takes to reach average ones.
2. The more trained you are, the more you have to lose and the longer it takes to regain the degree of stamina that was lost.

AVOIDING INJURY

Some individuals simply exercise too much. If a little is good, more is not necessarily better. Those who exercise more than an hour a day may significantly increase the likelihood of injury *without* much added improvement in aerobic capacity. A large ongoing study of male college graduates indicated that those who continued to be physically active (whether or not they had been athletes in college) tended to be healthier. However, significant added positive health benefits were not observed once activity exceeded the expenditure of approximately 2,000 calories per week.[8]

Data collected at the Institute of Stress Medicine shows an interesting association between maximal aerobic capacity and the degree of response to mental stress. Very highly trained individuals who had maximal MET levels of 13 or over were often Hot Reactors. Indeed, we have found that when presented with low-stimulus mental challenges, marathon runners show greater heart rate and blood pressure responses than do healthy nonrunners of similar ages. Often excessive running becomes a form of stress that can induce increased cortisol production with its associated complications. Thus, like any good medicine, there are limits to using exercise as a way of controlling mental stress. You can overdose on it.

Another example of overdosing on exercise involved the executive of a major corporation who came to us for a complete evaluation. He exercised daily within his target heart rate, was aerobically fit, and consequently did very well on the treadmill test. However, when we gave him the math stress test, we discovered that he was a moderate Hot Reactor. Other psychometric tests also suggested that stress was a major contributor to his peaks of high blood pressure. The solution came when we analyzed his daily exercise routine and learned that he was engaging in an excessive amount of weight lifting with strain. This was a major contributor of stress in his life and was causing an elevation of total systemic resistance. After receiving biofeedback training, reducing the degree of strain in his weight lifting, and adding aerobic exercise, his math retest resulted in normal levels of cardiovascular reactivity.

Too much exercise can result in *significant* pain with little gain.

You can also exercise at the *wrong time*. Serious repercussions can occur, for example, if you exercise too soon or too hard after an illness or a long period of inactivity. As you ease back into your exercise program, be sure that you never exceed your target heart rate. You can gradually increase exercise until you have achieved your previous level. Use your target heart rate as a guide.

Never exercise *during* an illness, especially if you have a fever.[9] If you are experiencing frequent colds and upper respiratory infections, you might be compromising your immune system by overexercising. In this case it will be prudent for you to reduce the duration or intensity of your exercise program temporarily.

Strenuous exercise can also provoke severe allergic reactions that can lead to life-threatening conditions such as anaphylactic shock in certain susceptible individuals. It's usually advisable to wait an hour after a meal before beginning strenuous exercise; however, those prone to food allergies should wait *two* hours. This is especially true for those with shellfish or celery allergies.[10]

A WORD OF CAUTION

You can avoid exercise-related injuries or complications if you "listen" to your body and become aware of any discomfort or other symptoms of intolerance to exercise. It is advisable to stop exercising immediately or skip the workout if you feel that your heart:

- palpitates or skips a beat
- suddenly seems to race or beat extremely fast
- feels as if it is fluttering

You should also be on guard for other signs and symptoms, such as pain or pressure in the chest, arm, back, throat, or jaw area that occurs during exercise or soon thereafter. Dizziness, light-headedness, confusion, cold sweating, or blue-colored fingernails should also be taken seriously and brought immediately to your doctor's attention. A rule of thumb is: Whatever your exercise, you should be able to carry on a conversation during it. If you are too breathless to talk, you are training beyond prudent fitness.

SPECIAL PROBLEMS WITH JOGGING AND RUNNING

Jogging and running, particularly for very long distances as in marathons, have been popularized and promoted by some as a maintenance method that can almost immunize a person against cardiovascular disease. The medical literature shows that it cannot. I know of nothing that will. Additionally, this level of exercise may impose other important risks to your health: heat stroke; anaphylactic reactions; musculoskeletal injuries such as stress fractures; dog, and bug bites; as well as being struck by moving objects—including cars. In addition, many medical practitioners have been concerned that intense exercise can become compulsive. Particularly in women, such compulsion can lead to anorexia. Many metabolic changes occur with extreme exercise, including: potassium and magnesium deficiencies, hormonal changes, and (in women) menstrual irregularities.

Our studies have shown that runners have significantly more illness immediately after completing marathons. Other research done at the University of California concluded that while joggers had a lower overall risk of cardiovascular disease than did sedentary persons, they also had a greater risk of sudden cardiac death during or just after exercise. Those at greatest risk for exercise-related death were men engaged in strenuous exercise when they were not accustomed to this kind of exertion.[11] In other words, they tried to do too much, too soon, and their bodies could not rise to the challenge.

For those joggers or runners who have simply converted their cardiovascular risks to orthopedic problems, it may be advisable to shift to a low-impact exercise (such as cycling or cross-country skiing). Reducing the impact on knees, ankles, feet, and hips may control or possibly reduce musculoskeletal complications.

OPTIMAL EXERCISE

Walking at your target heart rate is my personal recommendation for the near-perfect exercise. Walking can be a lifetime pursuit for a large portion of the population. Best of all, it's a conditioning activity that is sociable, applicable in a variety of settings, and requires only proper walking shoes. If you find walking boring, listen to your favorite tape or radio station.

> **"Walking is man's best medicine."**
> **—Hippocrates**

The following precautions can reduce the hazards of walking (and jogging):

- If possible, do not walk after dark. If you do, wear reflective material on your clothing.
- Walk *against* traffic, so that you face oncoming vehicles.
- Walk in single file on roadways.
- Wear proper footwear.
- Wear clothing suitable to the weather conditions.

After exercising, you should take a warm, not hot, shower or sauna. Extreme heat can dilate blood vessels and cause a marked drop in the amount of blood returning to the heart. This may lead to fainting, arrhythmia, or death. We've all heard about Scandinavians who go roaring out of a hot sauna and jump into an icy lake; but physiologically, this is like driving at 60 mph and suddenly jamming on the brakes while throwing the transmission into reverse. No wonder 10 percent of all sudden deaths in Finland are sauna related!

When you exercise, extremes of both heat and cold can add stress to the body. Cardiac patients especially should avoid this stress; for them, even swimming in cold water can be a hazard. If you *must* exercise in extreme temperatures, dress suitably and drink plenty of clear fluids (preferably water) before, during, and after exertion. This is especially true if you are perspiring profusely. In cold weather, it's best to wear layers of clothing so that you can remove a piece at a time as you warm up. Furthermore, it's important to wear something on your head (such as a stocking cap) since this is the site of the body's greatest heat loss (25 percent!).

Exercise is necessary for optimum health, but too much can be as bad as not doing any at all. Increasing the frequency, intensity, or duration of exercise beyond the levels recommended here can have additional benefits, but the price in time, effort, and risk is high for the added degree of improvement. As with other recommendations, moderation—combined with a safe, pleasurable approach—is the key. Consider exercise to be a potent medicine that must be managed like any other strong medicine if it is to be both safe and effective.

BASIC STRETCHING EXERCISES

This guide is divided into three sections. The first section illustrates stretches that are recommended *before* exercises that primarily use leg muscles, such as walking, jogging, and cycling. The second depicts stretches that are recommended *after* walking, jogging, and cycling. The third presents additional stretches that are suggested *before* and *after* exercises that also require the involvement of the arms, such as swimming, running, cross-country skiing, aerobics, and stationary cycling with arm motion.

The recommendations for stretching before and after exercise differ. Stretches done before exercise are designed to lightly limber up the major muscles that will be used by vigorous activity. Extensively stretching a cold muscle may result in injury to the muscle itself. As a result, only light stretching should be done before exercise by just "walking through" the different stretching postures. After exercise, however, the muscles are warm and stretch easily. Consequently, the flexibility of the muscles can be greatly improved by holding a relaxed sustained stretch.

I. STRETCHES TO BE USED BEFORE EXERCISE

Walk through each of the stretches listed below. Hold each position only one to two counts. Do the stretches in the order they are listed. Repeat both stretches three times for each leg. Light stretching done before exercise has been shown to result in greater freedom of movement as well as reducing muscle soreness and injury.

1. CALF STRETCH (stretches back of lower leg)

A. Stand so that your left foot is in a straight line behind your right foot.

B. Bend your right leg until the knee is over your toe.

C. Keep your left leg straight and the heel of your left foot on the ground.

D. If needed, move your left leg back to increase the amount of stretch.

E. Switch legs and repeat.

2. HAMSTRING STRETCH (Stretches Back of Upper Leg)

A. Put your right foot on an object that is at a level *lower* than your hips.

B. Lean slightly forward from the chest with your chin up

C. If needed, lean farther forward to increase the amount of stretch.

D. Switch legs and repeat.

II. STRETCHES TO BE USED AFTER EXERCISE

Without bouncing, hold each of the stretches described below in the order they are listed. Gently lean into the stretch until a light tension is felt. Breathe and relax into the stretch. After the tension has diminished, lean farther until a light tension is again experienced. Breathe and relax again into the stretch until the tension has subsided. Then hold that position ten to twenty counts. Repeat all four stretches three times for both legs.

Stretching after exercise increases flexibility and range of motion as well as preventing muscle soreness. Stretching leg and back muscles has also been shown to reduce the risk of lower back pain and injury.

1. CALF STRETCH
   Refer to instructions in Section I.

2. KNEE HUG (stretches groin and lower back)

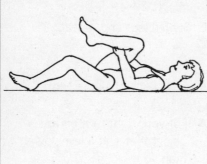

   A. Lie on your back with both knees slightly bent.

   B. Gently hug your right knee to your chest by reaching under your upper leg.

   C. Pull your right leg closer to your body to increase the stretch.

   D. Switch legs and repeat.

3. HAMSTRING STRETCH (stretches back of upper leg)

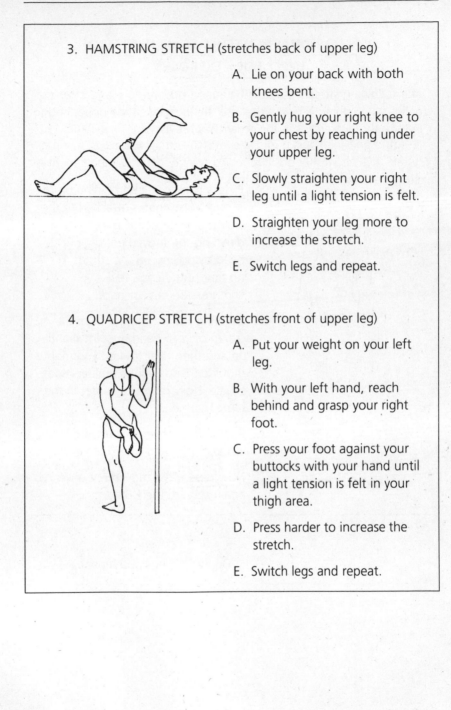

A. Lie on your back with both knees bent.

B. Gently hug your right knee to your chest by reaching under your upper leg.

C. Slowly straighten your right leg until a light tension is felt.

D. Straighten your leg more to increase the stretch.

E. Switch legs and repeat.

4. QUADRICEP STRETCH (stretches front of upper leg)

A. Put your weight on your left leg.

B. With your left hand, reach behind and grasp your right foot.

C. Press your foot against your buttocks with your hand until a light tension is felt in your thigh area.

D. Press harder to increase the stretch.

E. Switch legs and repeat.

III. ADDITIONAL STRETCHES TO BE USED WITH
UPPER BODY EXERCISES

The following stretches should be added both before and after exercise when doing activities that use the muscles of the upper body. Do the three stretches in the order they are listed.

1. HEAD TILT (stretches neck muscles)

A. Picture someone else holding on to a long string that is attached to the crown of your head. The person is directing the movement of your head by pulling on the string. At no time should you feel compression in your neck.

B. Initiating the movement from the crown of your head, first lift slightly up and then over toward your right shoulder. Relax your shoulders and exhale. Now return to center in the same manner.

C. Repeat the movement toward your left shoulder and return to center.

D. Now repeat the movement once again toward the front.

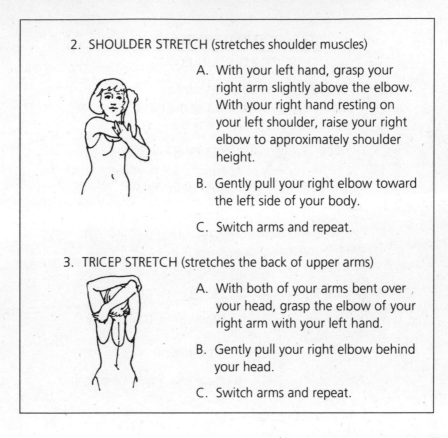

2. SHOULDER STRETCH (stretches shoulder muscles)

   A. With your left hand, grasp your right arm slightly above the elbow. With your right hand resting on your left shoulder, raise your right elbow to approximately shoulder height.

   B. Gently pull your right elbow toward the left side of your body.

   C. Switch arms and repeat.

3. TRICEP STRETCH (stretches the back of upper arms)

   A. With both of your arms bent over your head, grasp the elbow of your right arm with your left hand.

   B. Gently pull your right elbow behind your head.

   C. Switch arms and repeat.

BASIC EXERCISES FOR ABDOMINAL STRENGTH

In addition to warm-up and cool-down exercises, the following abdominal strengthening exercises are commonly prescribed by the Institute of Stress Medicine. They are a first-line defense against lower-back problems, 85 percent of which are either caused or aggravated by stress. You can be aerobically fit and still have back problems. The muscular tension and pain associated with back problems contribute directly to elevated blood pressure. A healthy back reduces tension, reduces blood pressure, and increases your ability to function aerobically.

ABDOMINAL EXERCISES

Work to master crunch 1 A-C. When you can successfully complete this sequence, move on to crunch 2 and finally to crunch 3.

1A: STRAIGHT CRUNCH

1. Lie on the floor with your knees bent and hands behind your head. Tuck your feet in close to your buttocks.

2. Slowly curl your head and shoulders straight off the floor while reaching with your chin toward the ceiling.

   Exhale with lifting.

   Work up to 10 repetitions.

1B: LEFT CRUNCH

1. Place your right ankle against your left knee.

2. Keeping your right elbow on the floor, lead with your left elbow and bring it toward your right knee. (It is not necessary to touch.) Your chin should reach toward the ceiling. Exhale on effort while lifting.

   Work up to 10 repetitions.

1C: RIGHT CRUNCH

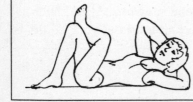

1. Place your left ankle against your right knee, repeat steps for crunch 1B (above).

   Again work up to 10 repetitions.

When you can easily complete all three phases of crunch 1, begin working up to ten repetitions for crunch 2 and finally crunch 3.

2. CRUNCH

1. With legs lifted, cross your ankles and bend your knees toward your chest.

2. Holding your knees stationary, curl head and shoulders straight off the floor while reaching with your chin toward the ceiling. Remember to exhale with effort. Work up to 10 repetitions.

3. Now add left and right crunches as you did for crunch 1, lifting the elbow opposite the leg that's on top.

   As you gain strength you will be able to work up to 10 repetitions for both the left and the right knees.

3. CRUNCH

1. Repeat the process above with both legs up and knees just slightly bent.

   Again, work up to 10 straight repetitions, 10 to the left, and 10 to the right.

EPILOGUE

A NEW APPROACH TO WELLNESS

Fifty-five percent of America's corporations with more than five thousand employees now have wellness programs, and an increasing number of smaller companies are also opting for such systems.[1] Wellness programs are highly effective at reducing the health bill, even though most efforts target only fitness and nutrition. The comprehensive tenets of Stress Medicine, identified in this book, add the missing dimensions and allow us to move beyond the accomplishments of existing wellness programs.

We can now reach the apparently healthy individual who is the walking time bomb so commonplace in corporate corridors. Surprisingly, many such individuals will fail to show up "at risk" on cholesterol screenings. This is not to say that cholesterol consciousness and control are unimportant parts of medicine. Rather, it is to say that we must look beyond cholesterol HDL, LDL, and triglyceride levels alone. These measurements do not identify the individual whose artery walls are being invisibly pummeled by the pile-driving surges in blood pressure that go undetected in the protected atmosphere of the doctor's office. In this remarkable David and Goliath life-and-death combat, high pressure blasts of Hot Reacting are pitted against the delicate membrane struggling to protect the artery from invasion and blockage by accumulated blood fats. It is in this inappropriate, all-out mortal combat setting that we also find the tiny ruptured heart muscle fibers (contraction band lesions) that can lead to electrical short circuits and sudden death.

Our comprehensive approach can now be added to other wellness and prevention efforts, providing the 24-hour physiologic control of blood pressure needed by the more than 60 million Americans who already have high blood pressure and the 20 million who are on their way to getting it. Unquestionably, the invisible, progressive destruction of heart muscle and blood vessels leads to immeasurable human and corporate costs—costs that could be contained by detecting and defusing otherwise unsuspected walking time bombs.

At this time, 95 percent of the overburdened American health dollar is being spent on medicine after the fact—*after* the disease has been identified, or, as I like to put it, after the patient has fallen off the cliff. Redirecting 5 or 10 percent of the health dollar into a general pot called "prevention" is *not* the solution either. Rather, the wonders and advances in tertiary care medicine deserve whatever funding can be obtained. My kind of fence-building medicine can pay for itself in many large corporations, organizations, and hospital chains. Decreased absenteeism and increased productivity are but two of the fringe benefits. To this end, large corporations and hospital chains are now providing funds for Health Maintenance Organizations (HMOs) that identify and plan for patient health needs *before* they become emergencies.

We at the Institute of Stress Medicine work with corporations, organizations, and individuals to control the $250 billion annual productivity waste of stress and to reduce the high cost of unnecessary illness and absenteeism. Our approach combines the high-tech and high-touch philosophies discussed in this book.

For large corporations, preservation of one key individual at any level (with enormous savings in insurance dollars) can pay and has paid the costs of an entire stress medicine program for as much as a decade. Additional benefits include improved productivity and morale (factors that are admittedly difficult to measure on a cause-and-effect basis) and increased incomes (a more apparent gauge of bottom-line success).

Finally, the principles of Stress Medicine fit beautifully into existing rehabilitation programs, as individual patients recovering from heart disease or heart surgery often seek opportunities to understand how they can convert their stresses into strengths. These anxious and highly motivated individuals want to achieve a good quality of life

259

while reducing their risk of recurrence and/or complications. They want complete answers to "Why me?" and "Why now?"

Our ability to identify our invisible weights and to lighten our loads is fundamental to taking care of ourselves, rather than waiting for treatment and heroics by others. Much of this new kind of medicine is a matter of teaching and empowering the individual to change his or her point of view. The result is *healthier perceptions,* which can improve the prescriptions the brain writes for the body in small, steady, reasonable steps.

Bringing this type of medicine to the public and the medical profession has been a real privilege and pleasure for me. Its continued development and extension will require help from all parts of our society. Those who see its value can help to find ways to reward practitioners who want to learn about and utilize it in their daily practice. These efforts include the identification of new, innovative sources of funding. Qualified health professionals who are eager for such knowledge and commitment need to be trained. The sources for such funds can include HMOs, self-insured corporations, employee-incentive award programs, unions, professional societies, and government agencies, among others. Whatever the source, funding must be a win/win team effort.

The choice is ours. If we value Stress Medicine, we will find ways to build it into our personal and professional lives and into our homes, businesses, and social structures. You don't, however, have to wait for our health system to change in order to benefit from Stress Medicine. I have written *From Stress to Strength* to give you the basic tools for your own personal journey. I hope you will want to return to this book often to pause and recheck your bearings—to reflect, review, and renew your commitment to a safe, healthy, and rewarding trip through life.

NOTES

CHAPTER 1   THE HOT REACTORS

1. Associated Press (Tokyo), *Omaha World-Herald*, June 29, 1989, p. 4. See also Chihara, et al. "Job Stress: The 20th Century Disease," *World Labor Report*, Geneva, Switzerland: ILO Publications, 1993.
2. Friedman, Meyer, and Ray Rosenman. *Type A Behavior and Your Heart.* New York: Knopf, 1974. See also Friedman, Meyer. "Modification of Type A Behavior in Post-Infarction Patients," *American Heart Journal*, 95, no. 5 (1979).
3. American Heart Association. *Silent Epidemic: The Truth About Women and Heart Disease.* Dallas, TX: American Heart Association, 1989.

CHAPTER 2   THE KILLER WITHIN

1. Phibbs, Brendan P. *The Other Side of Time: A Combat Surgeon in World War II.* Boston: Little Brown, 1987, pp. 309–10.
2. Lapin, B.A., and G.M. Cherkovich. "Environmental Changes Causing the Development of Neuroses and Corticovisceral Pathology in Monkeys," *Society, Stress and Disease: The Psychosocial Environment and Psychosomatic Diseases,* ed. L. Levi. London: Oxford University Press, 1971, vol. 1, pp. 266–79.
3. Von Holst, D., E. Fuchs, and W. Stohr. "Renal Failure as the Cause of Death in Tupaia Belangeri (Tree Shrews) Exposed to Persistent Social Stress," *Journal of Comprehensive Physiology and Psychology,* 78 (1972), p. 236.
4. Baroldi, G., G. Falzi, and F. Mariana. "Sudden Coronary Death: A Postmortem Study in 208 Selected Cases Compared to 97 'Control' Subjects," *American Heart Journal*, 98 (1979), pp. 20–31.
5. In the fall of 1992, I met with a former Soviet heart researcher, Michael Klibaner, M.D., Ph.D., FCAP, who showed me his extensive data, which confirmed and extended many of our laboratory findings. I have now added his slides and data to my medical presentations.
6. The medical community formally recognized this process in 1987 at the First International Conference on the Brain, Stress, and the Hemodynamics of Hypertension, which was conducted by the Inter-American Society of Cardiology in cooperation with the International Stress Foundation. Twenty international high blood pressure experts presented their research and their reactions to the subject. As symposium co-director, I had wondered whether the outcome would be chaos or consensus. Whenever science enters a new field, there is no way of knowing what will happen; but

in this case, there was uniformity of opinion. We knew then that we were moving in the right direction, and our conclusions were published in a special supplement to the *American Heart Journal*. See Mason, D.T., Editor-in-Chief, and R.S. Eliot, Guest Editor. "Hemodynamics and Stress Factors in Evaluation and Management," *American Heart Journal*, 116, no. 2, part 2 supplement (August 1988).

7. Personal communication with the late Daniel D. Savage, M.D., Ph.D., National Heart, Lung, and Blood Institute investigator, Bogalusa Heart Study. See also Soto, L.F., D.A. Kikuchi, R.A. Arcilla, D.D. Savage, G.S. Berenson. "Echocardiographic Functions and Blood Pressure Levels in Children and Young Adults from Biracial Population: The Bogalusa Heart Study," *The American Journal of the Medical Sciences*, 296, no. 7 (1989), pp. 271–79.
8. Friedman, M., R.H. Rosenman and V. Carroll. "Changes in the Serum Cholesterol and Blood Clotting Time in Men Subjected to Cyclic Variation of Occupational Stress," *Circulation*, 17 (1958), pp. 852–61.
9. Eliot, Robert S., M.D. "Stress and the Heart: Mechanisms, Measurement, and Management," *Postgraduate Medicine*, 92, no. 5 (1992), pp. 237–48.
10. Riley, Vernon. *Perspectives on Behavioral Medicines*, ed. Stephen M. Weiss, J. Allen Herd, and Bernard H. Fox. New York: Academic Press, 1981.
11. Bishop, R.W., et al. "Depressed Lymphocyte Function After Bereavement," *The Lancet I* (April 16, 1977), pp. 834–836.
12. Schleifer, S.J., et al. "Suppression of Lymphocyte Stimulation Following Bereavement," *Journal of the American Medical Association*, 250 (1983), pp. 374–77.
13. Ibid.

CHAPTER 3   ALL THAT ASSAULTS US

1. Marmot, M.G., and S.L. Syme. "Acculturation and Coronary Heart Diseases in Japanese Americans," *American Journal of Epidemiology*, 104 (1976), pp. 225–47.
2. Wolf, S. "Psychosocial Forces and Neural Mechanisms in Disease: Defining the Question and Collecting the Evidence," *Johns Hopkins Medical Journal*, 150 (1982), pp. 95–100. See also Wolf, Stewart, and John G. Bruhn. *The Power of Clan: The Influence of Human Relationships on Heart Disease*. New Brunswick, NJ: Transaction Publishers, 1993.
3. Personal communications with the late Daniel D. Savage, M.D., Ph.D., National Heart, Lung, and Blood Institute investigator, Bogalusa Heart Study. See also Soto, L.F., D.A. Kikuchi, R.A. Arcilla, D.D. Savage, G.S. Berenson. "Echocardiographic Functions and Blood Pressure Levels in Children and Young Adults from Biracial Population: The Bogalusa Heart Study," *The American Journal of the Medical Sciences*, 296, no. 7 (1989), pp. 271–79.

4. Syme, S.L. "Environmental Factors and the Epidemiology of Stress-Related Cardiovascular Disease." Paper presented at the Stress and the Heart Seminar, Grand Teton National Park, July 1–3, 1985.

5. Haynes, S.G. "Job Control and CHD," *Medical World News,* February 11, 1985, pp. 16–17.

6. Personal communication with Robert C. Rosenloff, M.D., Clinical Professor of Medicine, University of Nebraska.

7. "Women and Heart Disease: An Equal Opportunity," *Johns Hopkins Medical Letter—Health After 50.* Baltimore, MD: Medletter Associates, 1990.

8. Kahn, Steven S., et al. "Increased Mortality of Women in Coronary Artery Bypass Surgery: Evidence for Referral Bias," *Annals of Internal Medicine,* 112 (April 1990), pp. 561–67.

9. McKinlay, John, Deborah Cutter, and Ralph D'Agostino. "Evaluating Physicians' Cardiopulmonary Decisions," The New England Research Institute Pilot Study for National Heart, Lung and Blood Institute Grant R18HL37762, 1988. Excerpted from "Women and Heart Disease: An Equal Opportunity," op. cit.

10. Haynes, Suzanne, and Manning Feinleib. "Women, Work and Coronary Heart Disease: Results from the Framingham 10-Year Follow-Up Study," *Women: A Developmental Perspective,* ed. Phyllis Berman and Estelle Ramey. Bethesda, MD: National Institutes of Health Publication #82–2298, 1982.

11. Pearline, L.I., M.A. Lieberman, E.G. Menaghan, and J.T. Mullen. *Journal of Health and Science Behavior,* 22 (1981), pp. 337–56.

12. Frankenhauser, Marianne. "Stress On and Off the Job as Related to Sex and Occupational Status in White Collar Workers," *Journal of Organizational Behavior,* 10 (1989), pp. 321–46.

CHAPTER 4   THE NEW STRESS MEDICINE

1. Dimsdale, J.E. "Wet Holter Monitoring: Techniques for Studying Plasma Responses to Stress in Ambulatory Subjects," *Biobehavioral Bases of Coronary Heart Diseases,* ed. T.M. Dembroski et al. New York: Karger, 1983, pp. 175–84.

2. Pickering, T.G., and R.B. Devereux. "Ambulatory Monitoring of Blood Pressure as a Predictor of Cardiovascular Risk," *American Heart Journal,* 114 (1987), p. 925.

3. Pickering, T.G., et al. "Comparisons of Blood Pressure During Normal Daily Activities, Sleep, and Exercise in Normal and Hypertensive Subjects," *Journal of the American Medical Association,* 247 (1982), pp. 992–96.

4. Data from the Framingham Heart Study led researchers to the conclusion that for every 10mm rise in Mean Arterial Pressure (MAP), there is a 30 percent rise in cardiovascular risk. See Kannel, W.B., J.T. Doyle, A.M. Ostfeld, C.D. Jenkins, L. Kuller, R.N. Podell, and J. Stamer. "Optimal

Resources for Primary Prevention of Atherosclerotic Diseases," Athero-sclerosis Study Group, *Circulation,* 70 (1984), pp. 155A–205A.

5. Pickett, B.R., and J.C. Buell. "Usefulness of the Impedance Cardiogram to Reflect Left Ventricular Diastolic Function," *The American Journal of Cardiology,* 71 (1993), pp. 1099–100.

6. Keys, A., H.L. Taylor, H. Blackburn, et al. "Mortality and Coronary Heart Disease Among Men Studied for 23 Years," *Archives of Internal Medicine,* 128 (1971), pp. 201–14.

7. Farnett, L., et al. "The J-Curve Phenomenon and the Treatment of Hypertension," *Journal of the American Medical Association,* 265, no. 4 (1991), pp. 489–95.

8. Eliot, Robert S., "Relationship of Emotional Stress to the Heart," *Heart Disease and Stroke,* 2, no. 3 (1993), pp. 243–46.

9. Ornish, Dean. *Dr. Dean Ornish's Program for Reversing Heart Disease.* New York: Ballantine, 1990.

10. Eliot, Robert S., M.D. "Lessons Learned and Future Directions," *American Heart Journal,* 116, no. 2, part 2 supplement (August, 1988), pp. 682–86.

CHAPTER 6   IDENTIFYING YOUR STRESSES AND STRENGTHS

1. Berkman, L.F., and S.L. Syme. "Social Networks, Host Resistance and Mortality: A Nine-Year Follow-Up Study of Alameda County Residents," *American Journal of Epidemiology,* 109 (1979), pp. 186–204.

2. Nerem, R.M., M.M. Levesque, and J.F. Cornfield. "Social Environment as a Factor in Diet-Induced Aortic Atherosclerosis in Rabbits," *Science,* 208 (1980), pp. 1475–476.

3. Magid, Ken and Carol McKelvey. *High Risk: Children Without a Conscience.* New York: Bantam, 1988.

4. Berkman, L.F., and S.L. Syme, op. cit.

5. Seeman, T.E., and S.L. Syme. "Social Networks and Coronary Artery Disease: A Comparison of the Structure and Function of Social Relations as Predictors of Disease," *Psychosomatic Medicine,* 49 (1987), pp. 341–54.

6. Berkman, L.F., and S.L. Syme, op. cit.

7. Kohut, H. *How Does Analysis Cure?* Chicago: University of Chicago Press, 1984.

8. Friedmann, Erika, et al. "Animal Companions and One-Year Survival of Patients after Discharge from a Coronary Care Unit," *Public Health Report,* 95, no. 4 (July-August 1980), pp. 307–12. See also Friedmann, Erika, et al. "Social Interaction and Blood Pressure: Influence of Animal Companions," *Journal of Nervous and Mental Disease,* 171, no. 8, (1983), pp. 461–65.

9. Holmes, T.H., and R.H. Rahe. "The Social Readjustment Rating Scale," *Journal of Psychosomatic Research,* 11 (1967), pp. 213–18.

10. Benson, Herbert, and M. Kippler. *The Relaxation Response.* New York: Avon, 1976. See also Ornish, Dean, *Dr. Dean Ornish's Program for Reversing Heart Disease.* Ballantine, 1990.
11. Kimble, C.P. "A Predictive Study of Adjustment to Cardiac Surgery," *Journal of Thoracic Cardiovascular Surgery,* 5 (1969), pp. 891–96.
12. Williams, Redford. *The Trusting Heart: Great News About Type A Behavior.* New York: Random House, 1989. See also *Anger Kills.* New York: Times Books, 1993.

CHAPTER 8   VALUES

1. Bennett, Robert F. *Gaining Control.* Utah: Franklin International Institute, Inc., 1987.
2. I was introduced to some of these tests by Karl Gretz, Ph.D., Senior Training Consultant, Merrill Lynch, Inc., at a seminar in 1989.
3. Modified to fit our clinical approach from Raths, L., H. Merrill, and S. Sidney. *Values and Teaching.* Columbus, OH: Charles E. Merrill, 1966.

CHAPTER 9   THE POWER OF PERCEPTION

1. Ellis, Albert. *Growth Through Reason: Verbatim Cases in Rational-Emotive Therapy.* Palo Alto, CA: Science and Behavior Books, 1971.
2. Murray, Henry A. *Explorations in Personality: A Clinical and Experimental Study of Fifty Men of College Age.* New York: Oxford University Press, 1953.
3. Penfield, Wilder, et al. *The Mystery of the Mind: A Critical Study of Consciousness and the Human Brain.* Princeton, NJ: Princeton University Press, 1975.
4. Beck, Aaron T., et al. *Cognitive Therapy of Depression.* New York: Guilford Press, 1979, pp. 330–31.
5. Dubovsky, Steven L. *Concise Guide to Clinical Psychiatry.* Washington: American Psychiatric Press, Inc., 1988, p. 2.
6. Ibid.
7. Beck, Aaron T. *Cognitive Therapy and the Emotional Disorders.* New York: New American Library, 1979. See also Dobson, Keith S., Albert Ellis. *Growth Through Reason.*
8. Ellis, *Growth Through Reason,* op. cit. p. 4.
9. Ibid., p. 6.

CHAPTER 10   TIME MANAGEMENT

1. Boorstein, Daniel J. *The Discoverer: A History of Man's Search to Know His World and Himself.* New York: Random House, 1983.

CHAPTER 11   NUTRITION

1. Callaway, C. Wayne, with Catherine Whitney. *The Callaway Diet*. New York: Bantam, 1990.
2. Bray, G.A., and D.S. Gray. "Obesity: Part I. Pathogenesis," *Western Journal of Medicine*, 149 (1988), pp. 429–42.
3. Friedman, M., R.H. Rosenman, and V. Carroll. "Changes in the Serum Cholesterol and Blood Clotting Time in Men Subjected to Cyclic Variation of Occupational Stress," *Circulation*, 17 (1958), pp. 852–61.
4. Ornish, Dean. *Dr. Dean Ornish's Program for Reversing Heart Disease*. New York: Ballantine, 1990.
5. Olson, Robert E., M.D. "Point of View, Cholesterolmania—Is It Bad For Us?" *Nutrition and the M.D.*, November 1992.
6. Ornish, Dean. "Can Lifestyle Changes Reverse Coronary Heart Disease?" *Lancet*, 336 (July 1990).
7. Ibid.
8. National Academy of Sciences, National Research Council, Food and Nutrition Board. *Diet and Health Implications for Reducing Chronic Disease Risk*. Washington, D.C.: National Academy Press, 1989.
9. Rader, J.I., R.J. Clavert, and J.N. Hathcock. "Hepatic Toxicity of Unmodified and Time-Release Preparations of Niacin," *The American Journal of Medicine*, 92 (1992), pp. 77–81.
10. Stare, Frederick J. and Virginia Aronson. *Your Basic Guide to Nutrition*. Philadelphia: George F. Stickley, 1983, p. 155.
11. National Academy of Sciences, op. cit.
12. U.S. Department of Agriculture, U.S. Department of Health and Human Services. "Nutrition and Your Health: Dietary Guideline for Americans," Home and Garden Bulletin #232, 3d ed., Washington, D.C.: U.S. Government Printing Office, 1990.

CHAPTER 12   EXERCISE

1. Brody, Robert. "Addicted to Fitness," *Chicago Sun-Times*, November 6, 1990, section 2, p. 41.
2. American College of Sports Medicine. *Guidelines for Exercise Testing and Prescription*, 3d ed. Philadelphia: Lea & Febiger, 1986, p. 34.
3. Evans, W., and I.H. Rosenberg. *Biomarkers: The 10 Keys to Prolonging Vitality*. New York: Fireside (Simon & Schuster), 1991.
4. American Heart Association. *Exercise Testing and Training of Individuals with Heart Disease or at High Risk for its Development: A Handbook for Physicians*. Dallas: The American Heart Association, 1975.
5. Pollock, M.L., J.H. Wilmore and S.M. Fox III. *Exercises in Health and Disease*. Philadelphia: W.B. Saunders, 1984.
6. Karvonen, M.J., et al. "The Effects of Training on Heart Rate, A Longitudinal Study," *Ann. Med. Exp. Biol. Fenn.*, 35 (1975), p. 305.

7. Saltin, B., et al. "Response to Exercise after Bedrest and after Training," *Circulation,* 38, suppl. 7 (1968), pp. 1–10.
8. Paffenbarger, R., et al. "Physical Activity. All Cause Mortality and Longevity of College Alumni," *New England Journal of Medicine,* (1986), 314, pp. 605–13.
9. Zohman, L.R. *Beyond Diet: Exercise Your Way to Fitness and Heart Health.* Englewood Cliffs, NJ: Mazola Products, 1974.
10. Kidd III, J.M., et al. "Food-Dependent Exercise-Induced Anaphylaxis," *Journal of Allergy and Clinical Immunology,* 71 (1983), pp. 407–11.
11. Bairey, C.N. "Exercise and Coronary Artery Disease—What Should We Be Recommending to Our Patients (and Ourselves)?" *Western Journal of Medicine,* 144 (1986), pp. 205–11.

EPILOGUE A NEW APPROACH TO WELLNESS

1. "Health Management: A Survey of Company-Sponsored Wellness Programs," Survey released by Coopers & Lybrand, Washington, D.C., February 1991.

INDEX